CONTENTS

PHILOSOPHY FOR A BETTER WORLD

FLORIS VAN DEN BERG

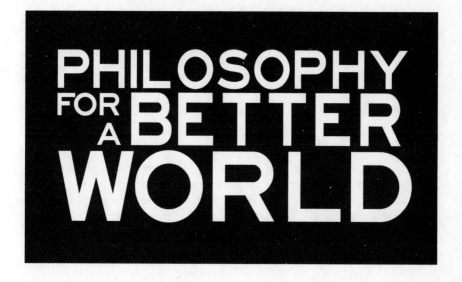

PHILOSOPHY FOR A BETTER WORLD

TRANSLATED FROM THE DUTCH BY
MICHIEL HORN

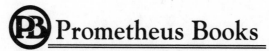

Prometheus Books

59 John Glenn Drive
Amherst, New York 14228–2119

Published 2013 by Prometheus Books

Filosofie voor een betere wereld
© Floris van den Berg / Houtekiet / Linkeroever Uitgevers nv 2009
Houtekiet, Katwilgweg 2 bus 3, B-2020 Antwerpen

This publication has been made possible with the financial support of the Dutch Foundation for Literature.

Cover design by Liz Scinta
Cover image © 2012 PhotoDisc, Inc.

In an effort to acknowledge trademarked names of products mentioned in this work, we have placed ® or ™ after the product name in the first instance of its use in each chapter. Subsequent mentions of the name within a given chapter appear without the symbol.

Inquiries should be addressed to
Prometheus Books
59 John Glenn Drive
Amherst, New York 14228–2119
VOICE: 716–691–0133 • FAX: 716–691–0137
WWW.PROMETHEUSBOOKS.COM

17 16 15 14 13 • 5 4 3 2 1

Library of Congress Cataloging-in-Publication Data

Berg, Floris van den, 1973-
    Philosophy for a better world / by Floris van den Berg ; translated by Michiel Horn.
        [Filosofie voor een betere wereld. English]
            pages cm
    Includes bibliographical references.
    ISBN 978-1-61614-503-3 (pbk.) • ISBN 978-1-61614-504-0 (ebook)
    1. Philosophy and social sciences. I. Title.

B63.B5513 2013
199'.492—dc23

                                                                    2012048979

Printed in the United States of America

For Annemarieke

CHAPTER 1
INTRODUCTION TO A BETTER WORLD

On the whole, we don't take the ethical and ecological consequences of our daily activities into account: taking the car to work, eating meat, flying to our holiday destination, wearing cotton shirts, buying strawberries in winter, acquiring hardwood garden furniture, eating fish, using plastic bags in stores. There are ethical and ecological objections to each of these examples. Without our being aware of it, our lifestyle does an immeasurable amount of damage to human beings, animals, and nature. Everyday actions therefore have to be assessed on the basis of their moral acceptability. Alas, the conclusion is that almost nothing we do can stand up to an ethical analysis. And that is frustrating. A lot of (unnecessary) suffering attaches to our way of life. The ethical investigation of your own lifestyle can lead to a disturbing experience, an ethical gestalt switch. Suddenly you're no longer the hero of your own life story but the villain.

The job of philosophers is searching for blind spots in our knowledge and epistemological methods on the one hand, and for blind spots in our ethics on the other. Philosophers are explorers in the realm of ideas.[1] During the last few decades their explorations have turned up many new ethical blind spots. That has led to emancipation movements and action groups on behalf of homosexuals, women, unbelievers, animals, the environment, and future generations. But how do you find such blind spots? After all, you can't perceive your own. By searching actively, with the help of guidelines and theoretical insight, you can succeed in finding new moral blind spots. When such a blind spot has been located, it is important to solve the problem. For example, in his book *Animal Liberation* in the early 1970s, the philosopher Peter Singer focused attention on the suffering of animals in intensive factory farming.

LESS SUFFERING, MORE HAPPINESS

This book explains the theory of what I call *universal subjectivism*. This is an ethical theory that everyone can apply quite simply to the search for blind spots and to finding the ways of making them disappear. The point of departure is *the capacity for suffering*. The issue is to diminish suffering and promote happiness.

The summit of 2500 years of philosophical writing is a three-word sentence in a footnote in a book by the English philosopher Jeremy Bentham (1748–1832): "Can they suffer?" These three words are the most profound and important words in all of the history of philosophy. Bentham points to the essential issue in ethics, that is, the capacity for suffering. What matters is not the possession of certain faculties, such as thinking or speaking, but the capacity of being able to suffer.

Bentham concludes that, from this perspective, the way human beings treat animals is unethical: "The day *may* come, when the rest of the animal creation may acquire those rights which never could have been withholden from them but by the hand of tyranny. The French have already discovered that the blackness of the skin is no reason why a human being should be abandoned without redress to the caprice of a tormentor. It may come one day to be recognized, that the number of the legs, the villosity [hairiness] of the skin, or the termination of the *os sacrum* [the large heavy bone at the base of the spine], are reasons equally insufficient for abandoning a sensitive being to the same fate. What else is it that should trace the insuperable line? Is it the faculty of reason, or, perhaps, the faculty of discourse? But a full-grown horse or dog is beyond comparison a more rational, as well as a more conversible animal, than an infant of a day, or a week, or even a month old. But suppose the case were otherwise, what would it avail? The question is not, Can they *reason*? Nor, Can they *talk*? But, Can they *suffer*?"[2]

Human society could be arranged a good deal better than it is. This book investigates how the world could be made more pleasing, better, more just, more beautiful, happier, healthier, freer, more prosperous, more peaceful, and more sustainable than it is now. How could there be less suffering and more happiness? For this purpose, I have designed a politico-philosophical theory called universal subjectivism. This theory is a stepping-stone toward looking at the world and exposing problems. Contemporary philosophers such as John Rawls, Peter Singer, A. C. Grayling, Paul Cliteur, and Paul Kurtz are an important source of inspiration. This theory is not a panacea for *every* problem. It can make many problems visible and it can also be used to solve them. That there will be problems left over is yet another reason to keep looking for solutions. My concern is to decrease suffering and to promote happiness. Universal subjectivism offers a guiding principle for ethical action.

The need for a theory is urgent, but the need for action is even more pressing. There is an unbelievable amount of suffering in the world, and a great deal of that suffering is easily preventable provided there is a collective will to do so. One of the greatest moral problems in the United States, as in other western countries—factory farming—could be solved simply by immediately passing a law prohibiting factory farming while simultaneously stimulating and subsidizing small-scale and environmentally friendly raising of cattle and other animals. Every day people die of starvation, although there is enough food to feed the population of today's world; everyday people die because of a lack of medication, although the medication could have been supplied easily. A huge problem is the future: humans are ruining the earth on an unprecedented scale, and the limits of the earth's capacity will soon be reached. It is five minutes to twelve. The time has come for action and for establishing priorities. The human lifestyle has to change drastically. How and why—that is what I will examine in this book. This is an urgent ethical appeal. If, after reading this book, the reader continues with business as usual, it means the message hasn't registered. Come on: wake up! Do something!

REEVALUATING EVERY VALUE

Aided by ethical reflection, I want to show that the basic intuitions that people have with respect to ethics and the good life are untenable in the light of reason. By means of thought experiments, striving for moral consistency, and looking beyond one's own culture and traditions, it will become apparent that the average person's behavior is deeply immoral. Does this grave accusation frighten the reader off from reading further? Galileo claimed that Earth circles around the Sun and not the other way around. Galileo was right, but no one saw it or dared to see it. That is partly because it was counterintuitive: it seems as if the sun is circling us; it rises in the east and goes down in the west.

Is it not absurd to say that almost everybody behaves unethically? The ancient Greeks with their democracy, whom we admire, were deeply immoral because their culture was based on slavery. Even the great philosophers did not discuss the matter. It was a huge blind spot. Looking back, therefore, it is clear that all Greek democrats behaved unethically. In today's society the blind spots are well known: the environment, animals, future generations, low-income countries. And yet we continue to ignore them. This book is a re-evaluation of every value. That is, after all, the risk of thought: you can end up with conclusions you had not expected or even ones that are not in your own interests. Philosophy is a quest for the true, the good, and the beautiful. Along the way I have thoroughly adjusted my ideas and my lifestyle, re-examining my opinions and behavior in the light of reason.

The Enlightenment Project

Thinking for ourselves about how together we can make the best of things in the here and now is the essence of the Enlightenment. This intellectual current flowered in Europe in the seventeenth and eighteenth centuries. It was a movement in which thinkers reacted against church and civil authorities and tried to study the world autonomously and to rearrange society. The term Enlightenment—*Aufklärung* in German, *Lumières* in French—points to the light of reason that shone after the darkness of the Middle Ages. In 1784 the philosopher Immanuel Kant (1724–1804) wrote an essay in which he investigated what the Enlightenment consisted of. He concluded that the Enlightenment meant that people, with the help of reason, needed to drag themselves out of the ignorance they had imposed on themselves, and that courage was needed to apply reason. Kant spurred people on to a further Enlightenment with the Latin saying: *sapere aude* (dare to think for yourself). The Enlightenment was a process of secularization: to varying degrees, religion was placed outside the domain of ethics, politics, and science. In the areas of morality and science, the role of religion was pushed back. Criticism of religion was one of the pillars of the Enlightenment.

The Enlightenment had a critical and a constructive side. The critical side criticized institutionalized belief and irrationality. The constructive side involved the search for new knowledge (science) and new social structures whose objectives were justice, democracy, and human rights. Tolerance for ideas, the struggle against oppression, individual autonomy, and self-determination were core values of the Enlightenment. These elements are prominent in the *magnum opus* of the Enlightenment, the *Encyclopédie* (1751–73) edited by Denis Diderot and Jean D'Alembert.

It is customary to differentiate between the early, radical Enlightenment, of which Baruch Spinoza was the most important representative—an irreligious and antireligious, atheistic current—and a more moderate version in which religion, having been modernized and watered down, isn't seen as an obstacle to progress. The Enlightenment cleared the way for the scientific revolution and the explosive growth of knowledge. The modern Western world, supported by science and technology, is directly descended from the traditions of the Enlightenment. And yet religious people sometimes deny the influence of the Enlightenment and ascribe wars in general, and the horrors of the Second World War in particular, to the decline of religion in society. The contemporary philosopher A. C. Grayling sees the Enlightenment as one of several movements in Western history in which reason and humankind had a leading role in the here and now. In his book *What Is Good? The Search for the Best Way to Live*, Grayling sees the ancient world, the Renaissance, the Enlightenment, the scientific revolution, and finally the human-rights discourse of today as shoots of the same humanistic trunk, wherein the individual and reason take a central place.[3] Freethinkers and secular humanists (for example, Paul Kurtz in *Toward a New Enlightenment*[4]) locate themselves explicitly and emphatically in the tradition of the radical Enlightenment. Historian of ideas Jonathan Israel sums up what the Radical Enlightenment entails:

> democracy; racial and sexual equality; individual liberty of lifestyle; full freedom of thought, expression, and the press; eradication of religious authority from the legislative process and education; and full separation of church and state. It sees the purpose of the state as being as the whole secular one of promoting the worldly interests of the majority and preventing vested minority interests from capturing control of the legislative process. Its chief maxim is that all men have the same basic needs, rights, and status irrespective of what they believe or what religious, economic, or ethnic group they belong to, and that consequently all ought to be treated alike, on the basis of equity, whether black or white, male or female, religious or nonreligious, and that all deserve to have their personal interests and aspirations equally respected by law and government. The universalism lies in its claim that all men have the same right to pursue happiness in their own way, and think and say whatever

they see fit, and no one, including those who convince others they are divinely chosen to be their masters, rulers, or spiritual guides, is justified in denying or hindering others in the enjoyment of rights that pertain to all men and women equally.[5]

Organized humanism seems to be somewhat more in the tradition of the moderate Enlightenment, that is, it expresses some support for critical review of religion and intolerant cultural practices and institutions, but in other parts seeking reform and accommodation.[6]

THE GOOD SOCIETY

The fundamental question of political philosophy is: what is a good society? This general question can be split into four specific questions, the four basic questions of political philosophy, namely:

1. For whom?
2. By whom?
3. What for?
4. By what means?

1. *For whom does a political order actually exist?* A common answer is: "For the people who live in a certain nation." A glance into a historical atlas reveals that national boundaries are historically unstable and contingent. Nations come and go. The present border between the United States and Mexico dates only from 1853, after all, and who knows how long it will last? Besides, there is also the question of for whom the laws of the nation exist. How are the interests of ethnic minorities dealt with? Turkey, for example, has Kurdish inhabitants who don't have a state of their own and whose interests are not optimally looked after by the Turkish state. Is the political order focused on the interests of adult, non-handicapped, heterosexual, non-dissident, conservative males,

or on the interests of all inhabitants? What is the situation for the interests of the physically or mentally handicapped, fetuses, future generations, dissidents, animals, the environment, and so on? The democratic answer is: a state is of the people, by the people, for the people. And "the people" means all inhabitants. All adult, mentally capable inhabitants are allowed to make their voices heard and represent also those who cannot or cannot yet make their voices heard, such as children and the mentally handicapped.

2. *By whom are the rules of society made?* The simplest model is a dictatorship: the dictator's will is law. As Louis XIV is supposed to have said: "L'état, c'est moi!" ("I am the state!") Rules and laws exist to serve the tyrant's interests. Everything and everyone is subordinated to the whims of the sole ruler. A party (as in communism), or a small group, as in an oligarchy, can also exercise dictatorial rule. In a democracy the rules are generally made indirectly by means of elected representatives of the people. The *trias politica*, the separation of powers between the legislative, executive, and judicial branches, is intended to guarantee that the rights of the individual are not violated and that democracy does not slide toward a dictatorship by the majority. In a democracy the very first concern is with the people who happen to have been born in the country and who have its nationality. Future generations, foreigners, and animals count for little if anything, or do so to a lesser degree. Since 2006 two members (out of 150) of the Dutch Parliament represent the Party of the Animals. This is unique in the world and in history.

3. *Why do states exist anyway?* Aren't they simply a pain? All those rules and those damned taxes.

THE PARABLE OF THE UNINHABITED ISLAND[7]

Suppose an airplane makes a crash landing in the Pacific Ocean. The passengers survive the crash and wash up on an uninhabited, hitherto undiscovered island whose chances of ever being discovered are small (after all, this is a thought experiment). The airplane carries, in separate compartments, Israeli Jews, Palestinian Arabs, Muslim Indians, Hindu Indians, Tibetans, Chinese, Americans, and Iranians. In short, people who have a lot of difficulty accepting each other's convictions. All of them wash up on that one small, undiscovered, uninhabited island. What now? They can make life hard for each other, or they can try to split the island up into compartments (just as in the real world, where the compartments are called countries), or they can try to make the best of the situation together. One way of doing that is to sit in a circle on the beach and to establish minimal rules for living and divide tasks fairly so that in the end everybody is better off and living in peace with the others. After five years the island is discovered. To the great astonishment of the media, the island dwellers are living together peacefully and have made the most of the modest means available to them. "An example to the world," the newspaper headlines shout.

4. *What means are used in trying to achieve the chosen objectives?* In a totalitarian society things are simple: anything goes. No provision is made for the interests of others to reach a certain goal. In this context, Leon Trotsky is said to have made the appalling statement that "human beings are the manure on the fields of the future." In short, human beings may be sacrificed in the present so that an ideal society, the communistic welfare state, can be established in the future. However, anyone who puts the individual at the center, as in individualism, liberalism, and humanism, will never sacrifice individuals to a greater goal. The road to Utopia must not be paved with corpses. Power and the monopoly of violence are closely linked. Whoever has a monopoly of violence has power. In the democratic, liberal, constitutional state in which the individual is central, the protection of individuals from violence is the sole legitimization of the state's monopoly of power. What is the goal that a political order strives toward? Is it social justice,

security, equality, a social safety net, happiness, permanence, or a combination of these and other ideals? What criteria can be used to judge a political or social order? When can politicians relax in the knowledge that the criteria have been met? And on what basis do people choose the criteria? In practice two factors play an important part. First, there is tradition: human beings do things in a certain way because things have always been done in that way. Second, there is political power. And power is a means of imposing your will on someone else.

For human beings to be able to live together on the planet, a minimal consensus about basic rules is necessary. These rules can be generated by means of the hypothetical thought experiment of universal subjectivism. What will become apparent, however, is that those basic rules are a lot more comprehensive than you might think. The minimal consensus about basic rules excludes a great deal, namely, all practices and traditions that stand in the way of individual freedom.

UNIVERSAL SUBJECTIVISM IN A NUTSHELL

Universal subjectivism is a thought experiment in which you yourself can determine how society is organized. You can determine the laws and rules. You're allowed to regulate everything that can possibly be regulated. You have access to an enormous control panel with all kinds of dials and sliding switches. For example, there is a dial marked "taxation" that you can turn higher or lower. And a dial marked "social welfare." There are big dials and small dials for fine-tuning. For example, fine-tuning affects the school-leaving age. There is a dial or switch for anything you can think of and that you might want to make rules for. You're sitting in a sky box with the control panel in front of you, and you arrange the parameters of society according to your own views. However, there is one important given: it is certain that you yourself will end up in the society that you have organized, only you don't know in what capacity. You don't know whether you will be a woman or a man, whether you will be intelligent or not, you don't know your skin color, your sexual preference, or what part of the world you will land in, etc. The strength of the thought experiment is that it is a way of determining how society may be arranged as favorably as possible, keeping in mind the worst possible situation (being handicapped, for example). What is at issue here is the maximization or optimization of the worst possible situation. The universal subjectivist model is a procedure that anyone can carry out whenever they wish. In order to do this rationally one needs to consider or allow for the worst possible situation (such as being gay in an Islamic society).

The procedure of universal subjectivism therefore means choosing a situation that is as bad as it can possibly be, and then, sitting at your control panel, changing the world in a way that you believe optimizes the circumstances of that worst possible situation. After that, you picture for yourself how it is working and you make adjustments if you think the situation can be improved. That is the feedback loop. Universal subjectivism is a dynamic process in which your thoughts jump toward different existential possibilities. It is a moral voyage of the mind. This book shows several examples of how some worst possible situations can be optimized: a handicapped person, a woman in a misogynist society, a homosexual in a homophobic society, a cow in a factory farming system, a poor person in a low-income country, and an inhabitant of the earth in the year 2511.

Universal subjectivism can be applied in two ways. First, it is applied as a *hypothetical theory of social contract.* This is the thought experiment whereby you have to determine the basic organization of society by yourself from behind a veil of ignorance. Second, universal subjectivism can be used as an exchange of identity with someone else. How would you like to be treated if you were someone else? This is universal subjectivism as role-playing. And role-playing is something you can practice. Stage acting is a good exercise in empathy. To be able to see the world from someone else's perspective does have to be linked to a reflection about morals and the will to act ethically. Whoever takes the fortuitousness of existence seriously, by which I mean the coincidence of being who you are, that you could have ended up in someone else's shoes, is bound to act ethically.

THE FORTUITOUSNESS OF EXISTENCE

The method of universal subjectivism makes you conscious of the fortuitousness of existence. It is by coincidence that you are who you are, since it could also have been otherwise. You didn't earn the place you find yourself in. Universal subjectivism is at odds with the ideas of reincarnation (Hinduism, Buddhism, and New Age) and predestination (Calvinism). In predestination as in reincarnation, there is a reason for who you are and where you are born. In reincarnation the soul migrates upon death to its next existence. On the basis of your accomplishments in this life, you can be either promoted or demoted. In predestination, God has a predetermined plan for you. God propels you into the world and watches whether you do well. In the case of predestination life is a survival test. In both instances it is not fortuitous that you are who you are. But if you don't believe in these hypotheses, than you are simply coincidentally (in professional jargon: contingently) the person you are. If you're born into a rich household you're simply luckier than if you are born into the Kibera slum of Nairobi.[8] Neither the poor nor the rich have deserved their places. Fate has decided, and fate is not a person. Speaking about "fate" is just a clumsy way of expressing statistical probability without a higher plan at its basis.

THE PARABLE OF THE EXCHANGED PRINCE

From my childhood I remember a fascinating animated film, in which a poor boy changes places for a day with a prince who is of the same age. The prince is curious to know what life outside the palace is like. However, when the "real" prince wants to get back into the palace in the evening to change places again, he is kept out by the guards. The film then deals with the adversity experienced by the prince, who is trying to show that he is the real prince. You tend to empathize with the prince who is suddenly poor and invisible. The philosophical question is: does anyone who has certain privileges by the accident of birth have more right to them than another? Many people believe intuitively that you are defined by where you are born: the idea is that there is a real and a fake prince. Is there a real prince, and if so, who is he?

Thinking about the fortuitousness of existence can perhaps be compared with the feelings of insignificance and futility that you may experience when you begin to think about the size of the universe. It is an overpowering emotion. When you find yourself in a favorable situation, you can feel happy, just as you can be happy when you win the big prize in a lottery.

Subjective, but Universal

Universal subjectivism is universal because the model can be applied to everyone in the same way. It is subjective because you and your feelings determine (when these have been hypothetically transposed to another existence) what has to be changed about society and its institutions in order to make life more bearable and, hopefully, more pleasurable. It is you who have to imagine yourself in the various worst possible situations. The paradox, to be sure, is that the model is subjective but the result is nevertheless universal. The ethical axiom is that all rational individuals would want the same thing in the worst possible situation. This ethical theory is not relativistic. There is a minimum concerning which everyone must share a consensus, for example: you can't desire for yourself that you should be tortured. Except for that minimal consensus, there is freedom and diversity. A sociopolitical order has to make room for that freedom and has to facilitate the possibility of diversity.

This model can be used in different ways: at the level of the individual as an ethical guideline, as a method for developing policies (such as a collective insurance system, medical care, and a social safety net), and as a method for making moral comparisons between societies.

In the first place, individuals can use it as an ethical guideline for themselves. When you are confronted with a moral problem, you mentally change places with the other person and imagine yourself in their situation. You can rationally will yourself to be in that situation. These are a few points to check: a handicapped person, a woman, a gay person, a cow, a future inhabitant of the world.

Aside from this personal response there is a social and political level. The model of universal subjectivism can be used to test how just a certain society or culture is and to change it in a positive direction.

Universal subjectivism seeks to maximize the freedom of the individual, not of the group, because it is always conceivable that some people in the group won't want what the group wants. That is why the state must guarantee and promote maximum freedom for the individual. But there are limits to this freedom. Individual freedom serves the freedom of other individuals. Individuals must not limit the freedom of others. That should happen only when compelling reasons exist, as in the case of compulsory education. Paradoxically enough, education, or at least secular, liberal education, is an interchangeable situation. Most adults agree that their parents were right in insisting that they go to school (this is postponed interchangeability).

The idea of interchangeability, in other words, the contingency of every form of existence, limits the domain of the possible options. This theory is based on the point of departure that you cannot rationally want to occupy the worst possible situation or, to put it differently, that you can't want to be tortured. In the case of pedophilia, for example, there are victims. When there are victims, exchangeability is irrational and self-destructive. Most people are not rational, or at least they are not rational all the time. But within the ethical play of the model of universal subjectivism it is assumed that people are rational. Ethics means the testing of a given situation for the possibility of exchangeability.

In the Western world we live in a utopia. If there is a paradise on earth, since the 1970s the Netherlands has resembled it. There is freedom and prosperity for almost everyone. Even homeless people are better off here than in other countries and at other times. In other words, geographically and temporally we live in a paradisiacal oasis. Whoever isn't happy in the Low Countries won't be happy anywhere. If God existed I would humbly thank that being every day that I came into the world here and now and in this place.

I am a somewhat misanthropic do-gooder. I would like to decrease the suffering in the world; most of all I would like to remove it altogether. In fact, I would also like there to be more nice people, nice not only to me, but nice to each other, so that I could feel less misanthropic. I am also a realist. I know that people make life hard for each other and that this will continue. The twentieth century was the bloodiest century ever. Never before did human beings create so much suffering. Among the reasons for this is that in the twentieth century the technologizing of society led to an exponential increase in the number of people on earth. The twenty-first century will also have a lot of misery in store for us, among which will be ecological disasters that will disrupt societies or perhaps even spell the end of the human race. At this moment a number of civil and international wars are going on, such as those in the Sudan, Kenya, Afghanistan, and Iraq. It is more than conceivable that a new war involving Israel will break out in the Middle East. Can a person who stays abreast of the human caused suffering in the world not be a desperate misanthrope?

Lessons from Utopia

In England in 1535, the high official Thomas More (1478–1535), who had fallen into disfavor, was beheaded on grounds of high treason.

Four hundred years later, in 1935, the Catholic Church rewarded More with canonization. The fact that in his book *Utopia* More made a plea for assisted suicide, something the church opposes adamantly, does not seem to be held against him. As a politician, More is known only among historians, but *Utopia* (1516) remains a classic in the literary canon. The book is interesting, however, not only on literary but also on philosophical grounds. It is a pleasant, readable book that stimulates thought about how a society may be organized. According to More, the most important human motive is greed. On the basis of his ideas about this, he creates a blueprint for a society that, in More's vision, brings forth the best in human beings and banishes the bad. Does More's design for an ideal society guarantee the happiness he emphasizes? Does More not overestimate the malleability of human nature? *Utopia* can be used as a springboard for reflection on a society that is as good as it can possibly be.

Utopia is a frame story. More claims to be writing down the tale of the sailor Raphael Nonsenso, whom he has met in Antwerp and who tells a small group of men, among them Thomas More, about his five-year sojourn on the island of Utopia. This literary device allows More to express social criticism by hiding behind the person of Raphael. The beautiful literary style contributes to the book's success. If *Utopia* had been given the form of a political-philosophical treatise, it would probably have been much less popular than it now is (although admittedly dry-as-dust, unreadable books like the Koran or Martin Heidegger's 1927 work *Sein und Zeit* [*Being and Time*] can gain cult status). After two introductory letters that make up the frame of the story, *Utopia* consists of two books—nowadays we would say chapters. Book 1 is a critique of English society at the time, of its criminal law, of private ownership, and of human exploitation. Raphael has a theory about crime that looks modern to us: crime is caused by poverty and unemployment. The solution to crime, as Raphael sees it, does not rest in punishing hard and often, but in social measures that reduce unemployment and poverty. Book 2 is the description of the social order in Utopia. Book 2 therefore offers the solution to the social problems signaled in Book 1. How *Utopia* is read depends on where you are situated. The point is to draw a comparison—at least if you want to read reflectively and not just for entertainment—between the society in which you live and Utopia. Reading this work, and also reading about other utopian designs[9] and about other cultures, such as works of cultural anthropology, stimulates reflection about comparisons among societies. To be able to determine whether a society is a paradise or a hell on earth, or where it is located between these extremes, you need a criterion that allows you to judge utopian designs. One way is to look at how the people who are in the worst possible situations fare in them: the poor, criminals (and who are the criminals?), women, children, homosexuals, foreigners, the handicapped, the sick, the aged, and dissidents.

Above everything else, More's Utopia offers a solution for the problem of poverty. The poor get a good deal in Utopia. It is a more or less egalitarian society, in which only the managers and directors enjoy privileges. It is certainly not a society of equals: women are subordinate to men, and children must obey adults.

Would I want to live in Utopia? No, absolutely not! Would I want to have lived in More's England? Not likely, unless I belonged to the high nobility. Would I want to live in the Netherlands of today? Yes, absolutely. Today's Netherlands is closer to a realized Utopia than has ever existed before in history. The Netherlands, Sweden, and a few other utopian islands are located in a sea of injustice, poverty, and oppression that is the rest of the world.

More does two things in *Utopia*. In the first place, he criticizes the societies of his time, and more particularly English society. These societies were unjust, not free, demonstrate a great gap between poor and rich, and were unstable, undemocratic, and cruel. If you were anachronistically to use the list of human rights in the Universal Declaration of Human Rights of 1948 as a moral criterion, you would find that English society at the time of More would score very low. That is not surprising, because, except for several countries in the modern western world, not a single society conforms or ever conformed to the ideal of human rights. Thomas More's Utopia doesn't either. Yet on a number of points Utopia is an improvement with respect to the society existing at that time, and on a number of other points it us a change for the worse. It is an instructive process to take all the points of Utopia into consideration and to compare them with the society at More's time; with our society today; with the Universal Declaration of Human Rights; and, finally, with other moral and political-philosophical standards. This chapter provides a few examples.

Aside from More's analysis of the problems in his society, for which he suggests a utopian solution, he also postulates a theory of human motivation. More claims to know what human nature is and what motivates people, namely, greed. People want possessions, not just for themselves but especially to show others what they possess. This is also known as conspicuous consumption. More is of the opinion that human greed is caused by fear of want and that when the problem of want has been solved, greed disappears as well: "No living creature is naturally greedy, except from fear of want—or in the case of human beings, from vanity, the notion that you're better than people if you can display more superfluous property than they can. But there's no scope for that sort of thing in Utopia."[10] More has a radical proposal for banishing this motive, which in his opinion leads to a lot of misery, namely, the abolition of private property. So there is no private property in Utopia, and there is no money. This is far more radical than the communist states in the twentieth century, where there was still a certain measure of private property, and money had not been abolished. More focuses on the elimination of hunger and poverty. In More's society, the conditions of life and work for a large part of the population were abominable. Only a small segment of the population lived a life of luxury and abundance. More analyzes a fundamental dichotomy: those who own property (land and money) and do nothing, and those who have no land and (little) property yet work like crazy to stay alive and have to give up a significant part of their income to the possessing class. In contrast, in Utopia this dichotomy has been abolished and everyone lives at roughly the same level, although supervisors (managers) and priests do enjoy privileges, which are reminiscent of the privileges enjoyed by the officials of the Communist party of the Soviet Union. And everyone has to work. The working day in Utopia is six hours—something that hasn't been attained yet even in the richest, most prosperous welfare states (I'm rather in favor of that, and in my view it should be possible). You could say that *Utopia* is a greatly expanded collective agreement for better working conditions. A large part, in fact, deals with work and conditions of work: "They never force people to work unnecessarily, for the main purpose of their whole economy is to give each person as much free time from physical drudgery as the needs of the community will allow, so that he can cultivate his mind—which they regard as the secret of a happy life."[11]

In More's time, a serious crisis had arisen in England because landowners were enclosing common grounds—hitherto used by small farmers to grow crops and graze their cattle—and were grazing their sheep on them. Raphael analyzes this tragedy of the commons as follows: "In those parts of the kingdom where the finest, and so the most expensive wool is produced, the nobles and gentlemen, not to mention several saintly abbots, have grown dissatisfied with the income that their predecessors got out of their estates. They're no longer content to lead lazy, comfortable lives, which do no good to society—they must actively do it harm, by enclosing all the land they can for pasture, and leaving none for cultivation. They're even tearing down houses and demolishing whole towns—except, of course, for churches, which they preserve for use as sheepfolds. . . . Thus a few greedy people have converted one of England's greatest natural advantages into a national disaster. For it's the high price of food that makes employers turn off [dismiss] so many of their servants—which inevitably turns them into beggars or thieves."[12]

It seems to be a universal human characteristic that rich people want to become richer and that "enough is enough" is not part of their worldview. In our Western world, captains of industry eagerly reach for more when the opportunities present themselves. Even when their employees are put out on the street in large numbers, these rich people have no scruples about cutting themselves in on additional millions. One of the arguments used is "that this is quite normal at the upper levels of the business world." This is, at the very least, a strange kind of normality. I often ask myself how people justify that to themselves. What kind of rationalizations do these greedy people offer for their behavior? More thinks it is simple avarice.

Why would I not want to live in Utopia? There is guaranteed security of existence, with work, education, a stable sociopolitical order, leisure time, food, and drink. Why don't I want that? Although there are worse states (and not just imaginary ones), Utopia is in fact a collectivist and totalitarian society that provides little or no room for deviant behavior or opinions. In Utopia human behavior, individual freedom, and the scope for developing one's potential are greatly constrained. Utopia resembles a humane penitentiary. Furthermore, slavery is tolerated in Utopia, and women are subordinate to men.

The British philosopher Bertrand Russell (1872–1970) rejects the utopian idea, but he is remarkably mild in his assessment of *Utopia*. Russell praises the liberal aspects of More's work, such as the conduct of war, religion and religious toleration, criticism of the killing of animals during hunting, and the mild criminal law. He concludes: "It must be admitted, however, that life in More's Utopia, as in most others, is intolerably dull. Diversity is essential to happiness, and in Utopia there is hardly any. This is a defect of all planned social systems, actual as well as imaginary."[13]

More is at his strongest in criticizing the prevailing abuses in society. Sometimes he offers good alternatives, but often his alternative, as noted above, is far from just. More's basic idea is to reform human beings from egotistical, violent, cruel, and above all greedy monsters into peace-loving, egalitarian, altruistic people. Instead of everybody seeking only their own interest, at the expense of others, the inhabitants of Utopia would seek the common interest. That is the collectivism of Utopia. More does not consider other possible kinds of society, such as a capitalist system that is driven by self-interest, linked to a social democratic welfare state in which a partial redistribution takes place so that those who are worst off are still better off than without such a system.

The avarice More identifies as the cause of social misery is a problem in a capitalist welfare state as well. But the problem is of an entirely different order than in More's time, namely, the steady increase in the ecological footprint, which is driven by greed and facilitated by increasing prosperity. It seems that More has a steady-state economy in mind. The idea of a steady-state economy seems to be a necessary condition for a world that is being overburdened by human economic activity. The only growth identified by More is population growth, and he solves that problem by founding colonies. In Utopia, effective management has led to a structural surplus in production that is exported. The money earned this way is used to hire mercenary soldiers who may be needed in case Utopia comes under attack.

Human behavior may be influenced in several ways, in which two different strategies can be distinguished. On the one hand, you can try to change people (for example, by means of child-rearing, education, information and propaganda), and on the other hand, you can arrange society in such a way that people will spontaneously do the right thing. The latter is a *procedural* approach.

THE PARABLE OF THE AMSTERDAM SUBWAY

When the Amsterdam subway was opened in the 1970s, everybody could enter freely: there were no conductors, no ticket takers, and no barriers. People were expected to buy tickets for themselves. The assumption was that people were not toddlers but responsible citizens who would understand that it is necessary to pay for public transportation. Fairly soon the subway system became something of a no-go area, and except for the most virtuous citizens, no one was paying to use the subway. There were even people who thought the subway was intended to be free. The high-minded, utopian ideals of the designers evidently foundered on the rather less exalted behavior of travelers. There was also a self-reinforcing process: if no one around you buys a ticket, next time you tend not to buy a ticket either. Through the introduction of turnstiles (which since then have been replaced by electrically operated sliding gates), the problem was solved quickly and almost completely. The method— the placement of gates—made it impossible to use the subway without a valid ticket.

When I was in Japan some years ago, I noticed a simple gadget to prevent speeding on the highway. The speed limit is seventy mph, and as soon as you drive faster, an irritating bell starts to ring. The car can easily go faster than seventy, but you have to have nerves of steel to withstand that bell. And most Japanese are too conscientious to have the bell disabled. It is strange, actually, that most cars can go much faster than the speed limit. It's possible, but it's not allowed. In an open society people have to restrain themselves. Those who can't control themselves risk getting a speeding ticket. Many people often drive too fast all the same. A procedural solution that does not allow people to exceed the speed limit, either by doing something to the car or to the road (such as speed bumps in residential areas or traffic circles where roads intersect), means that you don't have to address the inner motivation of people: the type of social engineering used compels the desired behavior.

Taxation departments have long been aware of the success of the procedural ethic. In principle, everybody is supposed to be in favor of taxes. After all, we have opted for them via our elected representatives. It's just that everybody would really prefer to pay lower taxes themselves. Although tax evasion does take place, a lot of taxes are collected automatically. When you go shopping, sales taxes are simply added to the price. If, after every purchase, people were asked to put the sales tax in a jar next to the cash register, without a cashier's supervision, the proceeds would be a lot lower than the amount of taxes due. We don't need to wait for social-psychology research to verify this.

In a country where permits to carry handguns are difficult to obtain and the sale of firearms is closely controlled, the number of murders is significantly lower than in countries where firearms are widely available. So there is an enormous difference between the homicide rate in the United States, where in many states it is legal to carry handguns, and in Canada, where few people are licensed to carry handguns. The film-maker Michael Moore demonstrates this uncomfortably in his documentary *Bowling for Columbine*.

Strategy #1 (hoping that people will observe the rules) is much less effective than strategy #2 (using social engineering to compel the desired behavior). Exhorting people to behave a certain way is generally less effective than enforcing that behavior.

Utopia has a planned economy, and it is in many ways reminiscent of the Soviet Union. There are collective farms with managers. This resembles the kolkhoz system of collective farms which were top down imposed in the former Soviet Union after the October Revolution of 1917, as an antithesis of family farming. The planned economy sounds wonderful on paper: "The authorities of each town work out very accurately the annual food consumption of their whole area, but they always grow corn and breed livestock far in excess of their own requirements, so that they've plenty to spare for their neighbours."[14] The twentieth century has demonstrated on a grotesque scale the failure of the communist planned economies, such as the former Soviet Union and China under Mao Zedong.[15] More's vision of the planned economy evidently does not work in the real world. There it leads to poverty, hunger, corruption, and misery. However, More's conception was a reaction to the phenomenon of famine in England: even though the granaries were filled, the wheat was not brought to market in the hope that prices would rise. That is indeed a terrible and absurd result of a market system. Yet when the market is liberalized, and there are no more monopolies, the chances of similar situations occurring decrease: experience shows that liberal societies don't have famines. But societies of that kind did not yet exist in More's time.

It sometimes seems that not only Stalin but also the abhorrent Chinese dictator Mao studied *Utopia*. According to Mao, everybody is a farmer first of all. That was imposed with an iron hand in China: intellectuals had to work on the land. In Utopia the regime is milder, but we can nevertheless speak of compulsion: "There's one job they all do, irrespective of sex, and that's farming. It's part of every child's education."[16] Another similarity between Mao's China and Utopia is the uniform: "They have no tailors or dressmakers, since everyone on the island wears the same sort of clothes—except that they vary slightly according to sex and marital status—and the fashion never changes."[17]

In Utopia factory farming has already been introduced: "They breed vast numbers of chickens by a most extraordinary method. Instead of leaving the hens to sit on the eggs, they hatch out dozens at a time by applying a steady heat to them—with the result that, when the chicks come out of the shells, they regard the poultryman as their mother, and follow him everywhere!"[18]

Some simple sentences make me shudder with dread. "They go to bed at 8 p.m., and sleep for eight hours."[19] The problem with this statement is that it reveals a serious measure of paternalism and compulsion. Suppose I don't want to go to bed at eight, or that I want to sleep for nine hours or six? Philosophers Hans Crombag and Frank van Dun have called this the "utopian temptation," the notion that it is permissible to impose your own ideals on other people.[20] Sometimes these ideals are in harmony with the ideas of those who have to acquiesce in them, but sometimes they aren't. The utopian temptation implies that leaders and utopian thinkers tend to meddle increasingly in more and more aspects of the inhabitants' lives, because they claim to know what is good for them. The inhabitants of Utopia get up very early: at 4 a.m. There's not a lot of freedom. The philosopher Karl Popper (1902–1994) expresses the importance of freedom this way: "Every man should be given, if he wishes, the right

INTRODUCTION TO A BETTER WORLD   33

to model his life himself, as far as this does not interfere too much with others."[21]

Big Brother is present in Utopia: "Wherever you are, you always have to work. There's never any excuse for idleness. There are also no wine-taverns, no ale-houses, no brothels, no opportunities for seduction, no secret meeting-places. Everyone has his eye on you, so you're practically forced to get on with your job, and make some proper use of your spare time."[22]

The British philosopher John Stuart Mill (1806–1873) analyzed the role of authority thoroughly. He pointed out that the exercise of government power over the individual can be justified only when the individual's freedom is threatened by another individual or group. In his liberal manifesto *On Liberty* (1859) he writes: "The only purpose for which power can be rightfully exercised over any member of a civilised community, against his will, is to prevent harm to others. His own good, either physical or moral, is not a sufficient warrant."[23]

This point is crucial, because Utopia and other utopian projects, both in theory and practice, do precisely that: the authorities coerce people ostensibly for their own well-being/happiness/salvation/ spiritual welfare/virtue. The essence of a liberal, open society is that people are free to do what they want, so long as they cause no harm to others. So if people want to spend their free time in idleness, that is their own choice, which the government has no right to change by using coercion. At most it can try to persuade people to engage in "more worthwhile" activities such as reading or jogging.

The social order in Utopia is hierarchical and static. Social relations coincidentally conform to those of Confucianism: "Each household [. . .] comes under the authority of the oldest male. Wives are subordinate to their husbands, children to their parents, and younger people generally to their elders."[24] Later More adds: "Husbands are responsible for punishing their wives, and parents for punishing their children, unless the offence is so serious that it has to be dealt with by the authorities, in the interests of public morality. The normal penalty for any major crime is slavery."[25] Sexual morality is severe and narrow-minded: "Any boy or girl convicted of premarital intercourse is severely punished, and permanently disqualified from marrying, unless this sentence is remitted by the Mayor."[26]

In Utopia religion plays the role of a social binding agent as well as a motive for acting morally. Although there is a measure of religious freedom, that freedom does not extend to atheism.[27] According to Raphael's explanation, an unbeliever has withdrawn from the foundation of society. "Anyone who thinks differently has, in their view, forfeited his right to be classed as a human being, degrading his immortal soul to the level of an animal's body. Still less do they regard him as a Utopian citizen. They say a person like that doesn't really care a damn for the Utopian way of life—only he's too frightened to say so. For it stands to reason, if you're not afraid of anything but prosecution, and have no hopes of anything after you're dead, you'll always be trying to evade or break the laws of your country, in order to gain your own private ends. So nobody who subscribes to this doctrine is allowed to receive any public honour, hold any public appointment, or work in any public service. In fact such people are generally regarded as utterly contemptible."[28]

At first sight Utopia seems to be a secular society, in which religion does not play a dominant role. All the same, it is apparent from the quotation above that religion is regarded as the guarantee of acting morally. According to Raphael, alias More, without a minimal quota of religion people will behave badly. In fact, this is a statement that can be examined empirically: are religious folk better citizens than unbelievers? A large part of the Dutch population consists of unbelievers, and many of them are atheists, yet anarchy does not rule in the Netherlands, and you can generally go out alone safely in the Netherlands. The idea that religion is a necessary condition for acting morally is a stubborn misconception. In the United States it is the case that a vocal atheist has no chance of achieving high political office.

The secular character of Utopia with an emphasis on rational management and a planned economy turns out to be a farce. Upon closer examination, Utopia is a narrow theocracy with a religious morals police. Utopia is not utopia but a dystopia. "Priests are responsible for conducting services, organizing religions, and supervising morals."[29] There is even a Council for impiety, an inquisition of a kind that nowadays exists only in Iran.

During the Second World War the philosopher Karl Popper wrote the book that later became famous as *The Open Society and Its Enemies*. Against expectation, he did not squarely oppose fascism, Nazism, and communism in it; instead, he took a close look at the traditions in political philosophy in which the collectivist idea had its origins. Popper discusses three great enemies of the open society and individual freedom: Plato, Georg Hegel, and Karl Marx. The list of thinkers who are enemies of the open society is long. Thomas More certainly belongs on that list. About dangerous thinkers and the utopian idea, Popper writes: "Even with the best of intentions of making heaven on earth it only succeeds in making it a hell—that hell which man alone prepares for his fellow-men."[30]

In their book *The Utopian Temptation*, philosophers Crombag and Van Dun point out the danger of utopias. Their book is in line with Popper's *The Open Society and Its Enemies*: "What the true-blue utopian wants above all to make clear is that his blueprint is realizable, that Utopia will also turn out to be perfect when it becomes reality. . . . People have to be malleable, so that the society may be achievable. . . . Utopia is presented to us as an efficient and effective happiness machine, which leaves the inhabitants no other choice and therefore forces them to be happy by making them undergo the good life."[31]

More wants to create a new human being, a human being without avarice, without jealousy, and without the desire to dress up and show off. With such a new human being living in a rigidly ordered society, Eternal Bliss would be guaranteed. But it is nearly impossible to change the human character. People just happen to have a certain measure of greed and the tendency to want to distinguish themselves from others. Another strategy is applied in the modern welfare state, namely, the partial channeling of that greed. By means of a progressive taxation regime, everyone benefits (in principle) from those who earn a lot (and therefore pay high taxes). An ideal motive for a better world is, in fact, "enlightened self-interest," as Bertrand Russell argues, the pursuit of self-interest without harming others[32] and thereby actually helping others along. Think of the baker baking bread. He does not do this in the first instance on altruistic or philanthropic grounds but to earn money. A social regime needs to establish preconditions designed to channel the self-interest and greed of people. On the subject of business ethics it is emphasized that self-interest and the mutual benefits of cooperative work and life are linked.[33] Philosopher Robert Philips writes in an article on business ethics: "Whenever persons or groups voluntarily accept the benefits of a mutually beneficial scheme of co-operation requiring sacrifice or contribution on the parts of the participants, and there exists the possibility of free-riding, obligations of fairness are created among the participants in the co-operative scheme in proportion to the benefits accepted."[34] Agreements have to be reached to ensure that *everyone* benefits and that the problem of free riders is dealt with. In this way a framework for political and economic activity will be able take form, because, as the philosopher A. C. Grayling writes, at present "the boundaries of legal permission in all capitalist economies lie outside those of moral acceptability."[35]

In an open society, i.e., a liberal, democratic society in which the rights of the individual are respected, in which there is a capitalist economy, and in which the state ensures just preconditions for economic activity and a social safety net, enlightened self-interest may well be the ideal motive. "Enlightened interest is, of course, not the loftiest of motives," Bertrand Russell writes, "but those who decry it often substitute, by accident or design, motives which are much worse, such as hatred, envy, and love of power."[36]

CHAPTER 2
LEARNING TO THINK PHILOSOPHICALLY

Everybody thinks like a philosopher at some point, alone or with friends. You can practice this kind of thinking by consciously learning certain techniques and applying them. Philosophy is asking questions about those things that people take for granted. For example: Why do countries have laws? Why is democracy good? What is good? It's easy to think of philosophical questions, and posing questions is the path to thinking philosophically. But this is not the same as randomly throwing out thoughts or venting opinions. The important thing is to support a position with arguments as best you can, or to counter a position with critical questions. An example of this is the Socratic dialogue. Philosophy and science have a similar structure of argumentation: what counts is presenting arguments supported by evidence. In the natural and social sciences the domain is fixed. Biology studies animate nature, physics and chemistry study inanimate nature, psychology studies the human psyche, and sociology the interaction among people. Philosophy, however, has no fixed domain. Every subject is suitable for philosophical consideration. Philosophy has been the source of many branches of science and quite probably of scientific thinking in general. As soon as philosophers address a subject, as Newton did with mechanics, this subfield is freed to become an independent science. In the course of the centuries, this is how physics, biology, sociology, and psychology came into being. In the twentieth century, the search for artificial intelligence originated in philosophy, but now it is a largely autonomous discipline. Logic, the science of valid argumentation, has been part of philosophy from olden days, since Aristotle, but in the course of the past century it has, through interaction with mathematics and information science, become an independent discipline.

Taking a helicopter view of the world, daring to think about fundamental questions, is not meant for everybody. You need nerve to do it. Who's up for it?

ABOUT PHILOSOPHY

Thinking like a philosopher begins with amazed curiosity. Asking yourself why things are the way they are, why human beings do what they do, why things happens the way they do. This curiosity leads to questions. Questions to yourself: why *is* it like that and not some other way? Questions to others: why are things the way they are? When free inquiry is not hampered, curiosity sets into motion a process that is called philosophical thinking and that partly overlaps science. All the same, curiosity and the investigations it inspires are not enough. After all, some people are curious about and amazed by crop circles, UFO's, ghosts, gnomes, and other "mysterious" phenomena. People who are curious about these sorts of things tend to look for a supernatural explanation and to accept it readily. Extraordinary claims require extraordinary proof, however: a blurry photo of something that resembles a flying saucer does not prove that earth is being visited by aliens. Ideally, rational consideration and a rigorous scientific method keep us from straying outside the natural framework. A rational, logical-empirical, scientific method is essential for philosophical thinking. Critical thinking is essential for philosophy. In nonscientific matters, such as ethical questions, or in areas where science cannot provide an answer, philosophical thinking is the correlation of all relevant information and the weighing of the arguments.

Philosophy is diametrically opposed to religion. Strangely

enough, this is not an undisputed statement. There are people who call themselves philosophers and are at the same time believers. Philosophy is rooted in rational consideration and the acceptance of propositions on the basis of a sufficient number of strong arguments. And these don't exist for religion. Faith means accepting things as true for which sufficient proof happens to be absent. Philosophy therefore begins with atheism. A pious philosopher is like a married bachelor. It would be entirely possible to write an alternative history of philosophy that left out philosophers whose view of religion was positive. The French philosopher Michel Onfray did something comparable in his six-volume *Contre-histoire de la philosophie* (*Counter-history of Philosophy*),[1] in which he discusses philosophers who have not neglected "the pleasures of the flesh" the way the dominant currents in Western thought have. I am undertaking to do something similar but from an ethical perspective: which thinkers or activists advocated morally sound causes, such as the equality of men and women, individual freedom, pacifism, veganism, the abolition of slavery, animal welfare, and the protection of nature? This will overlap the traditional history, with figures such as Philo of Alexandria (one of the few philosophers who argued against slavery); Jeremy Bentham (animal rights); John Stuart Mill (individual freedom, women's rights); Bertrand Russell (opposition to nuclear arms); and Peter Singer (animal welfare, war against poverty); but also other names such as Olympe de Gouge and Harriet Taylor (women's emancipation); Vera Brittain (opposition to the Allied bombing of cities during the Second World War); John Muir, Aldo Leopold, Bill McKibben, and Arne Naess (human-environment relations); Henry Spira (animal welfare); Dos Winkel (sea life conservation); and Paul Watson and his struggle against whaling.

Science and religion are fire and water. But the human intellect is capable of accommodating huge inconsistencies, and so it can happen that people who excel in scientific research are nevertheless religious. The phenomenon of combining two mutually exclusive systems of thought is known in psychology as cognitive dissonance.

People search for rationalizations in order to justify the inconsistencies and contradictions that exist. The biologist Stephen Jay Gould has suggested that science and religion deal with different subjects, the so-called nonoverlapping magisteria (NOMA). According to Gould, the sciences deal with the world and religion deals with meaning and morals.[2] But even superficial examination of this suggestion reveals that it cuts no intellectual ice but is, rather, a politically correct sop to believers. Many religions do have the presumption to make pronouncements about how the world fits together and how it came into being. From the religious side there is opposition to the theory of evolution, because believers are of the opinion that this is in conflict with the story of creation. To assign meaning and ethics to religion is to sell your soul to the devil, as it were. Religion does not exactly have a good name with respect to ethics; think of the centuries of the Inquisition, censure of the arts and sciences, discrimination against and oppression of women and homosexuals, the indoctrination of children and the exclusion of other religious groups. In itself science can't help with questions of meaning (from a scientific perspective life is ultimately meaningless) or with ethics. Science can only try to explain ethical and moral acts at several levels, from the standpoint of biology, neurology, sociology, psychology, anthropology, and history. By itself science can't design a system of normative ethics. It is up to everyone to discover what is right and wrong, and how to live with each other in the best possible way. Science can help provide knowledge about the nature of human beings. Ethicists are specialists in thinking about moral problems, about what is good and bad, and how we can live together successfully. However, ethicists have no authority. At most they can try to shore up their propositions as best they can with arguments that will stand the test of critical evaluation.

Philosophy is a meta-reflection on the foundations and philosophical consequences of the various sciences. The history of philosophy is one of the places where solutions to problems can be found. The chances are small, however, that it will offer much help with respect to the problem of the environment. After all, the history of philosophy is a history of errors. Either the questions were mistaken or nonsensical, or the answers were wrong or unjust. Above all, the history of philosophy shows us how *not* to do things. Easily the largest part of philosophy is hogwash, crazy, and often dangerous nonsense. Those who want to know how the world works would be well-advised not to study the history of philosophy. Studying the natural sciences, or even reading works of popular science, such as Bill Bryson's *A Short History of Nearly Everything* (2005) or Christopher Lloyd's *What on Earth Happened?* (2008), offers a better approach to insight into the world. An exception to this general rule is the excellent historical introduction to philosophy offered by the Ghent University philosophers Etienne Vermeersch and Johan Braeckman. In their 2008 book *De rivier van Herakleitos* (*The River of Heraclitus: A Freethinking History of Philosophy*) they show what we can learn from all those mistakes and glean wisdom from the nonsense. The history of philosophy is the history of human thought throughout the centuries. Many moral philosophers from both past and present are downright dangerous. Plato sought a totalitarian state ruled by philosophers; Augustine favored a Christian theocracy in the style of the Taliban. Nietzsche loathed democracy; Heidegger was a Nazi philosopher. Those who think about ethics are often prone to totalitarian tendencies.[3]

Another way to approach philosophy is systematic or thematic philosophy. The following disciplines are often distinguished from each other: ethics, social and political philosophy, philosophical anthropology, logic, metaphysics, philosophy of science, epistemology, philosophy of mind, esthetics, and applied ethics (which includes environmental philosophy). Aside from this there are many "philosophy of . . ." fields, such as philosophy of biology, mathematics, law, natural sciences, medicine, etc. Systematic philosophy focuses primarily on problems such as what is consciousness? This is a central question in the philosophy of mind. Systematic philosophy does not only look backwards but tries to make a contribution to the solution or in any case clarification of the problem under current consideration. It is unfortunate that many academic philosophers are directed inward. They address the game of philosophy, an academic game that is well removed from the world. The greater part of systematic philosophy has no social relevance.

SCIENTIFIC PHILOSOPHY

Thinking philosophically begins with reflection, and those who reflect on things will discover for themselves that God does not exist. A first step in philosophy is atheism. "Test everything; hold fast to what is good." First Thessalonians 5:21 is the self-referential Bible verse that Vermeersch and Braeckman quote with some irony in their book *The River of Heraclitus*. In their "freethinking" history of philosophy they make it clear that they reject religion. Nevertheless, they are able to find a biblical citation that applies to fervent atheists as well.

Philosophy is the only study whose domain isn't fixed. A person who writes a history of philosophy thereby creates an image of what philosophy was, is, and should be. There are countless definitions of and diverging conceptions about what philosophy is, and these are subject to constant change.

Braeckman and Vermeersch approach philosophy from the rationalistic, scientific perspective of freethinkers. Looking at the history of ideas through this optic makes an exciting image visible. There are many thinkers and ideas that more or less make up the established philosophical canon and that are treated in all overviews. A history of philosophy without Plato, Aristotle, and Immanuel Kant is unthinkable, but the identification of countless scientists, freethinkers, and activists is characteristic of the stimulating approach used by Vermeersch and Braeckman. For example, Albert Einstein and Charles Darwin are presented as philosophers.

Philosophy differs from science in the sense that scientists don't need to know the history of science or of their own specialization. Science is directed to the future: you use the data and conclusions of your immediate predecessors and don't bother with old, superseded ideas. In the case of philosophy it is unthinkable for a practitioner not to have a comprehensive knowledge of the history of the discipline. Knowledge of the history of philosophy is important for two reasons. First of all, in order to be aware of the questions that have been asked, a number of which, notably the nonmetaphysical, are still of interest, such as how should I live? and what is a just society? Second, it is important to find out what errors have been committed. The history of philosophy is largely a chain of failures, especially with respect to the grandiosely failed metaphysical project, occasionally interrupted by important insights, such as the refutation of the rational proofs of God's existence (Kant), the categorical imperative, the philosophical version of the golden rule (also Kant), the idea of toleration (John Locke), the social contract (Locke, Thomas Hobbes, John Rawls), and utilitarianism (Jeremy Bentham and John Stuart Mill). Those who want to go on in the history of philosophy have to guard against the blunders from the past. Pursuing philosophy is like wandering through a maze in search of knowledge and wisdom. The history of philosophy reveals which paths are dead ends so that it is possible to get ever closer to the truth.

According to Braeckman and Vermeersch, "philosophy . . . is the study of problems that we can't yet solve using the scientific method. . . . In philosophy [in contrast with science] you can hardly find a problem that every philosopher would answer in the same way. Philosophers don't even agree about the question of *what* philosophy is and how we should practice it."[4] Yet this definition of philosophy excludes a great deal of what people traditionally understand by philosophy: namely prescriptiveness. Philosophy does not only seek to know what the world is, but also how people should live (together). Ethics, esthetics, and political and social philosophy are outside the reach of this definition of philosophy.

How a society can be put together in the best possible way and what forms part of the good life are questions that can never be answered by means of the scientific method. Of course it is important to use scientific knowledge as input, but prescriptiveness cannot be derived from scientific facts. All the same, the authors devote a lot of attention to ethics. Their case study is slavery.[5] Few figures in the history of thought condemned slavery: "Before the sixteenth century not a single philosophical or religious authority, Jewish, Christian, or Muslim, matched the ethical level of Philo of Alexandria (20 BCE–50 CE), and you can count the exceptions before 1750 on the fingers of one hand."[6]

"Philosophy is always an activity aimed at the acquisition of knowledge," Vermeersch and Braeckman write, "a kind of scientific knowledge in the broad sense of the term."[7] They then provide their definitions of knowledge and science. "As *knowledge* we regard every depiction, every conception, and every conviction about which we can assume that it corresponds to a certain 'reality'. . . . As *science* we understand a human activity aimed at obtaining systematic and trust-worthy knowledge. . . . For parts of their world view, scientists can still feel the need for myths or dogmatic systems."[8] The book is a plea for rationality, freethought, science, and atheism. The authors make every effort to show that there is nothing more on earth and in the universe than can be known through science. They are *scientific naturalists* and explicitly reject all claims for the supernatural, and they are not reticent in attaching concrete conclusions to this: "People who believe in astrology are also irrational because this is in conflict with the undeniable laws of genetics."[9] And they emphasize human credulity: "In the course of history, humankind has given evidence of a distressing credulity, and due to bad habits of thought opinions were disseminated that have caused untold suffering, such as wars of religion, witch hunts, and racism."[10]

The history of mathematics and the sciences gets a lot of attention in the book, and with reason. The sections about the origins and doctrine of Christianity are enlightening. In the light of analytical reason, faith vanishes like snow before the sun. "During the last few decades, that form of scepticism that focuses on the critical analysis of pseudo-sciences, intellectual fallacies, misleading language use and so on, has been developing into an autonomous philosophical discipline that in the Anglo-Saxon world is called *critical thinking*. An example of a manual in this field is Robert Todd Carroll's *Becoming a Critical Thinker*.[11]

In his pioneering 1988 work in environmental ethics, *De ogen van Panda* (*Panda's Eyes*) Vermeersch attributes environmental problems to the trinity of science, technology, and capitalism. He and Braeckman note that this combination has serious negative side-effects: "An essential part of this seems to be the coupling of micro-rationality to macro-irrationality. In solving individual problems the system exhibits an astounding efficiency, but as a total system it is irrational. Its development has no goal of its own and is marked above all by an unlimited expansionary drive even while functioning within a world with limits."[12] Theirs is the first book about the history of philosophy I know that pays broad attention to environmental philosophy, and quite rightly, too. The greatest problem for humanity right now consists of the threat of environmental disasters and the destruction of the ecosystem: ecocide. The authors stake their position out clearly on another issue: "We are of the opinion that the extrapolation from human to animal suffering and from human rights to animal rights can and even must be assimilated into our ethical outlook."[13] They pay even more attention to bioethics, to which they make their own contribution. Just like environmental philosophy and animal ethics, bioethics is a form of applied ethics that has emerged since the 1970s. Within bioethics there are many collisions between philosophy and religion. Vermeersch has made himself useful by successfully working for the liberalization of euthanasia legislation in Belgium. The book correctly points to the pernicious influence exercised by the Roman Catholic Church: in 1968 Pope Paul VI issued the encyclical *Humanae Vitae* "which re-emphasized that all means of contraception (with the exception of periodic abstention) were morally inadmissible."[14]

ALL HANDS ON DECK

Does philosophy have a "most important problem"? In any case, there is the approaching ecological crisis that will threaten humanity as a whole in the near future. Many philosophers are facing backward: with their gaze fixed on past philosophers; they don't see what lies ahead. It is time for philosophers to turn around and to spot the abyss we are heading for. The traditional big questions of philosophy, such as what is knowledge? what is true? what exists?, what is consciousness?, what is the good?, what is the meaning of life? and "who am I? all take second place to that one great common problem, the ecological disasters that threaten us. Philosophers should leave Martin Heidegger and Thomas Aquinas and Plato and David Hume and Friedrich Nietzsche and Jean-Paul Sartre and Jacques Derrida for what they are—why are there ever more new monographs about persons who have already been described *ad nauseam?*—and turn their attention toward environmental philosophy and activism. The alarm bells are ringing. We are faced with the greatest problem that has ever confronted humankind: the destruction of the ecosystem of the earth by human action. Everyone will have to help: both by drastically adjusting our lifestyles and by helping to look for solutions. If philosophy is supposed to concern itself with a consideration of the most fundamental problems but fails to concern itself or barely concerns itself with the problem of the environment, then philosophy is irrelevant to the highest degree. Only a small number of academic philosophers are concerned with environmental philosophy. It's time to wake up. The realization that we are headed for our collective destruction has not yet penetrated to the musty library of the Titanic. Because of their disinterestedness, philosophers should be particularly well situated to make a contribution to the solutions. Moreover, science itself cannot create normativeness. It is important that people think sensibly about norms and values, without reverting to all kinds of nonsense, such as religion. As soon as the coast is clear, and I doubt that will be the case, philosophers will be able to pick up the thread of their work and puzzle about the "the Beingness of beings" and the deconstruction of texts. It is as though we are at war, when everyone works together in solidarity to defeat the enemy. In effect we are at war now, only the enemy is inside us, in our way of producing and consuming. As cartoonist Walt Kelly's Pogo says: "We have met the enemy and he is us."[15] The crisis is here, and all hands must be on deck to help. Or are we fatalists who believe that fate cannot be averted and that we will go down, wearing blinkers while we party? I, however, am pleading for an "all hands on deck" approach to philosophy. Philosophers ought to exert themselves *en masse* to help solve the environmental crisis.

THE *MAN-ON-THE-MOON* PARABLE

In 1961 President John F. Kennedy delivered a famous speech in which he said that he wanted to see a man on the moon within a decade.[16] *Man on the moon* was a clear message, an enormous budget was available for it, and it became perhaps the greatest technological project ever, to which many thousands of people contributed. And it succeeded: on July 20, 1969, two men stood on the moon. A similar project should now be started to discover and develop durable sources of energy, or to make solar or wind energy cost-effective. Hope is focused on President Barack Obama and his positive, inspiring slogan: *Yes, we can!*

HOW TO BECOME A PHILOSOPHER WITHOUT READING KANT

"Enlightenment is man's emergence from his self-imposed nonage. Nonage is the inability to use one's own understanding without another's guidance. This nonage is self-imposed if its cause lies not in lack of understanding but in indecision and lack of courage to use one's own mind without another's guidance. *Dare to know!* (*Sapere aude*). 'Have the courage to use your own understanding,' is therefore the motto of the Enlightenment. Laziness and cowardice are the reasons why such a large part of mankind gladly remain minors all their lives, long after nature has freed them from external guidance. They are the reasons why it is so easy for others to set themselves up as guardians. It is so comfortable to be a minor. If I have a book that thinks for me, a pastor who acts as my conscience, a physician who describes my diet, and so on—then I have no need to exert myself."[17]

This is the beginning of Immanuel Kant's famous essay: *Answer to the Question: What Is Enlightenment?* Written in 1784, it not only expresses the essence of philosophy but also exhorts people for once to think for themselves. To respond to this exhortation is the Enlightenment project. But how do you go about thinking for yourself?

It isn't necessary to have a thorough knowledge of the history of philosophy in order to think philosophically yourself. Knowledge of the history of philosophy *is* required if you want to join in the academic game of philosophizing. A good construction worker doesn't need to be aware of the history of his craft from the ancient Egyptians to the present. By thinking philosophically I mean critical thought about claims to knowledge and about the good life. A philosopher is a critical thinker who does not allow himself to be tempted into transcendental nonsense or unethical practices. What follows is a mini-course: learning how to think philosophically in ten steps.

1. *Think: sapere aude* (dare to know). The essence of philosophy is thinking independently and critically, and forming a judgment on the basis of considered arguments. Critical thought and reflection are difficult. Perhaps they are even unnatural. It is much easier not to think, or at least not to think deeply, about consequences, alternatives, the long term, justification, coherence, consistency, logical validity, desirability, etc. Thinking is less a question of "being able to" than of "daring to." Very intelligent, highly educated people

can do stupid, immoral things. Less highly educated people, on the other hand, can quite possibly lead ethical lives, without paying heed to religion and the whole supernatural kit and caboodle. You must dare to think.

2. *Look*: look for information. Be open to what you accidentally come across (serendipity), and think about how and where you look for information. Heuristics is the study of information-finding. This is an important skill that deserves a prominent place in the curriculum. Students should be able to look for information on their own and to be able to judge the trustworthiness of sources.

3. *Read*: read widely, various newspapers, magazines, fiction and nonfiction, join book clubs. Wisdom doesn't drop from the sky. Critical thought is like athletics, maybe even at the highest level. Reading is a key form of training, but it has to be both critical and extensive. Reading should serve the purpose of broadening your horizons, of acquiring knowledge about the world. A book club can be a stimulant to read books and reflect on them. You can get more out of a book if you reflect on it, think about it, write about it, or discuss it. It's important to read widely rather than reading a lot about a single subject. For specialized scholars, too, those who know a lot about a little, it's important to look beyond the horizon of their own field. Yet it's not the case that everything is equally valuable. Those who want to think philosophically would do well to read journals of opinion, book reviews, and to keep track of the state of knowledge or in any case to know what's current. This can be done, for example, by reading *Nature*, *New Scientist*, or *Scientific American*.[18]

4. *Discuss*: discussion programs, discussion evenings, well-ordered discussion offer the possibility of adjusting your opinions and weighing arguments.

5. *Associate*: make *mind maps*,[19] think freely, brainstorm. Think outside the box. Our socialization can limit our horizon of

possibilities. It is important to dare to think outside traditional categories. Thinking is hard work. Thinking freely is an attitude to life.

6. *Analyze*: make a list of your arguments. Weigh these arguments. Check the meaning of words. Beware of ambiguity.

7. *Argue*: use good arguments. Think about logic and persuasiveness (rhetoric).

8. *Reflect*: create distance from your subject. Look at it in as many ways as you possibly can. Look for information and counterarguments. Try to make the strongest possible case for your opponent and for the interpretation of his or her arguments.

9. *Reconsider*: remember that knowledge is liable to error. Ask yourself: is it really this way? Long-cherished ideas can be mistaken, too, and long-established patterns of behavior can be morally wrong.

10. *Act*: Adjust your actions in accordance with your arguments. Thinking philosophically in such a way that it has no real effect on your life is just spinning fantasies. Is thinking and reflecting any use if you know before you begin that it won't change your behavior? Arguments have only limited power in bringing about behavioral changes. Social psychology would be useful here in finding effective ways of making people change their behavior.

THINKING PHILOSOPHICALLY IS NOT "ANYTHING GOES"

I am consistent and tenacious in my views, just as scientists are tenacious and consistent, and accept propositions only when the evidence for them is sufficient. People who are not consistent or logical will never get very far with deductive argumentation. My argument seems to fit into the Karl Popper–Paul Feyerabend antithesis and opposes the latter's maxim of "anything goes." According to Feyerabend, new theories (and he does not make a difference between scientific and non-scientific theories) come to be accepted not because of their accord with some scientific method, but because their supporters make use of any trick—rational, irrational, rhetorical—in order to advance their cause, and thus Feyerabend argues that there is no superior scientific method but that de facto 'anything goes' as a theory insofar as people believe in it. I am consistent not only in scholarship, but also in ethics and political philosophy. My basic premise or point of departure is: it is not permissible to tolerate intolerance. That is my "dogma," which cannot be tampered with. Individual freedom is the core value. That value is not transcendentally grounded, but is justified by simply imagining that you yourself are the one whose freedom of action is hindered by the beliefs of the group. Suppose you are gay in a rigidly religious environment, whether Christian, Muslim, or Jewish: all are equally intolerant with respect to homosexuality.

My point of departure where politics are concerned is that an open society that guarantees individual freedom is superior to other forms of social organization that do not do this. In that sense I am consistent, and, to adopt a sobriquet: an Enlightenment fundamentalist,[20] in the sense that all mathematicians are fundamentalists because they consistently observe the axioms. Thinking philosophically is not "anything goes."

LAWS, RULES, AND TRAFFIC REGULATIONS

Why do laws and rules exist at all? Would it not be a lot more pleasant if we were liberated from laws and rules? Without rules, after all, everybody can decide for themselves what they will do. They could choose to wear or not wear a seatbelt in the car. Traffic lights could simply be viewed as decorative lamps. Speed limits would be for each of us to decide. Taxation is theft: that, in any case, is the view of libertarians. Anarchists believe we are better off without the state and its laws and regulations.

Ideally, rules and laws exist so that we can live together as a group in the best and most just way possible.[21] Rules and laws are means of effectively regulating human society so that everyone is better off. Rules are made by people for people in the here and now. Lawyers sometimes tend to forget that rules are made by and for people and are not end in themselves. Alas, not even the Netherlands is an ideal society, and there are rules and laws that don't work or are even unjust, such as Article 23 of the Dutch Constitution dealing with the freedom and funding of faith-based education.

There are countries and regions, such as Egypt and southern Italy, where traffic regulations are regarded as optional. And on long stretches of the German *Autobahn* there is no speed limit. That does come at a price in the number of traffic fatalities and accidents. Someone who gets a ticket for driving at 60 mph in a 50 mph zone is apt to comment that the police, who supervise the observance of the regulations, exist chiefly to annoy people. "Why don't they go after the real speed demons?" But the speed demon who zips along the highway at 160 mph and is stopped by the police is apt to say: "Why are you stopping me? I was driving fast, but I was driving safely, and there was no one else on the road."

The Tragedy of Pluralism

Why do people on the continent of Europe drive on the right side? Why do all people there drive on the right, while in England—also part of the European Union—people drive on the left? This is an interesting question philosophically. Whether we drive on the left or on the right: it really makes no difference. It's a matter of what you are used to. The choice is has no moral significance. All the same, it is absolutely essential for people to be in agreement. Without a clear consensus about whether people drive on the left side or the right, chaos and accidents will result. Whether North American Indians who are walking along narrow paths have rules governing right-of-way when they pass each other is an interesting question. It would be a good subject for research in comparative anthropology. Wrong-way drivers on the highway are people who have made a mistake, usually with disastrous consequences. So we must choose a side. In the Netherlands and the United States, among other countries, it is the right side. In Britain and some former British colonies, it is left. It is tricky and dangerous to leave Saint Pancras Station in London, the Eurostar terminal, and cross the street, with traffic coming not from the left but from the right. And driving in England, if you come from a country where people drive on the right, is even more difficult. You constantly have to remind yourself to keep left. Your so-called muscle memory, that part of your memory that governs actions you have performed so often that you can do them without thinking, has a tendency to direct you to the right side of the road. Only staying actively aware can prevent this.

Wouldn't it be more convenient if everyone on earth drove on the same side of the road? And what if we had the same railway gauge, and uniformity with respect to currency, language, and rules? Yes, it might be a lot more convenient! As a dictator Napoleon could impose uniformity within his empire, such as the metric system and the legal code. Arranging matters from the top has its advantages. With democratic consultation things move laboriously. However, the introduction of the euro is a successful counterexample of how international agreement can be reached without a dictator. Without a dictator, but with the institutionalized international consultation structure of the European Union, a large number of European states have surrendered their national currencies in order to introduce the euro. But cooperation among different countries and groups is difficult. You could call this the *tragedy of pluralism.* Every nation decides for itself, without taking account of everyone's perspective. Each is for itself; none is for all. How much better could matters be arranged if agreements could be made at the global level to make things more uniform, so that international and transnational cooperation could proceed more smoothly, and people could really feel themselves to be citizens of the world?

Imagine for a moment that the United Nations decided that everyone should drive on the right. Very nice, we would say, now we can cross the road more safely at Saint Pancras Station, and we can drive more easily in Britain and Japan. But the Japanese and British would be angry: "Now our steering wheel is on the wrong side! Surely we can't all be expected to buy a new car on the spot, with the steering wheel on the other side, and change our entire infrastructure? That can't be done, it's impossible! Why don't *you* start driving on the left?" This is the tragedy and the trap of the historical fact: a preexisting structure exists that is hard to change. It would be easier to start from scratch. Or, like Napoleon, to be able to assert your will. But that can't be done. The result is that the world is organized much less conveniently than it might be.

A NEW GOLDEN RULE

In a number of religions the idea of the golden rule is an important ethical principle. This rule is: "Don't do to others what you would not have them do to you." So if you don't want other people to steal from you, you yourself shouldn't steal from others.

It is interesting to note that the golden rule, in the Christian version as in others, does not refer to a god. The golden rule puts the individual at the center. The subject, the central and fixed point of ethical action, is put into another person's shoes. The golden rule is a subjectivist ethical theory. Very different from that other ethical theory that is central in the Abrahamic religions: the divine command theory in which God commands Abraham to sacrifice his oldest son Isaac:

And he said, "Take your son, your only son Isaac, whom you love, and go to the land of Moriah, and offer him there as a burnt offering on one of the mountains that I will show you." So Abraham rose early in the morning, saddled his donkey, and took two of his young men with him, and his son Isaac; he cut the wood for the burnt offering, and set out and went to the place in the distance that God had shown him. . . .

Then Abraham reached out his hand and took the knife to kill his son. But the angel of the LORD called to him from heaven, and said, "Abraham, Abraham!" And he said, "Here I am." He said, "Do not lay your hand on the boy or do anything to him; for now I know that you fear God, since you have not withheld your son, your only son, from me."[22]

At the moment that Abraham is about to kill his own son as a sacrifice, an angel comes between them to restrain Abraham. Instead of his son he is allowed to sacrifice a ram that god has supplied. If we apply the golden rule to Abraham's action, we get this: "Don't do to others what you would not have them do to you." Suppose that the roles had been reversed and that Isaac would have to sacrifice Abraham, would Abraham have wanted this? It could be that Abraham would have had the kind of slave mentality that would have caused him to say: "If God asks my son to sacrifice me then I want it, too." Although it is possible that people exist who have this extreme sadomasochistic tendency, the vast majority of people will not want to be sacrificed to a god.

The golden rule appears in Judaism, Christianity, Islam, and Confucianism. Well may you ask yourself why there is nevertheless so much discord in the world. The golden rule has a positive (GR+) and negative (GR–) version. The negative version is best. An example of the positive version is: I would like the people I meet to massage my neck and shoulders. So, my wish would be for all people, when they meet, to massage each other's necks and shoulders. That is great so long as everyone likes it, but it becomes problematic when someone doesn't like it. In Japan it is actually quite common for colleagues to massage each other's necks, shoulders, and even hands. The positive version states: "Do to others what you would have others do to you." Even more problematic examples can be imagined. Suppose a man says: "I want to have sex with every attractive woman I meet," and he tries to have sex with attractive women. This fellow will be guilty of harassment if not outright rape. This is because he does not respect the wishes of others, and perhaps he cannot imagine that a woman may not want to have sex with men she doesn't know. Applying the positive version of the golden rule means imposing your own will, wishes, and preferences on others. That is coercion.

A great many cultures and traditions take their departure from this positive formulation but apply it by the group against the individual: "We consider homosexuality to be depraved, so you're not allowed to be gay." Or: "We, your parents, consider religion to be very important, so you, our child, have to observe the rules of our faith."

So, although the principle of the golden rule, including the negative version (i.e., the ethically sound version), has been known for centuries and even millennia in various cultures, the positive or paternalistic form often dominates. As well, the golden rule is generally applied to one's own group and is not valid for outsiders. Believers are often not especially kind to those of other faiths or to nonbelievers, or to those who fall outside the prescribed pattern, such as homosexuals.

Yes, the story of the Good Samaritan, who is prepared to help a stranger in need, does indeed appear in the Bible.[23] It is remarkable that this parable plays an important role in Christian ethics, because the Samaritan is *not a Christian*. A non-Christian thus serves as the preeminent example of Christian morality.

Not until the liberal tradition, beginning with the Enlightenment of the eighteenth century, and more particularly in the nineteenth century in the work of the philosopher John Stuart Mill (1806–1873), is the individual placed at the center, above the group. A morality that is not individualistic can easily repress individuals. Individualism is a necessary condition for true morality: it ought to proceed from the individual. Morality has to do with how people can live together in the best possible way. In the liberal tradition, in which the point of departure is individual freedom, morality means looking for rules that guarantee that all individuals who live together, or have to get along with each other, possess the largest possible measure of freedom. Some rules are essential given the logic of the situation: as I said, everyone needs to drive on a previously determined side of the road. This "denial of freedom," namely, requiring all drivers to use the left or the right side, guarantees the freedom of all individuals. But a rule like "red automobiles are prohibited," or "everyone must drive a Buick" unnecessarily limits that freedom. The first kind of rule, about which side to drive on, is an ethically relevant rule, just as rules and regulations about traffic safety are ethically relevant. The second kind of rule, about color and make of automobile, has no ethical relevance and is therefore unethical. Suppose I dislike red cars or have a financial stake in General Motors, do these reasons entitle me to force such rules on everyone? Yet that is what happens often, in fact too often. There are people who object to nudity, often basing this on religious grounds, and so there many countries that censure cultural expressions such as film and the visual arts with that objection in mind. The liberal position is totally different: as long as others are not interfered with in their freedom, everything is permitted, even things you yourself may not consider agreeable.

A Virtual Museum of Offending Arts and Censorship that illustrates this problem particularly clearly has been in existence since 2008.[24] Displayed in this virtual museum are works of art that have met two criteria: (1) they have given rise to controversy because people have been angered by them or have felt wounded or insulted; (2) there have been demands that they be censored. The offended often call for censorship and, ever more often, they are being listened to. But not everyone needs to think that a piece of art is beautiful or pleasant. Art may be wounding, insulting, or ugly, as long as people have the freedom not to be confronted with it excessively. Museums are open to people who choose to enter them, and as a visitor to a museum you run the risk of being confronted with something you would rather not have seen. In public spaces the issue is a bit more difficult. An enormous poster of a woman in a sexy bikini was displayed in Utrecht's city center a while ago. Some people, the members of a Christian student group in Utrecht, for example, found this offensive. It was difficult if not impossible to walk through the center of Utrecht without seeing the poster. You could just walk past it and shrug your shoulders, but some people got genuinely angry and did not wish to see such an "indecent" image, at least not in a public space. Are there limits to what may be shown in public? If it had been a really pornographic image, the protests would have been much stronger. In fact, the city would not have granted permission to display the poster. All the same, a right-thinking liberal would have said: so what? If you don't like it, just look the other way. Yet there is a degree of consensus about what is and is not permitted. In much of the "Western world," the opinions of religious people tend to deviate from what the majority considers acceptable.

Some liberals are of the opinion that just about anything should be tolerated in a public space. The only limit is that there must be no incitement to or threat of violence. That is absolutely not allowed. If this conception were to dominate, it would mean that in public spaces, on the streets, for example, you could be confronted with all kinds of images that you might find ugly, revolting, or offensive. As well, people might be able to do things in public that you would rather not see, public sexual intercourse, for instance. Most people, including a large number of liberals, would, after consulting each other, want to put some constraints on freedom of expression—but as little as possible.

One big difference of opinion has to do with places where gays can connect with each other. Religious people often consider these people to be depraved and are of the opinion that the authorities should prohibit them from interacting. Liberals are generally of the view that these persons should be able to decide for themselves if they want to have sex with each other in public places, but that the activity should not cause a nuisance to third parties. For example, it is inappropriate for such an area to be placed close to a children's play-ground in a public park. Moralists who want to impose their personal views on others, often because of religious conviction, would just as soon limit the freedom of individuals. Liberals would like to expand that freedom as much as possible. In practice attempts are made to create facilities for as great a variety of people as possible, including minorities. In many countries there is a subculture of nudists. In the Netherlands the authorities have set aside areas for nudist recreation on many of the North Sea beaches. In this way people who have an aversion to nakedness are not confronted with it, and people who enjoy walking around in the altogether have the opportunity to do so. The degree to which public provision is made for naturists is, in fact, a simple indicator of the degree to which a country is liberal and feels strongly about promoting individual freedom.[25] The same applies to women's topless sunbathing. In many countries this is subject to social taboos or even legal prohibition. Liberals say: it's up to women themselves to decide whether or not they want to wear a bikini top.

A large measure of individual freedom requires citizens to be able to deal with the freedom of others. People with a cultural background that pays little respect to individual freedom may sometimes have problems with the freedom of others. A distressing example is provided by physical attacks on gays by those—in the Netherlands they are often Moroccan youths—who disapprove of homosexuality. You're free to dislike homosexuality and you're free to state your opinion publicly, so long as you do not incite others to violence, but you're not free to molest gays. Another example is the verbal abuse directed by Moroccan youths in the Netherlands against topless sunbathing women. In this way they seek to restrict the freedom of women to determine for themselves how they want to sunbathe.

CHAPTER 3
UNIVERSAL SUBJECTIVISM AS THOUGHT EXPERIMENT

INTRODUCTION

John Rawls (1921–2002) is regarded as one of the most important philosophers of the twentieth century.[1] His greatest contribution is in the area of political philosophy. Characteristic of Rawls's work is the central position it gives to justice. This is true not only of his book *A Theory of Justice* (1971), but the call or the need for justice resounds in almost all his ideas. Rawls challenges his readers to think outside customary patterns, and for this purpose he uses the powerful instrument of the thought experiment. Rawls has designed a procedure to discover what justice is. The important thing is *procedural justice.* Rawls is an example of a philosopher's philosopher: unknown to lay people but known to all philosophers. With his political theory Rawls revitalized political philosophy and, above all, in combination with the Kantian idea of universal rules, the idea of a social contract. His theories are widely known among philosophers, but his books do not make for easy reading. Along with Karl Popper's *The Open Society and Its Enemies,* Rawls's book is a major contribution to twentieth-century political philosophy. The book is written in a rather inaccessible academic style, but his theory of justice is simple to explain and understand. Since the book's publication an entire Rawls school has come into existence. Every political philosopher has to take a position with respect to Rawls, whether for or against. Rawls designed the equipment and used it to construct a theory. It is possible to use Rawls's equipment to construct a larger, more inclusive theory. He himself applied his theory in a rather conservative fashion.

Peter Singer (1946–) is the most important philosopher of the twenty-first century.[2] He is one of the founders of applied philosophy, which has come strongly to the fore since the 1970s. He uses philosophy to improve the world. Singer shows in a disquieting way that the way of life of most people is unethical. His thought is a reevaluation of all values. First he tracks down distress and tries to dissolve it, both theoretically by designing a methodology and concretely through activism. At present he is the Ira W. DeCamp Professor of Bioethics at Princeton University. The method Singer uses is preference utilitarianism: good is what an individual considers to be good, bad what an individual considers to be bad. The point is that suffering is bad and pleasure good. Singer's method is therefore what I call pathocentric (from the Greek *pathos* meaning suffering or pain). The capacity to suffer is central. Wherever it is found and whoever experiences it, suffering is bad. Not all suffering can be avoided, but you can try to prevent as much of it as possible. Singer's approach can be compared to a lighthouse at night, with the lamp turning in the darkness. The rotating lamp is the preference utilitarianism that is being used to look for suffering. He writes: "I approach each issue by seeking the solution that has the best consequences for all affected. By 'best consequences' I understand that which satisfies the most preferences, weighted in accordance with the strength of the preferences."[3] In this way Singer keeps changing his focus, but always approaches his subject from the same perspective. He has shone his light on issues such as abortion and active as well as passive euthanasia, and on animal suffering, in the book *Animal Liberation*[4] and a series of books written in its wake. "Species is, in itself, as irrelevant to moral status as race or sex," he states. "Hence all beings with interests are entitled to equal consideration: that is, we should not give their interests any less consideration than we give to the similar interests of members of our own species. Taken seriously, this conclusion requires radical changes in almost every interaction we have with animals, including our diet, our economy, and our relations with the natural environment."[5] Singer also deals with environmental problems and future generations, notably in his book *One World*.[6] His recent book *The Life You Can Save* deals with the moral duty of the rich (including you and me) to donate a substantial part of our incomes in order to alleviate extreme poverty.[7] Singer wants us to improve the world. "In the world as it is now, I see no escape from the conclusion that each one of us with wealth surplus to his or her essential needs should be giving most of it to help people suffering from poverty so dire as to be life-threatening. That's right: I'm saying that you shouldn't buy that new car, take that cruise, redecorate the house or get that pricey new suit. After all, a $1,000 suit could save five children's lives."[8] Also: "If it is in our power to prevent something bad from happening, without thereby sacrificing anything of comparable moral importance, we ought, morally, to do it. By 'without sacrificing anything of comparable moral importance' I mean without causing anything else comparably bad to happen, or doing something that is wrong in itself, or failing to promote some moral good, comparable in significance to the bad thing we can prevent."[9] Singer's way of thinking philosophically leads to activism and changing your life to a more ethical one: "Discussion, though, is not enough. What is the point of relating philosophy to public (and personal) affairs if we do not take our conclusions seriously? In this instance, taking our conclusion seriously means acting upon it. The philosopher will not find it any easier than anyone else to alter his attitudes and way of life to the extent that, if I am right, is involved in doing everything that we ought to be doing. At the very least, though, one can make a start. The philosopher who does so will have to sacrifice some of the benefits of the consumer society, but he [*sic*] can find compensation in the satisfaction of a way of life in which theory and practice, if not yet in harmony, are at least coming together."[10] Taking Singer's arguments seriously leads, among other things, to veganism, opposition to most experiments on animals, donating a large part of one's income to the war on poverty, atheism, being pro-choice in abortion (advocating self-determination of women), pro-euthanasia, cosmopolitanism, and environmental activism.

Rawls Plus Singer

My theory of universal subjectivism is an expansion of Rawls's theory, in which the philosophy of Peter Singer has been taken into account. Universal subjectivism = Rawls + Singer.

Imagine that you yourself alone are able to decide how society is organized. You can determine what the laws and rules are, how taxes are collected, what institutions should exist, and how these are organized. You can regulate everything that can possibly be regulated. You have an enormous control panel within reach with all sorts of dials and levers. For example, there is a dial marked "taxation" that you can turn higher or lower, and a dial marked "social welfare." There are large dials and small dials for fine-tuning. For example, the age at which people are entitled to retire with a pension is a matter for fine-tuning. There is a dial for everything you can think up and make up rules for. You're sitting in the sky box behind the control panel and you adjust the parameters of society according to your own opinions. There is, however, one important fact: it is certain that you yourself will land in the society you have organized, but you don't know in what capacity. The thought experiment invites you to arrange the society in the best possible way, keeping account of the worst imaginable situations. The task is to maximize or optimize the conditions of those in the worst possible (minimal) situations. In political philosophy this is referred to as the maximin strategy.

There are four possible strategies for setting the dials: (1) minimin (those in the least privileged positions are worst off); (2) maximax (those in the most privileged positions are best off; this can be coupled with minimin); (3) minimax (the minimization of the maximum, which in theory is the strategy of communism; equality has to be achieved to the greatest possible extent, with the result that those who are most privileged get the least); (4) maximin (the maximization of the minima). This last possibility is the strategy of Rawls, one I follow (with a different interpretation of which people are "min"). Rawls sharpens the maximin strategy with the difference principle: inequalities among people can only be justified when those who are in the worst situations benefit from the inequalities.[11]

WHY ACT ETHICALLY?

Ethics is the search for the good life: how should I live? It is entirely possible to go through life without ever entertaining a moment of ethical reflection. But if it is possible to live without ethical considerations, why should I think about good and evil at all? Well, because life can be better, more just, finer, and happier than it is without ethical reflection. But what if I am happy and content, what reason do I have for reflecting ethically? It is difficult to persuade a nihilistic cultural relativist. Someone like that might say: "I don't approve of the way women are treated in Saudi Arabia, but that is just my opinion. Ethics is also merely an opinion. Anyway, there are lots of ethical theories that differ from each other about what is good and bad. Ethics solves nothing and leads to nothing. Why should I get worked up about ethics?" The only thing persons like that get worked up about is the maintenance of their lifestyles. Resistance to thinking is a common reaction.

Why should anyone carry out this thought experiment of universal subjectivism? If you are conscious of the fortuitousness of fate, then you can try to make the world more just by means of the procedure of universal subjectivism, *because you might have been the one stuck in a wretched situation.* Hypothetically you could have been in one of the worst possible situations yourself. Many people don't realize the ethical consequences of the coincidental nature of their fortunate existence; they are not prepared to surrender their privileges. Not wanting to apply this model means an end to or in any case a serious limitation of the ethical dialogue. Whether you want to become part of the ethical dialogue or not is a personal choice. It's a choice that everyone can and must make.

Education, and especially ethical education, is crucial. It is important to be able to imagine yourself in someone else's situation. How can this be done better than by reading literature? When you read a novel, you see the world through the eyes of a character in a book. You see and experience the world as it is seen from another person's perspective. If you can do this yourself, you can play the game and see the world from different perspectives.

Interesting documentaries are being made about all the things that are going wrong in the world. A good documentary makes a problem understandable. One way of doing that is to give scientific or scholarly experts the opportunity to speak, to add quantitative content, and to show the problem as explicitly as possible, with lots of detail. Documentaries can exhibit what is hidden, and they provide information. Nondocumentary films, on the other hand, can express social relations effectively and strengthen empathy with individuals.

The documentary *Our Daily Bread* (2005), for example, exhibits in an esthetic way the origins of a number of important food products. And that is quite shocking. It shows how animals who provide our meat are dealt with, and how tomatoes are cultivated industrially. The taste of vegetables and fruit vanishes, but they look good. And so the consumer buys them.

In *We Feed the World* (2005) we are shown how poor farmers in northern Brazil go hungry, even though the soil is fertile, because the big companies grow only soy beans, and how vegetables and fruits from Europe are dumped at low prices in African markets, so that African farmers can't sell their products. European farmers are still being subsidized to a scandalous extent by their respective governments. Discrimination may be illegal, and other than US presidents few will say it, but European governments act on the dictum: our own people come first. They couldn't care less that people in other countries and future generations will be the victims of their actions. In many ways the European Union is a fort—Fort Europe— in which the rich robber barons make common cause in order to be better prepared for their raids and to be able to compete better with other robber barons, most notably the United States.

To see the world from someone else's perspective is one thing, to feel empathy, putting oneself in someone else's shoes, is something else altogether. Operating from the perspective of universal subjectivism, you don't need to feel sympathy for someone else's fate, but only with your own fate, which can be anything at all. You need empathy to be able to prepare yourself for the worst possible positions. Sympathy you need to feel only for yourself. Universal subjectivism takes the moral importance of coincidence seriously.

Using examples, I shall show how universal subjectivism works. The examples of the worst possible situations are: being handicapped, living in a misogynist society, being homosexual, living as an animal in factory farming, and belonging to future generations.

THE EXPANDING CIRCLE OF MORALITY

Morality, or "principles of right and wrong in conduct," according to *Webster's Dictionary*, is often exclusive and applies only to a limited group. In some cultures a collection of healthy adult males from the same group (tribe or clan) count as the basis of moral status. Women, children, the handicapped, and people from other groups don't fall within the circle of morality. In his book *The Expanding Circle* (1981) Peter Singer points out that the history of humanity can be seen as an expanding circle in which, like a balloon, the circle can keep collapsing into a small core. In the course of history morality has expanded slowly and by small steps, and that process, in ideological terms as well as in practice, is still ongoing. In the often

admired Athenian democracy the circle of morality was limited to
a select group of adult, well-to-do, male citizens. Women, children,
slaves, and non-Athenians who lived in Athens, often for generations,
were excluded from the political order and had only a derived moral
status, in so far as it suited the male rulers. The course of history
exhibits long periods of stagnation, such as the Middle Ages, as well
as spurts of change during which the circle of morality expands.
With the French Revolution came the idea that all citizens are equal
before the law, as against aristocratic privileges. As well, slavery was
abolished in differing stages. At the outset of the twentieth century
the realization emerged that women are morally equal to men.
Some time passed before this translated itself into constitutional
reforms and women were both passively and actively enfranchised.
In democratic societies women have gained the vote, but the
proportion of female rulers (presidents or cabinet ministers) falls
far short of the 50 percent one might expect. Even the elimination
of institutionalized inequality is not enough to end the existing
inequality. The moral and thus legal equality of all human beings,
irrespective of which country they happen to have been born in, was
finally recognized in 1948. This Universal Declaration of Human
Rights is a milestone in the history of humanity. This is the most
beautiful and best document ever conceived by humankind.[12] It is an
example of an applied social contract that has been subject to active
negotiation. And there is actually a measure of consensus concerning
it, because a large majority of countries have signed the declaration.
That there is such a degree of consensus can be simply explained by
the fact that it concerns a declaration, not a treaty, and that there is
no legal obligation for countries to observe it.

The concentric circles of expanding morality could be the
following:

1. I (egoism)
2. Family
3. Group (religion) and friends (ethnocentrism)

4. Nation (nationalism)
5. All people who are currently living (anthropocentrism = speciesism)
6. Future generations (Martha Nussbaum and Peter Singer)
7. Primates and dolphins (*Great Ape Project*)
8. All adult higher mammals: consciousness is central (Tom Regan)
9. All beings that can suffer (pathocentrism, Peter Singer)
10. All life (Paul Taylor)
11. Biodiversity (E. O. Wilson)
12. Ecosystems (ecocentrism, Aldo Leopold, Arne Naess, Bill McKibben, "deep ecology")
13. Biosphere: Gaia hypothesis (holism, James Lovelock)

Everything begins with the I. Yet few people are purely and solely egoistic. Immediate family, friends, and group members show more consideration for each other than for outsiders. The ethologist Jane Goodall was taken aback by the behavior of groups of male chimpanzees that didn't hesitate to kill members of another group when they ran across them. That is roughly the standard tribal attitude between groups, including human beings. Quite possibly this is natural morality. Of course, saying that is not the same as justifying it. It is possible to rise above such inclinations. It may be unnatural, but no more unnatural than swallowing a pill when you have a headache. Ethnicity can be determined by race, language, and/or religion. How wide the circle of morality is depends on how you define your identity: are you a world citizen or a white Protestant American nationalist? The nation state is the default mode for the political and legal organization of today's world, joined by a few transnational cooperative arrangements, of which the European Union is the most successful. Peter Singer has argued that national boundaries are morally irrelevant: suffering is suffering, wherever it is found and whatever creature experiences it. Making suffering central leads to pathocentrism. At this point a scale of suffering becomes visible: the higher primates and dolphins score higher than other animals. The philosopher Tom Regan draws a rigid moral boundary at adult higher mammals. In his view, killing such animals constitutes murder, hence the slogan: "Meat is murder."[13] The idea of intrinsic value can lead to all living organisms being included in the circle of morality, or even biodiversity or, as in the Gaia hypothesis, the earth in its entirety. Future generations actually don't fit easily into this outline,[14] but I have nevertheless added them, because, as universal subjectivism shows, they can in fact suffer as a result of our actions.

Universal subjectivism is pathocentric: suffering occupies a central place. In this theory it's not possible to include biodiversity or an ecosystem directly in the expanding circle of morality. It can be done indirectly, however, because the quality of life is strongly influenced by ecosystems and biodiversity. Indirectly we can and must attach a lot of importance to a restrained, lasting relationship with what remains of nature.

I. SUPPOSE YOU'RE IN A WHEELCHAIR

Suppose you have a physical handicap and are in a wheelchair. You're part of the society that you yourself have conceived and arranged "up there," but there are no ramps to get into shopping centers, stores, and other buildings. For someone in a wheelchair this constitutes a serious problem. Yet it would be easy to devise a world in which this problem has been solved. In the thought experiment you can go back to your control panel, furnish the public spaces with facilities for wheelchairs, and return.

You can't exclude the possibility that you will end up in a wheelchair, because there are, after all, people with physical handicaps in this world. You can try to adapt society as closely as possible to the requirements of physically handicapped persons.

The same thing applies when you come into the world with a mental handicap, which could vary from a minor intellectual handicap to severe idiocy. This example makes it easy to see that we are engaged in a thought experiment. People with severe mental handicaps will never be able to think through the thought experiment themselves. But other people can. People without that intellectual handicap can imagine what it would be like to be handicapped that way. You don't even have to make an exact image of the world of the intellectually handicapped, you can picture the difference between being tied down on a bed or walking around freely and playing games.

In the 1970s a revolutionary change took place in psychiatrists' treatment of their patients, from being paternalistic and indifferent to a view that was more sensitive and empathetic. It is not the case that psychiatric care is well-arranged everywhere, but it is moving in the right direction. In the wonderful 2003 Italian film *The Best of Youth* (*La Meglio Gioventu*) the change in psychiatric practice plays a major role: from neglected patients who are chained to their beds and subjected to shock treatment to caring accompanied living projects.

You have to imagine the thought experiment as though you are your own guardian. How would you want to be treated if you were mentally handicapped yourself? That's not an entirely abstract idea: some people stipulate how they want to be treated if they should become legally incompetent or subject to excruciating pain. They register an emphatic wish for conditional euthanasia (in the Netherlands, at least). These people are thus imagining what it would be like to enter into a state where they are no longer able to cope. The thought experiment of universal subjectivism goes a step farther because you have to try to put yourself in the shoes of mentally as well as physically handicapped people. You don't have to imagine this in a detailed way. It's the principle that matters. If you were an architect and were asked to design an institution for the mentally handicapped, you would be well-advised to study the environment of these people closely. In that case you have to think yourself into the position of others to the best of your ability. There are many possibilities for imagining the lives of others. Scientific specialists can contribute to this in popular articles for magazines and in books.

With his novel *The Curious Incident of the Dog in the Night-Time* (2003), about an autistic boy, the novelist Mark Haddon has made an enormous contribution to our understanding of people with autism. The book is an international bestseller. It is fascinating to get inside the skin of someone with autism. The film *Rain Man* (1988) has also contributed to an understanding of and emancipation for autistic people.

For example, an architect could spend a couple of days in an institution as a patient, or as a prisoner if she has to design a prison. In principle designers should always want to use their own designs. The architect who designs a house in which she would never want to live is not working properly. There is a trick for motivating engineers to do their best possible work. For example, if airplanes are involved, you can establish the rule that the designers and technicians go along on the first test flight. This procedural arrangement ensures that the chance of accidents drops drastically.

It is desirable that you as an individual should be able to develop your capacities as fully as possible and participate in society as completely as possible without being treated paternalistically as an object of pity. The issue may be special provisions that allow handicapped people to participate in public life, such as providing elevators in public buildings for people who don't move easily, and ramps for people in wheelchairs. These ramps are also useful for people pushing baby carriages.

These provisions don't necessarily have to be supplied or required by government. Social acceptance and tolerance are required for everything that falls outside the range of what someone's fellow citizens consider to be "normal." How would you feel if your face was disfigured as a result of burns sustained in a fire? Whether you dare to show your face outside your house depends in part on how people treat you. If people speak to you normally, without constantly staring at you, you will go out in public more readily than if people behave oddly toward you. The same thing applies to little people (often referred to as dwarfs). For a long time they were outcasts.

And yet the emancipation of the handicapped, or people with an unusual appearance, is still far from complete. Can you imagine a cabinet minister whose face is disfigured, who is in a wheelchair, lacks an arm, or is hunchbacked? If the answer is "no," there is something not right in society.

Albino in Africa

People with albinism have an inherited aberration as a result of which their bodies produce little or no melanin, the pigment that colors skin, hair, and eyes. Their skins stay forever pale. Their hair is as white as milk or yellow as straw. The pale blue eyes lighten into red. Suppose you are born as an albino in Africa. The tropical sun burns your skin day after day. You are seen as witches' spawn. Nowhere does albinism occur as often as in Africa. Albinos are in a worst-case situation. Their handicap means they are sensitive to sunlight and run the risk of getting skin cancer. And sunblock is largely unknown in Africa. Dermatologists are few and far between and information about protecting yourself against the sun is not available. Aside from this, there are the social prejudices and accursed superstitions that ensure that albinos are treated as outcasts. Things are so bad, in fact, that albinos are murdered to turn their body parts into magical medicines. How is it possible that superstition and prejudice can flourish so widely and ruin the lives of so many, in this case albinos? In Zimbabwe albino women are raped because of a belief that sex with one will cure a man of AIDS. "In Tanzania, 25 albinos have been killed in the past year," a 2008 investigation by the British Broadcasting Corporation found: "The latest victim was a seven-month-old baby. He was mutilated on the orders of a witch doctor peddling the belief that potions made from an albino's legs, hair, hands, and blood can make a person rich."[15] In Burundi the members of a gang that murdered albinos for export to Tanzania is on trial.

In universal subjectivism you must take account of the possibility that you may end up as an albino in Africa, suffering from the sun and from discrimination and intolerance. How would you want society to deal with you? In the first place it should provide medical care (dermatology) and medical information about protection against the sun's rays through clothing and sunblock. Second, you would want society to accept you as a human being and you would not want to be subject to discrimination, rape, murder, and mutilation. It appears that in Africa there is a great lack of scientific knowledge about the world and about albinism in particular. Stories that AIDS can be cured by having sex with virgins make the rounds. Alternative therapies and magic flourish abundantly. How can this be changed? Good education can prevent a great deal of misery. Rich countries could invest in and donate to provide education. But it would have to be education of good quality, i.e., scientific and scholarly education, not hijacked by missionaries who want to replace local superstition with an institutionalized form of their own religious myths. Tolerance toward people who look different has to be actively promoted. Education about human rights and the Universal Declaration of Human Rights can function as a guideline.

2. SUPPOSE YOU'RE A WOMAN IN SAUDI ARABIA

Suppose you enter the world as a woman in a society that is unfriendly to women, such as Saudi Arabia. Probably you'll want to leave as quickly as possible or change the institutions so that no society oppresses women any longer. Societies, cultures, and peoples should not be misogynistic. In Islamic countries where women don't enjoy equal rights and where the freedom of women is severely restricted, men often say that it is actually a sign of respect for women to treat them in this way. These men belief in the values of Islam and they think that women are degraded when they are free to do as they please, like driving a car or going out without a veil. From the Islamic perspective these misogynistic men are virtuous men. However, these virtues turn out to be vices when analyzed ethically. Suppose some women would freely choose such a life (which is hard to believe), there will be women who don't want to be treated with that kind of "respect." You always have to imagine that you're the one who does *not* want what the group wants for you: you don't want to wear a hijab, a chador, or a burqa. You want to study, to find a job, drive a car, go out alone, have relations with men or women, go to the beach or the movies, and so on. Totalitarian repression of individual freedom, especially of women, invariably develops in countries where religious authorities have temporal power. The Taliban does not exist only in Afghanistan; imagine what society would look like if the Vatican or evangelical Christian Focus on the Family had absolute power. How would things be for those who have different beliefs or are nonbelievers, for women, for homosexuals, or for socialists?

As soon as religious denominations get social or political power they show evidence of misogyny. Whether we're talking about Islam, Christianity in Europe into the 1960s, Hinduism in India, or Orthodox Judaism: in every case women are the victims of misogynistic ideology. Female circumcision, honor killing, and suttee (the Hindu custom of widows burning themselves or being burned), which used to be practiced in India), are low points within religious hierarchies dominated by men.

I chose the obvious example of Saudi Arabia, but even in the liberal West you can imagine a situation in which a woman lacks freedom or a fair chance. Suppose you have an unwanted pregnancy and your family and social group won't allow you to get an abortion: would you want that for yourself? There are misogynistic subcultures even in Western Europe and North America, such as the polygamous sects that have their roots in Mormonism.

A PARABLE OF HORROR FROM AFGHANISTAN

Rahima was ten years old when she was contracted to marry a man of fifty. This was a case in which the father gave away his child in exchange for the man's sixteen-year-old daughter. For both men it was their third wife. Rahima became pregnant three times before she turned fifteen. Each time the child died at birth. The owner of a hotel in Mazar, where she sat alone in her room while her husband was doing business elsewhere, took her to the police. Her husband had abused her in a variety of ways, including anally. Nobody in her native province of Badghis gave her any support, not even the authorities.[16]

It is incomprehensible that some people, even some feminists, adopt an attitude of cultural relativism. These cultural relativists are of the view that it is impossible as well as undesirable to condemn other cultures. Positive judgments are allowed, but condemnation is not. This is a terrible train of thought. It means that victims of misogyny can't count on empathy and help. Strangely enough, culturally relativist feminists take the side of the dominant males instead of those who are being oppressed. According to feminists who take a nonconformist position, feminism as ideology is morally bankrupt because it has been infected by cultural relativism. This is the claim Phyllis Chesler makes in her 2005 book *The Death of Feminism*.[17] It is just as if environmental activists were to side with the oil companies and pay attention only to the statements of the big corporations.

A culture, society, or ideology in which there are victims is worse than a culture, society, or ideology in which that is not the case. There is a moral ranking in social orders. The ideology and culture of Nazism were morally pernicious. The regimes of Stalin (Soviet Union), Mao (China), Pol Pot (Cambodia), and the Taliban are also morally pernicious. You could say: the fewer citations in Amnesty International®'s annual report, the better the country, because there are fewer offences against human rights.

THE PARABLE OF WHEN IN ROME, DO AS THE ROMANS DO

Peter is a sales representative who travels widely. While he is on a business trip in an Arab country, his hosts take him along on an excursion. He is open to the customs of the countries he visits and goes along enthusiastically. However, as soon as he sees the gallows in the crowded square he turns pale. He hasn't counted on a public execution. He is acquainted with strip clubs and the like, but not this. But he quickly recovers himself and thanks his hosts for their hospitality. Peter is receptive to the cultures where he is a guest and he doesn't force his own opinions on others. In any case, he has faced more disagreeable situations: he recalls the time in Nigeria when he was allowed to witness the stoning of a half-buried woman. Peter found that really nasty. But in many countries the food is no joke either. With disgust he remembers how he managed to swallow some sheep's eyes and how in China he spooned up the brains of a still-living monkey. Peter is a man of the world. His guiding principle is: if you want to do business, you go along with your hosts and you don't condemn them. Business is business.

Abortion as Export Product

The foreign policy and development aid of Western countries should be directed toward helping people in difficult and perilous situations. One of the things helpful to women is the legalization of abortion. In many countries abortion is prohibited, with the consequence that women who become pregnant against their will are greatly burdened with the care and raising of unwanted children. Many women die as a result of illegal abortions. Foreign policy should be aimed at the dissemination of sexual counseling, including discussion of the number of children, and the distribution of birth-control information and contraceptives. Contraception prompts a decline in the birth rate and the risk of sexually transmitted diseases, and it strengthens the position of women. Nothing advanced the emancipation of women in the Western world as much as the introduction of the birth control pill in 1960.

The independent Dutch organization known as Women on Waves has a ship that operates in international waters and offers abortions to women in countries where abortions are illegal. In these countries, Portugal for example, abortions are performed in unprofessional and sometimes barbaric ways. There is a lot of protest against Women on Waves from the religious (Catholic) side. For this reason the government, or better yet, the United Nations, should support projects of this kind. Individual suffering should be the point of departure for external policy, irrespective of groups or organizations, such as churches, that in fact reinforce that suffering. In this case it is women with unwanted pregnancies who are desperately looking for a way out. What is important is that the women in question must be able to make autonomous choices. Individuals have to be protected against oppression by groups. The same considerations apply to female circumcision (the surgical removal of the clitoris and sometimes the labia).

Missionaries continue to be sent around the world, though on a smaller scale than some decades ago. I consider this to be a continuing black page in our history: the export of untruths that lead to oppression. The moralizing tone of the churches has been tempered these days and the accent has been put on development aid. The taboo that attaches to abortion in many non-Western countries is sometimes of Christian origin. That places an extra obligation on the West to help women who are subject to an oppressive religious morality.

Then there is still this question: is abortion murder? The embryo is in the process of becoming a human being. There is no magical moment after which we can talk about a human being. The whole perspective of the so-called categorical ban on murder leads from a ban on abortion to death: the death of women who undergo illegal abortions. If abortion is categorically banned (with the argument that it is murder), this will lead to the death of women in the case that abortion would be the sole treatment to save the life of the mother, and illegal abortion is much more dangerous than legal abortion. So a ban on abortion will lead to more cases of dangerous illegal abortions. The important thing is not the sanctity of life (what is sanctity?) but the quality of life. The embryo is not yet an individual with its own life, the pregnant woman, however, is. The woman's interests therefore weigh more heavily than those of the fetus. The more advanced the pregnancy, the farther the embryo has developed, the more heavily the interests of the human being-to-be start to weigh.

If the United States wanted to lead the world, there is an excellent opportunity here. It should launch an entire armada of government-financed abortion ships operating internationally. In this way the United States could help prevent the destruction of the lives of women with unwanted pregnancies.

3. SUPPOSE YOU'RE HOMOSEXUAL

Suppose you come into the world as a homosexual, but in the society you created, homosexuality is illegal. You, and not someone else, happen to be homosexual. Actually, there is a five-percent chance that you may be homosexual. The denial of someone's emotional and sexual development has serious consequences for psychological well-being and happiness. This is going to be a difficult thought experiment for stubborn homophobes, because they will have to imagine that they themselves are homosexual.

It is the homophobe who interferes with the life of the homosexual, not the other way around. And yet the homophobe will probably respond that he or she personally feels deeply insulted by the homosexuality of others. In an open society, however, you can be put off and feel disturbed by the behavior of others, but as long as others don't interfere directly with your behavior, you have to be able to put up with them, just as Muslims should be able to put up with cartoons of the Prophet and allow criticism that they may experience as insulting.

Individual Freedom

Universal subjectivism is a liberal theory, that is, the freedom of the individual is central. The thought experiment forces you, from the vantage point of your original situation, to take account of all possible situations and particularly those situations which, if you had the choice, you would rather not be in, such as in Kibera in Nairobi, one of the biggest slums in the world. Aside from not knowing in which social position you will land, you also don't know what your preferences will be. They could be anything. But suppose you have created a restrictive society in which almost nothing is permitted. Lots of people can't pursue or enjoy their hobbies and pastimes. If, in the original situation, you have taken account only of the way you are right now and have banned or hindered everything you dislike, you run the risk of landing in a society in which you are disadvantaged. Suppose I have designed a society in which soccer has been banned, at least no soccer fields can be created, no stadiums can be built, and no soccer games can be transmitted via television. A world without soccer doesn't seem all that bad to me. So I do everything to suppress soccer. But I subsequently end up in the society I have designed and chance has determined that I'm a passionate soccer player and fan. But there are no facilities for the sport, and furthermore establishing them privately is prohibited. A society like that would frustrate me immensely. I would say to myself: I don't harm anyone by playing soccer, do I? Who would be bothered if I play it? Fortunately it is a thought experiment, and I can return to the original situation and create a society in which soccer fans can enjoy themselves. The same thing goes for basketball, baseball, football, volleyball, tennis, swimming, music, dancing, jogging, art (museums and galleries), nudism, and so on.

In an open society in which the freedom of the individual occupies a central position, the government (and in the thought experiment that is you yourself) should provide two things. First, it should offer the greatest possible freedom of expression. This is called *nega-*

tive freedom. But you could also call it *cheap freedom,* because it costs government nothing. Government should prohibit as few things as possible. Government, with the police as its strong right arm, ought to guard the freedom of all citizens. So if someone limits someone else's freedom, the police should swing into action. Noise pollution is a simple example. If I crank up my sound system with the windows open, the chances are great that my neighbors won't appreciate it. When they have exhausted their patience, they can phone the police, who will order me to turn down the sound or put on headphones. It's all right to listen to loud music, in concerts and dance clubs or with headphones. This is a simple example, with which almost everyone can easily agree. Yet many people find negative freedom difficult to tolerate. The point is that everything should be allowed so long as it doesn't harm others. This includes matters we personally hate. The emancipation of the 1960s in large part had to do with the increase of negative freedom. It was a clash between the "solid citizens" and the "dirty hippies." The hippies wanted all kinds of things that self-appointed moral arbiters abhorred and still abhor: long hair for men, cheerfully colored clothes, sexual freedom, drugs, pop music, communes, loitering, and etcetera. The moral arbiters really wanted the hippies to become solid citizens, too. The hippies, on the other hand, rejected bourgeois values but lacked a proselytizing drive.

As long as no harm and suffering is done to others, animals included, everything is permitted. So free love among adults, the use of soft drugs, pornography (as long as there is no coercion and there are no children involved), communes, nudism, all these come under the umbrella of freedom of expression. Not the consumption of meat, however—in contrast to what is generally thought—because that does cause harm and suffering to others, namely, to (other) animals.

The First Law of Philosophy

The first law of philosophy, it is sometimes said, is that you can't say you agree with the premises but don't accept the conclusion. Thinking philosophically can therefore lead to uncomfortable conclusions. If you don't like the conclusion, you can reexamine the premises closely and run through the argument once more. But if that is all sound and you refuse to accept the conclusion, then what? The point of thinking philosophically lies in the search for truth, justice, and the good. If you find those and you don't want to accept them, what is the use of thinking philosophically? Compare this with a dictator's civil servants and advisors. The truth and conclusions of research are subordinated to the wish to please the dictator, because if you say something that doesn't suit him, you will be punished at once. In 1958–61 there was a great famine in China due to Mao's ill-conceived agricultural policy. Nobody dared to report the failure of the policy. On the contrary: glowing reports were written. A dream world of magnificent harvests took shape that was the very opposite of the reality.

Moral philosophy means that you analyze what is good and bad and apply it to today's world. Those who are happy and satisfied with their lives and have no problems with the suffering that others experience can sit back and live free of worries, without any moral reflection. Such reflection can act as a boomerang, however, for it could be that your own lifestyle does not agree with the conclusions of moral analysis.

Negative freedom centers on the freedom of the individual, the freedom to arrange your life according to your own insights, the freedom of expression. Hobbies, appearance, sexual behavior, choice of career and partner(s), and the freedom to express your opinions: that is the essence of an open society. Tolerance means permitting things for which you have no respect at all or which you hate. Some Dutch Christians recently wanted to prohibit a play in which there was sex on stage, as being against public decency. But if the sex is voluntary, and if the audience consists of adults whose decision to attend the performance is voluntary, there is no reason for banning it.

In some countries or cultures certain sexual practices are prohibited or taboo, such as anal sex, oral sex, same-gender sex, sex with menstruating women, group sex, sex theater. In every case the rule applies: as long as there are no victims, everything is allowed. Or everything should be allowed. Negative freedom is cheap and simple to obtain, namely, by lifting prohibitions and abolishing taboos. Many people object to the freedom of expression of others. You may have an unbelievable dislike of and revulsion against certain practices, but in an open society no one will force you to take part in them. However, many believers owe their identity to the enforcement of taboos, commandments, and prohibitions. Almost all religions, and in any case the Abrahamic religions, have prescriptions concerning diet and sexuality. Strangely enough, the believers generally apply the dietary rules only to themselves, while they want the *sexual* prescriptions to apply to others as well. I know no believer who gets excited when others eat pork, for example. But there are believers who get worked up about the homosexuality of others. Of course you don't have to become homosexual yourself. Moreover, you can repress your own inclination if you feel a conflict between it and your religion, but in an open society you can't force others to do so. Sexuality is an important point of conflict between people who favor negative freedom, such as individualists, liberals, libertines, libertarians, humanists and freethinkers, on the one hand, and paternalists, conservatives, and religious believers on the other. The aversion toward the liberal West felt by many Muslims results from the freedom enjoyed by Western women and homosexuals. We can hardly imagine a nudist colony or wellness center in Saudi Arabia or Iran. We can, oddly enough, imagine a conservative mosque in the Netherlands. In countries where religion has political power, the freedom of the individual and more particularly that of women and homosexuals is severely limited. To say it provocatively: the existence of a nudist colony is a criterion for judging whether a society is open.

As well, the existence of meeting places for homosexuals, in locations where they are not a nuisance, is a sign of civilization, because that is the essence of negative freedom.

Banning smoking in restaurants and bars is progress on the scale of negative freedom. It may sound strange that a ban involves an enlargement of freedom. But smoking causes harm to nonsmokers, those referred to as passive smokers who breathe in the smoke of others. It doesn't bother all passive smokers, but there are many nonsmokers who find it unpleasant and annoying to breathe secondary smoke. It stinks and is unhealthy. The liberal rule is that you shouldn't harass or harm others, and that is definitely what happens when you smoke in public places. A liberal government therefore must ban smoking in public places. However, it would be a violation of individual freedom to ban smoking altogether. When somebody smokes without hurting others, smoking is permitted. Even when people smoke at home or in their cars, they ought not to do harm to others, their own children included. The fact that smoking is bad for the smoker's health is of virtually no concern to the government. It is important to disseminate valid information about the effects of smoking, but individuals are fully entitled to ignore it and do things that are bad for them.

Negative freedom means not only that as many practices as possible are permitted, but also that practices that create victims are prohibited and that the police must actively try to prevent them. Negative freedom is about the protection of individuals. Examples of this protection are the banning of female circumcision and so-called honor killing. In most Western countries female circumcision is illegal.

Why? Would you, as a well-informed woman, want to be circumcised? Yet lots of women in the West are circumcised, either in the country their parents have migrated to or during a return visit to their or their parents' country of origin. Government can look the other way, but in that case the freedom of the women undergoing the practice is seriously impaired. It is the job of government to protect citizens, even against their own group and family. When Ayaan Hirsi Ali was a member of the Dutch Parliament, she made several practical proposals, such as the annual medical inspection of girls from high-risk countries. Forced marriage, honor killings, domestic violence, rape within marriage, female *and* male circumcision: it is the duty of government to prevent practices like these and, if that is unsuccessful, to track down the perpetrators and punish them. Aside from this, information campaigns and educational programs should be established to discourage such practices and to offer protection and help, over the long term if necessary. A liberal society fails badly when victims are ignored. It is the tragedy of a multicultural society when, under the guise of toleration, the freedom of individuals is limited and harmed because groups are given the freedom to limit the freedom of group members.

Positive Freedom

Positive freedom is more expensive. Through positive freedom government facilitates the wishes and hobbies of people by means of subsidies and permits. Positive freedom also means that the government protects individuals against the vagaries of fate by creating a social safety net. Providing hospitals, welfare, education, culture, sport, research: in most Western countries the government's task is broad.

Libertarians favor as wide a rule of negative freedom as possible; some say that libertarianism is about killing the beast of government. All government needs to do is take care that individuals observe the law. For this you need only a strong police force and a system of courts. Libertarianism stands for a minimal state, also referred to as the night watchman state. Citizens arrange almost all matters voluntarily. People who want to play soccer buy a field and play. People who want their children to go to school collect money and establish a school. As long as people are able to satisfy their needs and wants, there is no problem. However, as soon as they can't, such as when they become unemployed, there's a big problem. Quite possibly there are people who would voluntarily establish a fund for the unemployed, but most probably not. Would you want to trade places with someone who falls overboard in a night watchman state? Probably you would not. Proponents of a night watchman state are often people who are well able to look after themselves and who think that their tax money is being wasted on the indigent. Libertarians want low taxes and as little government interference and regulation as possible.

Liberals, on the other hand, want freedom and opportunities for personal development for all individuals. Ideally everyone should be able to develop themselves in various fields, depending on their ability, for example, occupationally, socially, creatively, sexually. This requires government to establish a social welfare net and to facilitate and subsidize opportunities for personal development in areas like education, culture, sport, and science. In the current political climate this does happen. Discussions take places about how tax revenue can be distributed so as to support the positive freedom of as many people as possible. That is the underlying concept of the welfare state. An open society has, simultaneously, maximum negative as well as positive freedom.

In the formerly Communist countries there was a limited degree of positive freedom, but certainly no negative freedom. In China negative freedom is still problematic: criticism of the authorities is put down forcefully. There is no freedom of expression.

Assisted by the method of universal subjectivism, you can test a society for both positive and negative freedom. To test a society for positive freedom you have to imagine what will happen to you if you are sick or disabled and you are not insured or if you lose your job— see, for example, Michael Moore's documentary *Sicko* (2007), which shows that positive freedom comes up short in the United States.

To test a society for negative freedom, you only have to look to see whether activities that don't harm others are prohibited, the so-called victimless crimes. You have to ask yourself why there are countless laws and prohibitions that patronize citizens, such as the compulsory use of seatbelts and of helmets while riding motorcycles, the setting of maximum speeds, and a ban on bareback sex parties during which gay men have unprotected sex and are therefore at risk of getting HIV and AIDS. Are citizens not autonomous enough to make choices and take the consequences? The traditional liberal vision is that when people have made a well-considered choice on the basis of sufficient and objective information, they should be allowed to do whatever they want, as long as they don't harm others. But in a complex modern welfare state the consequences of an autonomous choice that turns out badly are shifted to others, namely, the taxpayers. For example, someone who doesn't wear a seatbelt, and is seriously injured and disabled as a result, claims medical care, nursing, rehabilitation, and the social welfare net.

There are good reasons for even a liberal government to be paternalistic to a degree and to limit negative freedom: in the first place, to guard people against their own weak will. Safety regulations in the construction industry produce a decline in the number of accidents, but individual construction workers often think they can manage without a helmet, ear protectors, and sunblock. That is the difference between approaching the matter from the point of view of the individual and that of the government, which has an overview of the number of accidents and injuries.

The second reason justifying paternalistic regulations, such as building codes and fire safety regulations, is that they are supposed to protect people against unforeseen harm. It is often difficult for owners and managers in the hospitality and entertainment industry to meet requirements, and often everything goes well, but when things go wrong, as in the Station Nightclub fire in West Warwick, Rhode Island, on February 20, 2003, they go really wrong. When the tour manager of the band that was performing that evening set off some pyrotechnics, a fire started in the highly flammable foam insulation in the walls and ceiling surrounding the stage. In the absence of a sprinkler system the fire spread rapidly, and there were more than 300 casualties, with 100 deaths. Through universal subjectivism, you can imagine that you are a victim because of a building code that did not ban highly flammable building materials and did not mandate a sprinkler system. In the thought experiment, you would want to be part of a society in which better building codes and fire-safety regulations are imposed. This form of government compulsion is justified by the protection it offers to potential victims.

Third, there is an intuitive argument. Should we permit sports in which professional fighters sometimes kill each other, such as boxing or mixed martial arts (MMA)? If it concerns consenting adults who have made a considered choice and are not compelled financially to engage in the activity, I can't, as a liberal, think of an argument why government should ban it. Or can I? What matters here is the irreversibility if there should be deaths, or when participants retain lifelong disabilities as a result. A disabled boxer or MMA fighter can feel regret. A dead one can't even regret what happened, but from the vantage point of universal subjectivism you can imagine that the fighter feels regret just before the lethal blow. Government measures may protect individuals from themselves.

Even in a utopian, liberal, constitutional state there will necessarily be a certain measure of paternalistic interference by government, to protect citizens from themselves and their fellow citizens. However, the arguments for a limitation of individual freedom must always be approved democratically and should only be imposed upon consideration of real suffering and real harm to others. When government also begins to take seriously offenses to beliefs and feelings another kind of paternalism looms, one that leads to censorship and prohibitions on so-called victimless crimes, such as abortion and euthanasia. Arguments to limit the freedoms of others must not be based on ideological or religious grounds, but should be purely pragmatic. Citizens are not minors for whom the state can decide what is good. Religious paternalism of the kind we see in Iran, where Islam is the state religion, leads to enormous restrictions on individual freedom. The determination of reasonable limits on government interference is a matter for public debate.

4. SUPPOSE YOU'RE A
COFFEE FARMER IN ETHIOPIA

From a cup of cappuccino that may cost three dollars, a farmer earns three cents. The film *Black Gold: A Film about Coffee and Trade*, by Marc and Nick Francis, shows how the farmers in Ethiopia who grow some of the world's best coffee live: miserably, at an absolute subsistence level, on the edge of hunger.

Suppose you are born in a rural area in Ethiopia into a family of coffee farmers. You grow coffee of excellent quality that fetches a high price in the market, but you yourself receive so small a fraction of that price that you can barely provide for your family. Would you not want to receive a better, fairer price for your product? The price Western consumers pay for a cup of coffee is the end price for the product. You can put that price in a pie diagram to show in percentage terms who gets what. It involves a long chain: farmers, local merchants, exporters, shippers, roasters, wholesalers, coffee shops, until the product finally reaches the consumers. The absurd and unfair aspect of this trade is that those who do the most work—the farmers who grow the coffee—earn the least. The farmers, who are often unorganized because their government doesn't tolerate producers' unions, are in a weak position and because of this they are easily exploited.

Yet it is possible to correct the market morally and carry on the trade more fairly. The Fair Trade concept ensures that a higher percentage of the final sale price goes to the producers. One way of doing this is to shorten the trading chain. But Fair Trade products will only be available if enough consumers buy them. So when you order a coffee, think of who is at the other end of the production chain: for example the Ethiopian farmer who is mired in poverty.

Coffee is roasted in the consuming countries, not in the countries of origin. The roasting and grinding of coffee is highly profitable. Coffee not processed in the country where it is grown because there are tariff walls against processed goods. There is no international free trade. The tariff walls protect Western countries. In the West, farmers receive government subsidies, while Western pressure has meant the end of agricultural subsidies in Africa.

In a free-market economy, the consumer largely determines what the market supplies. Government can institute regulations, and that does indeed happen sometimes, but in the end the consumer rules. If we want a fairer, more stable world, we shall, as consumers, have to provide evidence of our wishes. Fair Trade products are part of a broader morally conscious consumption pattern that includes other things as well: reducing consumption (the reduction of our ecological footprint), buying organic products, and engaging in veganism.

The point is that you should always be able to change places with someone else without anything changing morally. Suppose you are in a restaurant, then you should be able to imagine yourself as waiter or chef. The same in stores: you, too, could be the sales clerk. A manager should be able to imagine what it is like to be an employee in her organization. A taxi user should be able to change places with a driver. In principle you should be able to change places with everyone without anything changing much morally.

You won't enjoy a lot of these jobs, and there are lots of things you can't do and won't ever be able to do, but the point is—and it's important to realize this—that *morally* nothing has changed. On the other hand, you would not want to change places with any of the millions of animals in factory farming. (Try thinking seriously about this for a minute.) There will be more about this in the next section.

But there certainly are relationships that are not reciprocal, that is, one side would absolutely not want to be in the shoes of the other. A torturer and his victim come to mind. The torturer does not want to be in his victim's place. The man who beats his wife would not want to reverse their roles. This is an important moral criterion. If you can, in principle, reverse the roles, there is nothing wrong in moral terms, or, better put, the situation is morally sound. As soon as two roles are not exchangeable, something is morally wrong.

In this way, you can measure a society as a whole by a moral yardstick, by examining whether there are relations that are not morally reciprocal. Are there groups of people who are structurally oppressed or disadvantaged? Look at the position of homosexuals, transsexuals, women, children, the religiously unorthodox, unbelievers, political critics, journalists, human- rights activists, ethnic minorities, animals, and so on. As soon as the position of people in a certain role is not reciprocal with that of others, you have hit upon a moral problem. For example, if homosexuality is officially banned or subject to a social taboo, it is hard to imagine that you would want to change places with an oppressed homosexual, regardless of whether you yourself are gay—the point is to see whether an ethical change takes place when the roles are exchanged. In Saudi Arabia, homosexuality is prohibited by law. In Egypt, homosexuality is subject to a severe Islamic taboo.

Cultures of Victimization

Many societies are cultures of victimization. In a culture of victimization there is a group that is systematically oppressed. That oppression becomes visible because the relationship is not morally reciprocal: people don't want to change places. A clear example is a culture or society that permits slavery: nobody wants to be a slave, neither the slaves nor the slaveholders.

This method of reciprocity can also draw attention to less obvious evils. A number of societies have pariahs or untouchables, that is, groups of people who have a lower social status by birth and face discrimination. Castes exist not only in India but also in Japan and other countries.[18] In Japan there is an underclass, the so-called *burakumin*. These people can't be distinguished physically from other Japanese. Yet they are subject to a great social taboo. In fact, if a couple are planning to marry, the parents of one or other of the prospective partners (or both) sometimes hire a private detective to make sure the future son- or daughter-in-law is not a *burakumin*. Should that be the case, heavy social pressure is exerted. This often results in the cancellation of the wedding. The problem is clear: which non-*burakumin* would want to change places with a *burakumin?*

The historical background of the *burakumin* helps to explain their treatment. There are two more or less national religions in Japan: Shintoism and Buddhism. Buddhist teaching forbids the killing of human beings and animals. But the Japanese like to eat meat. According to Buddhist teaching, once an animal is dead, eating it is not a problem. The *burakumin* were the executioners, undertakers, slaughterers, butchers, and leather workers. They performed work to which a strong taboo was attached and became "infected" in this way. In 1976 the Japanese government prohibited discrimination against the *burakumin*. Officially, therefore, there is no problem. Unofficially, however, discrimination is a fact of life. If you are born into a *burakumin* family, a stain exists that adheres to you for the rest of your life. The chances that you will go far are perceptibly smaller than if you are not a *burakumin*. The persistence of this discrimination damages Japan's moral stature. Japanese society is a culture of victimization, too: the *burakumin* are systematically disadvantaged.

The caste system in India has a long history that is interwoven with Hinduism. But that is morally beside the point. An appeal to reincarnation—even if it existed and that is certainly not the case, because people cannot continue to exist without their bodies—cannot justify injustice. It is also immoral if God, directly or through his representatives, gives orders to kill unbelievers, because the perpetrators would not want to change places with the victims.

The children of war criminals can't be held responsible for what their parents did. Germans born after the Second World War are not in any way to blame for Nazism or the Holocaust. Nor do Netherlanders today need to feel any guilt about the slave trade. But if the descendants of criminals have inherited property that has been acquired illegally, such as money earned in the slave trade, then this property has been acquired improperly and its ownership is invalid, at least on ethical grounds. For example, if you acquired an antique clock from your grandfather, and he once stole it, you can't make a lawful claim to that clock.

Getting back to India: in that country there are different castes, each possessing different social privileges. You can luck out by being born into a high caste, or crap out when you end up in a low caste. In the West you are in luck when you enter the world in a rich family. But the possibilities for personal development are more fairly distributed in the West: it is possible to work your way up the social ladder, and also to marry someone from a different social class. The caste system means that as an individual you are limited to the possibilities that give form to your life. In the low castes, freedom of movement is small, especially for women.

Not only Ethiopian coffee farmers are victims of an unfair economic system. For every product you buy as a consumer, you should be willing to change places with anyone in the production chain. If you buy bananas at a supermarket, you should be able to imagine that you are the stocking clerk, the shipper, the buyer, the sailor on the container ship and, at the end of that long chain, the banana farmer. And the same way for all products: cotton, consumer electronics, and so on.

How much responsibility do you have as a consumer? Do you really have to check, for every product, to see whether everything has been done fairly? Or whether it has been made in a durable and ecologically sustainable manner? No, but consumers do have to consider their choices: as soon as there are organizations that do the necessary research and make the results known to the public about the chain of production, then you as consumer have a moral obligation to act accordingly. The government could make regulations to make producers responsible and liable for products and ingredients that they buy to resell or process. At the moment it is nongovernmental organizations (NGOs), that is, noncommercial organizations founded by citizens, that regulate free trade and assign seals of approval.

It is difficult for an individual to distill information from the sea of information and to act appropriately. Many people find it frustrating that scientific information can change quickly in the course of time. Many people react fatalistically: "You're not supposed to do this, and then you're not supposed to do that. At a certain point you won't be allowed to do anything anymore!" This remark may be exaggerated, but it is true that consumption patterns should change radically, from the perspectives of ethics and health as well as sustainability. You have to inform yourself to the best of your ability. That begins with keeping an open mind. Reading a quality newspaper is helpful; so is reading periodicals like *Consumer Reports* and *Living Green Magazine*, and gathering information from the Internet. Many NGOs have their own magazines and websites. As a consumer you can and must do your best to constantly adapt your actions and patterns of consumption on the basis of new information.

If it turns out that a certain brand of sports shoes are made by children, that is a good reason for boycotting products by that company. Among corporations there is a tendency toward the Global Reporting Initiative (GRI).[19] Corporations are formulating ethical codes. This is rather comical. Suppose you go to a friend's home to bake a cake and you formulate a code in which you promise not to wreck the kitchen, not to hurt the cats, and, as long as it isn't too much trouble, to clean up everything when you're through. It is no more than normal that, no matter what you are doing, you don't inconvenience or interfere with others. Just like other activities, economic activities should cause no inconvenience to anyone, nor should they leave a mess. Apparently this basic ethical insight has been covered up in capitalism by unpunished and selfish behavior at the expense of others. It isn't true that taking account of the interests of all interested parties, including animals and future human generations, is at odds with economic activity and entrepreneurship. There are limits upon and rules applying to economic activities. Ethical codes and the GRI remind us of them and make the limits explicit. The question is whether corporations are actually prepared to observe them or whether it is a façade, *greenwashing* as it is called. Compare this with a book thief. Does he have the right to complain if stronger security measures put limits on his manner of "shopping"? Is it necessary for shoppers to formulate a Fair Shopping code stating that shoppers promise not to steal or damage goods? A code like that would be regarded as ridiculous. And so it is. Why, then, do business firms have to formulate an ethical code? That is suspect. As soon as corporations adopt an ethical code, it means at least two things: (1) that they have done things in the past that couldn't pass muster; and (2) that they want to decide for themselves which things can pass muster and which can't.

Here's one example: under pressure from the Dutch animal rights organization Wakker Dier, restaurants in the IKEA® furniture chain don't use eggs obtained from confined battery chickens any longer. Well done, Wakker Dier, but it is incomprehensible that it was necessary for an organization to point this out to IKEA. There is an enormous myopia among economists, politicians, managers, and entrepreneurs, who look only at costs and profit margins, and fail to take account of other factors, like the manner in which hens are housed. Wakker Dier, like WPSA (World Society for the Protection of Animals®) and PETA® (People for the Ethical Treatment of Animals),[20] is a pragmatic organization that continues to take steps to lessen the suffering that human beings impose on animals. One example is its continuing campaign against the production and consumption of *foie gras*, fat goose liver. To fatten the livers of geese and ducks, food is forced down the animals' throats, with the result that the livers swell up, reaching six to ten times their normal size. This method of production is so animal-unfriendly that it is prohibited in the Netherlands. At the request of Wakker Dier, a number of stores and restaurants have ceased to serve *foie gras*. Would you want to be a goose that is fed in that manner? If the production of *foie gras* is banned in the Netherlands because it is too animal-unfriendly, why is its importation and sale permitted? It is regrettable that restaurants have to be asked to take animal-unfriendly products off the menu. But consumers are guilty as well, because it is widely known how these geese are fed. Restaurants and businesses are evidently somewhat sensitive to the pressure exercised by NGO's like Wakker Dier. If things proceed along this course restaurants will use only organic free-range eggs, and will not serve white veal (from caged calves suffering from anemia), or fish. The final objective will be an organic vegan menu that involves as little animal suffering as possible and that is produced sustainably. But that is utopian. Greenwashing is taking place: businesses go along some distance under pressure from Wakker Dier, but the potential for backsliding is great. Consumers and producers soon respond to financial stimuli. It is said that organically raised meat costs too much, but the fact is that nonorganic meat is too cheap. Although the activities of Wakker Dier are noble *and* pragmatic, it would be best if government would ban the entire factory-farming industry at once, preferably at the supranational level in Europe and North America, or better yet, at the United Nations level. And consumers should accept responsibility and not purchase so naively. Buying means making ethical choices.

5. SUPPOSE YOU'RE A COW

Before you begin this section, first watch the People for the Ethical Treatment of Animals (PETA) video *Meet Your Meat* about animals in factory farming.[21] If that doesn't convince you to become a vegan, you can always watch the 95-minute film *Earthlings*, also available on the Internet.[22] "If I could show people one film, I would show them *Earthlings* (2005)," Peter Singer has said. I watched the trailer with great difficulty, and I shiver at the thought of having to watch the film in its entirety.[23] But if we can't face up to the world and how we behave, including cruel barbarism on an immense scale, simply for the sake of our own consumption, is there not something fundamentally wrong?[24]

Suppose you are a cow living under the hard and cruel conditions of intensive cattle breeding. Perhaps you have to be imaginative to enter into a cow's life, but you can try. Cows can suffer, and it is the capacity for suffering that determines whether a creature falls within the circle of morality. I'm not sure I can form a vivid image of what it is like to be a cow, but I can perceive the difference between a lush meadow and a dark, enclosed space.

If you travel through the Netherlands you see lots of green meadows with cows, sheep, or horses. Although I travel by train, I have never seen pigs or chickens anywhere. Are there actually chickens and pigs in the Netherlands? You bet! There are roughly 100 million chickens in the Netherlands, 57 million that are being raised for meat, while the remaining 43 million produce eggs. But if there are 100 million chickens, I don't see any. Where are they? They are in stables, barns, and cages. No fewer than 400 million pullets (young hens) are slaughtered annually in the Netherlands alone. In the documentaries *Our Daily Bread* (2005), by Nikolaus Geyrhalter, and *We Feed the World* (2005), by Erwin Wagenhofer, we get to see how chicks and chickens are treated. And that is not exactly benignly. It sounds hard, but the way "consumption animals" are treated is the equivalent of torture. Economic considerations prevail over animal welfare.

There were 12.2 million pigs in the Netherlands in 2012. Every year 18 million pigs are slaughtered—there are more animals slaughtered in a year then there exist at one point in time, because many pigs are slaughtered after six months. These millions of pigs are also removed from public view, just like the slaughterhouses. Who has ever seen or visited a slaughterhouse? Children are taken on school trips to a petting farm or a zoo. A petting farm may resemble farms in children's books, but they resemble nothing in the real world.[25] By exposing children on a large scale to a mistaken image of farms, children are indoctrinated with a falsehood. If education is concerned with the honest conveying of knowledge, children would have to visit factory farms and slaughterhouses. Parents don't find this a happy thought. The children would come home thoroughly upset. That is why we would rather give them a false picture of how people deal with animals than confront them with the reality. This is indoctrination.

Biologist Marian Stamp Dawkins writes: "Some animals undoubtedly have an advantage over others when it comes to arousing human sympathy."[26] As *New York Times* science columnist Natalie Angier has written, some animals benefit from the "cute factor."[27] The World Wildlife Federation exploits the tendency of people to judge animals by how cuddlesome they look: for example, the panda bear and the tiger. Reptiles are much less cute and so arouse less sympathy. Many so-called animal lovers are biased in their love of animals. People who cherish their domestic pets feed their beloved dog or cat with meat originating in factory farms. It doesn't matter to these animal lovers that animals have suffered to provide their pets with meat. It seems people can have large blind spots. This is called moral dissonance.

Peter Singer's book *Animal Liberation* is about the way human beings deal with animals. Singer is a utilitarian, that is to say, in his view ethics and life are about diminishing suffering and promoting well-being and happiness. Good is whatever contributes to reduced suffering and increased well-being. Bad is whatever causes or promotes suffering and stands in the way of well-being. From Singer's point of view, it doesn't matter who or what is suffering. Suffering is bad. End of story. And suffering is not just limited to human beings. Animals can suffer, too.

In philosophy and science it has long been denied that animals can suffer. Animals were conceived mechanistically as machines. The philosopher René Descartes (1596–1650) thought that way. According to this belief, human beings enjoy a higher status. Human beings were thought to have a soul, breathed into them by God, and animals did not have one. In this religious concept, humankind is the apex of creation, and animals exist for the sake of human beings. Singer describes the moral positioning of some animals (*Homo sapiens*) above others as discriminatory. Analogous to discrimination, sexism (discrimination on the basis of gender) and ageism (age discrimination), this form of discrimination is called "speciesism": one species discriminates against other animals. Singer acknowledges that there are differences among species. But these differences are gradual and not categorical.

In the world of science there is broad consensus about the fact that animals can suffer. In her book *Animal Suffering: The Science of*

Animal Welfare, the biologist Marian Stamp Dawkins has summarized the state of knowledge about the ability of nonhuman animals to suffer. There are four reasons for arguing that animals can suffer. The first is physiology, the "wiring" of animals. It is in fact almost the same as in human beings. All vertebrates have a central nervous system through which the body reacts to physical stimuli. The second reason lies in evolutionary development. Human beings are mammals and related to the higher primates. Why should human beings be able to experience pain and not the higher primates, or other animals? As well, there is the evolutionary function of suffering. Pain is painful in order to bring about a rapid and appropriate reaction. If you are insensitive to pain, cooking, for example, is mortally dangerous: you won't notice whether you are chopping not only the onions but also your fingers, or whether you have picked up a boiling hot saucepan. Without painful stimuli the chances of survival are a lot smaller. With many animals, the experience of pain is an evolutionary survival strategy. Third, there is the behavior of animals, their ethology. Animals exhibit the same behavior in response to pain stimuli as human beings, namely, withdrawal, avoidance, and flight. Finally, human beings, especially children, have an innate capacity for recognizing pain in others. Who doesn't know a child who is really anxious about a crippled bird? An important part of human culture consists of denying and unlearning the ability to recognize the capacity for suffering in other creatures and act accordingly. Culture is the acquisition of speciesism: only the suffering of people and domestic pets in your immediate environment is morally relevant, not the suffering of others (be they people or other animals).

Moral Status Value Scale

Whether an entity has moral status depends on its capacity for suffering. This capacity is not equally great for all creatures, however, and it is therefore possible to devise a moral status value scale. The question as to which creatures can suffer to what degree is a *biological* one. Biology, then, provides the input for determining which creatures should be accorded moral status. Below are a few examples arranged in order from no capacity for suffering to a great capacity for suffering:

- stones, rocks
- trees, plants
- brain-dead persons, zygotes, embryos
- insects
- crustaceans
- fish
- rats, household pets, farm animals
- human fetuses
- higher primates and dolphins
- mentally handicapped people
- babies
- children, men, women
- humans of future generations

If what matters is the capacity for suffering, stones have no moral status. As a result, if someone crushes a stone, you cannot call it an immoral act. But suppose this stone was Michelangelo's *Moses*. Is it not immoral to reduce an important work of art to rubble? Yes, that is immoral. But the statue, the stone itself, is morally indifferent. The stone that represents Moses can't suffer. It is possible for a lot of people to suffer, to be angry and sad that such a beautiful and important work of art has been destroyed. It is individuals who suffer as a result of the destruction of the statue. In that sense the statue has *indirect* moral value. For the statue itself it isn't bad to be destroyed, but for many people it is bad. Destroying or damaging things or objects can cause suffering to human beings or other animals. The construction of buildings on small islands is not morally harmful to the rock of which the island consists, but it can influence the birds whose breeding grounds have vanished. In that case construction on the island causes suffering to animals.

I have listed "women" separately on the moral status value scale. In many societies and cultures women are treated, by men *and* by women, as if they are morally inferior beings. Violence against women occurs in many cultures. Genital circumcision is a distressing example of the status of moral inferiority that is accorded to women in many cultures.

The capacity for suffering develops gradually from zygote through embryo, fetus, and baby to child. Without a nervous system there can be no question of suffering. In itself, therefore, a zygote or early embryo has no moral status. The further an embryo develops, the greater its capacity for suffering. That a toddler can suffer more than a newborn infant may seem counter-intuitive. But a toddler has a social relationship with the environment and particularly the mother. An infant is above all a body and not yet a person. The claim to protection (in case there should be a conflict such as: which of the two should I save from a burning daycare center) is greater in the case of a toddler than of a baby.

A brain-dead person is in fact a kind of plant. There is a form of living, but no conscious living and no interaction, or at best minimally, with the surroundings. But a brain-dead person (who therefore is no longer a person because what makes him or her a person is dead, only the body is still alive, like a plant) probably has family and friends. This has the result that a brain-dead person is treated as if it were a person. If the family is conscious of the fact that the person is dead and accepts the death, there is no good reason to keep the brain-dead person artificially alive. The deceased are not put into the waste disposal bin; they are buried or cremated because the survivors are suffering under the loss. Burials and cremations are rites of passage for the survivors so that they can make sense of the death of the loved one and cope with it. Death doesn't hurt the deceased, but it does hurt the survivors. Dying itself can be accompanied by physical and mental suffering. To mitigate this pain or even to prevent it, the affected person can, at least in some countries and a few states of the United States, opt for euthanasia (literally, good death), by hastening death with medical assistance.

If biologists were to learn that there are trees or plants that can suffer, i.e., are conscious of physical stimuli and exhibit fear and flight reactions, then these trees or plants need to be ranked higher on the moral status value scale, and this has ethical consequences. If it should appear that apple trees experience physical pain from apple picking, then it would be immoral to continue picking apples. On the other hand, if it should appear that a certain animal, the dolphin, for example, cannot suffer, then this also has ethical consequences, and we can henceforth treat the dolphin like a stone. It does seem that we human beings treat many animals as though they were at the bottom of the moral status value scale. It is also possible that human beings are well aware of the moral status of other creatures but nevertheless pay no attention to it.

One problem is the relationship between human beings and animals. Although a rat and a cat are biologically similar in their capacity for suffering, people generally attach more value to their cat than to a rat that enters their house. Rats are exterminated, cats are pampered. But if a rat has the same moral status as a cat, is it then not immoral to kill rats? Or is the method of killing the issue? Muskrats, many of which undermine dikes, are caught in underwater traps. As a result they drown. Not exactly a pleasant or easy death.

As a vegetarian I ate fish for a while. And that was stupid. Fish can suffer, too. Actually, I knew that, but I repressed the idea. Novelist Ian McEwan's novel *Saturday* (2005) contains the following trenchant passage. Henry Perowne, brain surgeon, reflects while he is shopping in the market and buys fish from a stall: "It's fortunate for the fishmonger and his customers that sea creatures are not adapted to make use of sound waves and have no voice. . . . It was once convenient to think biblically, to believe we're surrounded for our benefit by edible automata on land and sea. Now it turns out that even fish feel pain. This is the growing complication of the modern condition, the expanding circle of moral sympathy. Not only distant peoples are our brothers and sisters, but foxes too, and laboratory mice, and now the fish. Perowne goes on catching and eating them, and though he has never dropped a live lobster into boiling water, he's prepared to order one in a restaurant. The trick, as always, the key to human success and domination, is to be selective in your mercies. For all the discerning talk, it's the close at hand, the visible that exerts the overpowering force. And what you don't see. That's why in gentle Marylebone the world seems so entirely at peace."[28]

Where do species fit on the scale of suffering, the eel species or the tuna species? An individual eel and an individual tuna can suffer, but can the eel or tuna *species* suffer? In environmental philosophy and within ecological organizations, such as the World Wildlife Federation, value is often attached to species of animals. People are going to a lot of trouble to save pandas or tigers from extinction. But is it morally wrong if a species becomes extinct, whether as the result of human activity or not? Let me limit myself to the tuna species. This enormous fish has a quality, disadvantageous both for the species and for individual tuna, that human beings' mouths begin to water at the thought of its flesh, and therefore it is fished out of the seas at a rapid pace, with the result that tuna is on the list of species in danger of extinction, unless tuna comes to be commercially farmed. For whom is it bad if the tuna dies out? For every tuna the suffering done to it by human beings is morally unacceptable. But beyond that, is it bad if the species as a whole becomes extinct? It may be that the extinction of a species brings about the disturbance of an ecosystem and thus has all kinds of disadvantageous consequences for that ecosystem. There is also an aesthetic argument: there will not be any more tuna: not to see, not to taste. It looks as if the extinction of a species has moral consequences for human beings or other animals, but that the species has no moral value in itself.

Here the animal rights movement comes into conflict with environmental associations. For animal activists the issue is the individual animal with moral status. Ecological activists look at the ecosystem as a whole. An example of the conflict is the century-old Dutch organization *Natuurmonumenten* (Nature Monuments), which catches tens of thousands of wild geese annually and, over the protests of animal lovers, gasses them in order to protect what they have pictured as nature! Natuurmonument wants an ecosystem in which geese do not play such a dominant role at the cost of other species of birds.

Intensive Livestock Farming

If your only concern is animal suffering, you should eat crustaceans rather than fish, because crustaceans are lower on the evolutionary ladder and therefore lower on the moral status value scale. Better yet, eat jellyfish and algae.

If you limit the thought experiment of universal subjectivism to the United States, and you could be born as a human being or an animal, the chances of ending up in a factory farm would be greater than that you would be born as a human. This means that, for your own benefit, you would do well to limit, as much as possible, the suffering you would experience if you were to end up as a farm animal. In a positive sense this means that you should be able to satisfy all your natural urges. As a pig you would root around in the mud, as a chicken you would search for grain, as a cow you would graze in a meadow. The veterinarian and philosopher Bernard E. Rollin cites research indicating that the behavior of pigs born on a factory farm exhibit the behavior of wild pigs if they are released into the outdoors: "Generally the behavior of . . . pigs, born and reared in an intensive system, once they had the appropriate environment, resembled that of the European wild boar."[29] So, all those millions of pigs that never get to go outside from their animal prison are deprived of the possibilities to live a life according to their natural instincts.

Someone who looks at our modern industrialized society from the perspective of an industrial farm animal will be shocked. For human beings, matters are extraordinarily well arranged. No one falls through the cracks. We are free and live in prosperity. Holland, for example, is a paradise. Never before in the history of the world have societies existed in which there was so much freedom for *all* individuals, so much prosperity, so much comfort, so many opportunities for development and self-realization. But this is not true for animals. Since the industrialization of livestock-raising began, notably in the second half of the twentieth century, the number of animals has grown exponentially and animal welfare has shrunk in the same way. Someone who looks at Holland from the animal per-spective sees a hell on earth: concentration camps, torture on a hith-erto unknown scale. But hardly anyone cares. The animal welfare movement, inspired by people like Peter Singer and Tom Regan, is trying to do something about it. Several factors are complicating their efforts. First of all, people want many and inexpensive animal products, and, second, farmers want to earn money. The dynamic between supply and demand ensures that the interest and welfare of animals are subordinated to economic interests. Regulations con-cerning animal welfare do in fact exist, but in practice they are con-travened on a wholesale basis. There is, then, a large degree of social indifference. Now and then images showing the facts about factory farming trickle out to the media, as in May of 2011, when a news story about the maltreatment of Australian cattle in Indonesian slaughter-houses prompted outrage in Australia and a ban on the export of farm animals to Indonesia.[30] Incidents of this kind are reported often enough that no one can say: "We didn't know what was happening!" People know very well the miserable living conditions of the animals they consume, but they simply don't give a damn. Not, at least, when you see how they behave. Perhaps people won't say out loud that they don't care about the suffering of animals, but their purchasing behavior implicitly condones the abuses and ensures that intensive livestock-raising continues to exist.

Veganism as Solution

How can animal suffering be reduced? Governments could prohibit factory farming and permit the raising of livestock only when animal welfare can be guaranteed. The question is whether livestock can be raised that way at all. Seen from the perspective of universal subjectivism, so that you yourself would have to think up the rules for the original situation, you would end up with a prohibition on factory farming because you have to consider the possibility that you might land in the worst possible position, for example as a crated calf. But not only governments have responsibility. The citizen is responsible because consumers determine demand. If consumers ask for cheap animal products, the market will supply them. But consumers can also choose to buy only products to which no animal suffering is attached. That means buying no animal-unfriendly products at all. There is, therefore, a moral obligation to adopt veganism, the nonconsumption of animal products—no dairy products, eggs, or leather.

It is the meat-eaters who have to justify why they eat meat. Not the other way around, as is now often the case when a vegan is asked: "Why don't you eat meat?" The writer and animal rights activist J. M. Coetzee quotes Plutarch: "You ask me why I refuse to eat flesh. I, for my part, am astonished that you can put in your mouth the corpse of a dead animal, am astonished that you do not find it nasty to chew and swallow the juices of death-wounds."[31] If you do harm to human beings or animals, you must have a good reason. You don't need to excuse yourself if you don't harm or injure humans or animals. Suppose I am a vandal and set fire to cars at random. Do people have to elaborately explain to me at a party why they don't set fire to cars? Vegans are sometimes treated like pariahs, but it should be the other way around: people who don't care about animal suffering, but who are guilty of it by buying animal products, should be pariahs. When will we be able to welcome the first prime minister or president who is openly an ethical vegan? I mean that the reasons for veganism should be moral reasons, not religious reasons such as a Hindu. It would help, too, if film stars and other role models would identify themselves as vegans; a few, Paul McCartney for one, have done so. Many celebrities are vegetarians or vegans. Lists can be found at www .famousveggie.com and www.happycow.net.

Veganism is the simple solution to a complicated problem. The transformation of intensive, animal-unfriendly livestock-raising into animal-friendly, organic, extensive, and sustainable livestock-raising is much more complicated than ceasing to use animal products. This is the case even though it is probably more difficult to overcome people's psychological barriers than to make all those complicated and laborious regulations. Philosopher-veterinarian Bernard Rollin makes a plea for the complicated option: the transformation of the livestock industry—and the human-animal relationship more generally—into one that is more animal-friendly.[32]

There is much lack of clarity surrounding veganism. Not all vegans are worried about animal suffering. There are also health-conscious vegans. There are, indeed, good reasons for believing that a diet without animal products is healthier than the average eating habits of people who do consume animal products.[33] The scandals surrounding factory farming (the entire industry is a morally outrageous, but the media swoop down on it only when the health of human beings is at issue), among others mad-cow disease, chickens with high dioxin levels, and the use of hormones and antibiotics in livestock, have demonstrated that meat is not always healthy. There are large meat and dairy lobbies. Milk is widely advertised as an ideal food, but nothing matches the campaigns constantly waged on behalf of the hamburgers served by the major fast food chains. The propaganda machine insists that meat is good for you and even a requirement for being healthy and strong. That this is nonsense was proven by the Olympic sprint champion Carl Lewis, who was a vegan during his glory years.[34]

Ethical veganism means that people decide to eat no more meat on ethical grounds. Vegans don't consume any animal products. Vegans are more consistent than vegetarians. Vegetarians consume some animal like dairy, eggs and leather, all of which involve the harming and eventual killing of animals. Veganism demands a big change in lifestyle. You have to expend a lot of effort. This is because the entire society based upon animal consumption. And yet in recent years cautious changes seem to be taking place. Vegetarian and vegan restaurants are becoming increasingly common, and most restaurants have vegetarian dishes on the menu. Occasionally there is even a vegan option. And these days, people who send out dinner invitations ask whether anyone is vegetarian. As a vegetarian/vegan you are often treated circumspectly, a bit like someone who is mentally handicapped: "Yes, this gentleman here is vegetarian!" Many people find it an incomprehensible choice. Veganism is something else again. I am striving to be a vegan. I don't have leather shoes anymore, but vegan (non-leather) shoes.[35] I won't buy leather-upholstered furniture or leather clothing. Instead of animal milk I use organic soymilk. This is fine for cereal but not for a café latte. For a time I used organic milk to add to my organic fair-trade coffee. When I showed my students *Meet Your Meat*,[36] and I watched the video for the umpteenth time, the truth suddenly dawned on me: to obtain milk from a cow the calf has to be separated from its mother right after birth. The treatment of dairy cows with their heavy udders is not optimal either, and they are slaughtered in the end when milk production goes down. From that moment I stopped using milk or yogurt, and as a consequence I have stopped drinking lattes. It was difficult to stop ordering a grande latte or making one, but I persisted. It turns out that I do like my coffee black, and that is a nice break. After the fact, I don't understand why I did not take that step earlier, just as I don't understand why I did not become a vegetarian earlier. I have been a vegetarian for fifteen years and have strived to be a vegan for two years, but even before that time I was acquainted with the facts of factory farming. I'm ashamed about that now.

I know that veganism is ethically the superior option, and I aspire to that. It is important to be a vegan in your sleep as well. To sleep as a vegan you must not lie under a duvet made of eiderdown, which may have been taken off living birds.[37] Vegetarianism/veganism consists of a spectrum from part-time vegetarians at one end (fake vegetarians, actually, although reducing one's consumption is of course a step in the right direction) to vegans at the other end.

It is entirely possible to live a healthy life without eating animal products. Vitamin B12 is the only thing that is not easy to get in other ways than from meat or dairy. But B12 is added to many meat substitutes, and there's vitamin B12 in every bottle of multivitamins. Our two sons are being raised as vegetarians and for the past two years as vegans. We don't forbid them to consume meat or other animal products at other people's homes, but we don't buy animal products ourselves. The boys (9 and 10 years old) are thoroughly healthy. They are not overweight. People ask: what if they want to eat meat later? Well, we don't cook with it. So if our sons decide later that they do want to eat meat, it will have to be away from home. We won't forbid it, but we will continue to provide information. If they nevertheless eat meat, that is their own, well-informed choice. It is a choice I shall regret, but it won't influence our relationship.

Consuming Less

There are people who are consuming less and consciously consuming fewer animal products. The less we consume the products of animal torture, the better. However, in the prosperous Western countries the consumption of animal products continues to increase. A few decades ago it was common not to eat meat daily. Consuming less is not an example of morally elevated behavior, it is a lamentable minimum. You can compare it to the behavior of someone who usually speeds and who resolves to keep to the speed limit now and then, and congratulates himself for doing so.

Aside from eating less meat, it is possible to consume free-range meat and organic dairy products. In this case the animals are treated better than their counterparts in factory farms. A lot of confusion exists about the descriptions and terminology: "organic" and "free range" can apply to the way the animals are treated (animal welfare) as well as to the feed provided to the animals. Factory animals are given feed they would not eat in a natural environment. The farmers feed the animals whatever is cheapest, promotes the most rapid growth, and does not make them visibly ill, which means lots of antibiotics. It can happen that cattle feed contains protein made from cow carcasses, although cows are herbivores. This may have led to mad-cow disease. These days many animal products have quality trademarks and labels. The way factory-farming products are packaged can make it seem as if the animals led idyllic lives. Egg cartons may carry images of beautiful farms and meadows. Free-range chickens are not usually allowed to have their feed in the open air. No, it means that the chickens can walk freely in a barn without natural light, with an average area of one piece of letter-size paper per chicken. 'Free-range' turns out to be a misnomer. In Europe eggs are labeled from 0 to 3. The number 0 (organic free range) is best for the consumer as well as the chicken. But these eggs are also the most expensive. Number 3 eggs come from battery chickens. In poultry farming, battery cages are an industrial agricultural confinement system (factory farming) used primarily for egg-laying hens. The name comes from the lines of similar cages connected together, sharing common divider walls. Battery chickens live a miserable life, cramped into tiny metal cages. Because their toes must curl around the bars to stay upright, most cannot walk on a flat surface. The only thing they have to eat is chicken feed—no grass, no scraps, no insects, none of the food that free chickens like to eat. If you were a chicken—and by means of the thought experiment that is possible— what kind would you like to be? Any volunteers for being a battery hen? We need an awful lot of them, because 97 percent of all eggs are produced in that way, under the worst possible conditions.

Unfortunately there is a lot of hidden use of dairy products and eggs. Only a small percentage of eggs are sold in stores as eggs; the great majority of them are used in other products, such as cakes and cookies and other processed foods. How likely is it that a producer will choose free-range eggs? This means that even people who are consciously choosing to buy organic products are nevertheless consuming the products of animal torture. That is also true of restaurants. When it comes to animal suffering, fast-food chains are at the top of the list. A seal of approval is needed to encourage restaurants to use only organic animal products. Actually, it is strange that something like that should be necessary to indicate that restaurants use animal-friendly products.

THE PARABLE OF THE SUPER-TASTY HUMAN FLESH

Why do people eat meat? Is it because of its taste, habit, laziness, conceit, being macho? When I'm dining with people, I usually hear only the argument of taste: "This meat tastes so good." I don't deny it. I'll go further: I, too, like the taste of meat. The smell of grilled meat makes my mouth water. But suppose that human flesh were to taste much better than the most succulent piece of filet mignon, would that be an argument for cannibalism?

THE PARABLE OF THE HUMAN-EATING ALIENS

On November 14, 2014, alien scouts landed on planet Earth. The first things that caught their eye were the luscious, tender, two-legged mammals that were present in large quantities. The aliens wasted no time and undertook the colonization of planet Earth, in which they took steps to fatten up the erect bipeds on large farms. The aliens' advanced technology and high intelligence easily enabled them to domesticate the bipeds in human farms. To prevent screaming, which can cause a nuisance, newborns are put through the devocalization machine to remove their vocal cords. Human meat, human dairy products, leather, hair, and teeth are popular among the aliens, and therefore the production of humans has been stepped up. Women are inseminated artificially and have, on average, three to four children per delivery. The aliens also use the bipeds for all kinds of entertainment. For example, there are game reserves where the bipeds can be hunted. Some alien thinkers believe they can discern a form of rudimentary intelligence in humans and point out that they seem to be able to feel pain. The majority of the aliens don't worry about this, however: how can you have a proper barbecue without children's rump?

Outspoken Veganism

You can keep your veganism to yourself and treat it as something highly personal, never talking about it with others. But actually it is important to do so, to speak about it within the bounds of common decency. That is active veganism. As a vegan you aren't part of the problem but part of the solution to animal suffering and ecological damage, the philosopher Michael Allen Fox has remarked.[38] But it's not easy to adopt a minority point of view, to always be the exception, the one who is "difficult." Yet right is not always on the side of the big battalions. On the contrary: large groups are capable of great injustice. Fortunately vegans are not undergoing persecution. In fact, vegetarianism is more or less on the increase. Vegetarian dishes appear on menus and vegetarian products such as meat substitutes are available in stores. Will a time ever come when people look back with astonishment at the time when their ancestors ate large quantities of meat without shame or scruples, as we observe with amazement that human beings, even partly civilized peoples like the Greeks and Romans and, much later, President Thomas Jefferson, owned slaves without feeling shame? I hope so. But changes don't happen all by themselves. Slavery has been abolished; we are aware that slavery is morally pernicious. In the past it was otherwise. A moral reversal, a *Gestalt* switch, has taken place. The circle of morality has become larger. That is moral progress.

"Human beings are omnivores! They happen to eat meat. That's the way nature is. You can't change things just like that." These are oft-heard arguments and yes, human beings are, just like the other primates, omnivores. But humans can't digest raw meat easily, so it must first be roasted or grilled or cooked. Humans are not dependent on animal products for a healthy and all-round diet. It is more than possible to follow a healthy and tasty vegan diet. Meat-eaters sometimes say: "You can't turn a lion into a vegetarian, right?" No, that you can't do. Lions are carnivores; their diet consists entirely of raw meat. In ethics the issue is not what animals do among themselves, but what humans do with animals. Ethics as it relates to animals is about the human-animal relationship. Lions are bound to their nature. They can't do anything but eat meat. Humans are more flexible and can reflect on what they do and eat. Humans do a lot of unnatural things—brushing their teeth, for example. All culture is unnatural. Humankind is the most unnatural animal. Nature is cruel and a lot of suffering takes place.[39] That's the way it is. But humans are responsible for their actions. Humans can choose: they can treat other animals humanely or tolerate terrible suffering.

In times past, and in the Third World even today, humans depended and depend on animal products for survival. That changes the situation. If eating meat and fish is necessary for survival, then that is less immoral than if there is no such necessity. Furthermore, poor Africans dependent on eating meat often consume free-range animals that stay around their homes or are caught in the wild. These animals do not, as in the prosperous countries, originate in intensive livestock-raising or fish farms.

PARABLE OF THE NEW VEGETARIANISM: EATING INSECTS

In his 2010 TED (Technology, Entertainment, Design) talk, ento-mologist Marcel Dicke made a plea for eating insects instead of mammals, fish, and poultry.[40] Dicke addressed the abundant environmental, ethical, and economic advantages of eating insects. To support his point of view he outlines five arguments. (1) As humans, we are more distantly related to them than to the animals we (Westerners) eat, so there is less risk of diseases spreading from insects to humans. (2) Insects produce less polluting waste than, for example, cattle. (3) Insect farming is much more efficient than factory farming of cows, pigs, or chickens. It is therefore much more profitable. Ten pounds of feed produce one pound of beef, whereas ten pounds of feed can produce nine pounds of locusts. (4) Insects are full of proteins, minerals, and vitamins, and are therefore nutritious and healthy. (5) Insects have less capacity for suffering than vertebrates. They are invertebrates and it is widely believed that they respond solely to sensory stimuli (with the probable exception of octopuses and squid). Insects are capable of responding to pain, avoiding hurtful stimuli and limiting the use of injured body parts.[41] Evidence for the existence of emotions in insects, such as distress, anxiety, and suffering, is still absent. It is safe to say that insects are much lower on the scale of suffering than the vertebrates we eat. It should be added that insects are considered a delicacy in many Asian countries. With a growing population and a growing demand for meat, eating insects might be an alternative to vegetarianism. We will have to overcome our cultural abhorrence against eating insects. But what other viable options do we have? Meat production is an environmental and moral disaster.

Still, why eat animals at all if we can have a healthy vegan diet? Perhaps insects do suffer in one way or another. Using the precautionary principle, if you are not sure whether an animal can suffer, don't harm it unnecessarily. All of this will lead to intensive insect farming, as is now the case with bee farming. We don't need to do it. According to deep ecologists, we should restrain ourselves where animals and nature are concerned and tread lightly on the earth. Organic meat is better than factory-farm meat. Eating less meat is healthier than eating a lot of it. Eating insects is better than eating meat. Eating no meat (or insects) at all, and consuming an organic plant based diet, is best of all.

Who Is to Blame for Factory Farming?

Is it the consumers, the farmers, the shops and supermarkets, the slaughterhouses, the politicians, the engineers, or the veterinarians?[42] There isn't one specific group that can be designated as the most blameworthy. There is a chain of responsibility. Everybody shares in it. Since everybody has only a small role within the chain, the buck of responsibility and guilt can be passed on to somebody else. This is what I think of as the "pass-the-buck problem": who is responsible for what?

The farmers and shopkeepers say: there is demand for these products. Consumers say: it's available in the stores, isn't it? And, everyone is buying it. Government says: aren't the laws adequate? And, there is a strong demand. Veterinarians say: we're employed by the farmers. Engineers say: we are asked to design stables and slaughterhouses that are as efficient as possible. It's all understandable, but added together it leads to animal suffering on an inconceivably large scale. I have already made the argument for the moral duty to be vegan. Now I am going to focus on the role of the veterinarians, who claim to be concerned about the well-being of individual animals.

The philosopher Jerrold Tannenbaum, who specializes in veterinary ethics, states: "There can be no guarantees that ethical deliberation will always make life easier for beleaguered large animal practitioners."[43] In a dissertation done for Utrecht University, L. J. E. Rutgers quotes from a survey of veterinarians about the limits of veterinary action. Here are a few excerpts:

"If we give medical treatment to animals it may be necessary from the veterinary point of view, even though we don't support the objective or assist in the achievement of certain objectives. It is also necessary to persuade owners that their objectives for keeping animals may be wrong."

"There are calves in my practice. Many right-minded people have objections to the way these animals are kept. Me too, but I still try to keep these farmers as clients."

"Unfortunately veterinarians are usually asked to solve the problems inherent in techniques and systems. The question arises: do I leave the animal in its condition or do I try to help the animal survive the system?"

"Many stabling systems are far from optimal. It's unrealistic not to offer cooperation in these cases. The next fellow may think differently about this. Information and legal regulations should change the situation."

"There are systems that I think should in future be prohibited. The problem is that if you want to get the same results with the alternatives as with the traditional systems, the quality of livestock owners must be improved. That will happen only when the mentality of this group changes."

"There are many situations in livestock raising that need adaptation or complete change, but that doesn't mean that we should absolutely decline to cooperate. By withdrawing completely from systems, you can't exercise any further influence."[44]

The problems signaled here mostly concern intensive livestock-raising. Veterinarians are wrestling with the question of their role in the agrarian industrial complex. In the above quotations it is evident that the issue of responsibility for the welfare of animals is sloughed off to various other groups: the livestock owner, the consumer, the next fellow, and society.

Jerrold Tannenbaum, in his comprehensive guidebook *Veterinary Ethics* (1995), adopts a rather facile and conservative point of view:

A fundamental premise upon which all farm and performance animal practice rests is that people may sometimes[45] use animals for purposes such as food, fiber, and entertainment. This view is so widely and deeply held that one can assert it not just as a fact of life which any realistic approach to veterinary ethics must accept as a given, but also as a correct moral principle.[46] . . . Through the centuries, in diverse places and cultures, the overwhelming majority of humankind has consulted its basic moral intuitions—and has concluded that it is proper to use animals for food, fiber, draft, entertainment, and companionship. Abolitionists may prefer to think that this has been a giant, horrible prejudice. However, the fact that most people who have lived and toiled on this earth have arrived at the same general conclusion is powerful evidence of its correctness.[47]

Tannenbaum sees little point in a dialogue between proponents and opponents of the use of animals for the benefit of humankind, because "those who endorse abolitionism are no more likely to accept refutations of their point of view than the rest of us would be disposed to agree that an animal farmer is the moral equivalent of a slave owner, or that a meat-eater is no better than a cannibal."[48]

From the point of view of animal-welfare thought, such as that of Peter Singer, the livestock farmer is in some senses definitely comparable to a slave owner. According to Tom Regan, killing some kinds of mammals is equivalent to murder.[49]

The Animal Holocaust[50]

In J. M. Coetzee's 1999 novella *The Lives of Animals*, the protagonist, Elizabeth Costello, compares factory farming to the Holocaust. This book is a tract about animal suffering in novella form. The message is not new, but the reading audience is much larger and also includes readers who may not be acquainted with the works of Peter Singer and Tom Regan. "A stimulating and worrying book. It is hard to imagine anyone coming away from it without a new perspective on our relation not only to animals but to the natural world in general, and, indeed, to ourselves," John Banville wrote in reviewing the book in *The Irish Times*; the quotation appears on the cover of the novella. The story is about the feminist author Elizabeth Costello, who has been invited by an American university to give two lectures about the treatment of animals by humans. She shocks her audience by comparing the treatment of animals in factory farms (she calls them "production facilities") with the Holocaust. The guests' reactions during the ensuing dinner provide an overview of common replies and apologia. The novella's style resembles Plato's dialogues, and in particular the *Symposium*, in which a philosophical discussion takes place during a meal.

In her lecture Costello remarks that the production facilities have been well hidden: "I was taken on a drive around Waltham this morning. It seems a pleasant enough town. I saw no horrors, no drug-testing laboratories, no factory farms, and no abattoirs. Yet I am sure they are here. They must be. They simply do not advertise themselves. They are all around us as I speak, only we do not, in a certain sense, know about them. Let me say it openly: we are surrounded by an enterprise of degradation, cruelty, and killing which rivals anything the Third Reich was capable of, indeed dwarfs it, in that ours is an enterprise without end, self-regenerating, bringing rabbits, rats, poultry, livestock ceaselessly into the world for the purpose of killing them.[51]

Costello compares factory farming with the Holocaust and the psychology of cruelty. She points at a gigantic moral blind spot:

> The question to ask should not be: Do we have something in common—reason, self-consciousness, a soul—with other animals? (With the corollary that, if we do not, then we are entitled to treat them as we like, imprisoning them, killing them, and dishonoring their corpses.) I return to the death camps. The particular horror of the camps, the horror that convinces us that what went on there was a crime against humanity, is not that despite a humanity shared with their victims, the killers treated them like lice. That is too abstract. The horror is that the killers refused to think themselves into the place of their victims, as did everyone else. They said, "It is *they* in those cattle-cars rattling past." They did not say, "How would it be if it were I in that cattle-car?" They did not say, "It is I who am in that cattle-car." They said, "It must be the dead who are being burnt today, making the air stink and falling in ash on my cabbages." They did not say, "How would it be if I were burning?" They did not say, "I am burning, I am falling in ash." In other words, they closed their hearts. The heart is the seat of a faculty, *sympathy*, which allows us to share at times the being of another. . . . There are people who have the capacity to imagine themselves as someone else, there are people who have no such capacity (when the lack is extreme, we call them psychopaths), and there are people who have the capacity but choose not to exercise it.[52]

During the dinner a discussion develops about the mental capacities of animals, in particular about consciousness that is more or less exclusively human. In the comments that follow, Costello characterizes speciesism without using the term: "They have no consciousness *therefore*. Therefore what? Therefore we are free to use them for our own ends? Therefore we are free to kill them? Why? What is so special about the form of consciousness we recognize that makes killing a bearer of it a crime while killing an animal goes unpunished?" A fellow diner completes the thought for her: "Therefore all this discussion of consciousness and whether animals have it is just a smoke screen. At bottom we protect our own kind. Thumbs up to human babies, thumbs down to veal calves."[53]

Her opponent in the story is a professor of philosophy who introduces moral relativism: "When it comes to human rights . . . other cultures and other religious traditions quite properly reply that they have their own norms and see no reason why they should have to adopt those of the West. Similarly, they say, they have their own norms for the treatment of animals and see no reason to adopt ours— particularly when ours are of such recent invention. . . . As long as we insist that we have access to an ethical universal to which other traditions are blind, and try to impose on them by means of propaganda or even economic pressure, we are going to meet with resistance, and that resistance will be justified." To this Costello replies: "You are correct, of course, about the history. Kindness to animals has become a social norm only recently, in the last hundred and fifty or two hundred years, and in only part of the world. You are correct too to link this history to the history of human rights, since concern for animals is, historically speaking, an offshoot of broader philanthropic concerns—for the lot of slaves and of children, among others."[54]

The relativistic philosopher who tries to respect cultural differences and who shows respect for non-Western cultures ignores intolerance and cruelty. In terms of universal subjectivism you would have to ask: what is the worst possible situation? Are there victim situations? This is independent of any and all cultural traditions. Factory farming was developed in the West and has spread quickly around the world, just at the point that in the West a marginal protest movement against it is becoming culturally acceptable. The philosopher has yet another trump card that he now plays: animals don't fear death. "I do not believe that life is as important to animals as it is to us. There is certainly in animals an instinctive struggle against death, which they share with us. But they do not *understand* death as we do, or rather, as we fail to do. There is, in the human mind, a collapse of the imagination before death, and that collapse of the imagination . . . is the basis of our fear of death. That fear does not and cannot exist in animals, since the effort to comprehend extinction, and the failure to master it, have simply not taken place. For that reason, I want to suggest, dying is, for an animal, just something that happens, something against which there may be a revolt of the organism but not a revolt of the soul. And the lower down the scale of evolution one goes, the truer this is. To an insect, death is the breakdown of systems that keep the physical organism functioning, and nothing more."[55] The philosopher quite rightly puts the ability to conceive of one's own death and to fear it—specifically how someone's life comes to an end—on a scale. What the philosopher ignores is the evolutionary scale of the capacity to suffer, in which the fear of one's own death is not the sole parameter. Perhaps cows don't fear their own death (although cows don't enjoy going to the slaughterhouse), but cows can definitely suffer, and it is the suffering *caused by human beings* that is morally relevant. The issue is not consciousness (consciousness-centrism), nor is it life (biocentrism), but it is suffering (pathocentrism). After the second lecture, Costello's son remarks, "If I were asked what the general attitude is towards the animals we eat, I would say: contempt. We treat them badly because we despise them; we despise them because they don't fight back."[56] When you deal with the matter from the perspective of animal suffering, the perspective on our civilization alters dramatically: the peaceful "civilized" Western countries show themselves to be barbaric and cruel societies in which almost all citizens are willing executioners.

Costello says to her son John, "I seem to move around perfectly easily among people, to have perfectly normal relations with them. Is it possible, I ask myself, that all of them are participating in a crime of stupefying proportions? Am I fantasizing it all? I must be mad! Yet every day I see the evidences. The very people I suspect produce the evidence, exhibit it, offer it to me. Corpses. Fragments of corpses that they have bought for money. It is as if I were to visit friends, and to make some polite remark about the lamp in their living room, and they were to say, 'Yes, it's nice, isn't it? Polish-Jewish skin it's made of, we find that's best, the skins of young Polish-Jewish virgins.' And then I go to the bathroom and the soap-wrapper says: 'Treblinka—100% human stearate.' Am I dreaming, I say to myself? What kind of house is this? But I'm not dreaming. . . . Calm down, I tell myself, you are making a mountain out of a molehill. This is life. Everyone comes to terms with it, why can't you? *Why can't you?*"[57]

Will Coetzee's literary pamphlet bring about a moral Gestalt switch? But, as Henry Perowne, the protagonist of Ian McEwan's novel *Saturday*, shows, there is a difference between knowledge and acting on the basis of that knowledge. That is the immoral tragedy of the human condition.

Anti-fur Activism

In the summer of 2009 the action group Respect for Animals was active in Maastricht (Netherlands), targeting stores that sell fur. Activist Max Boon stated: "After actions in the 1980s and 1990s, fur had almost completely vanished from the streets. Now it's making a comeback. People walk around in the fur of mink, foxes and rabbits as if it's nothing."[58] The organization Fur Is for Animals, like PETA in the United States, is working for the abolition of the fur industry and against the wearing of fur. Animal activists agitate more often against fur than against leather products, because in the case of fur animals are raised only for their coats and then killed, and because there is no necessity at all for fur since there are plenty of alternatives. However, when you choose the pathocentric perspective and you look at the suffering done to animals, it makes no difference what objectives animals are used for. The AIVD, the Dutch Domestic Security Service, regards Respect for Animals as "the symbol of radical animal rights activism."[59]

Animal-Friendly Veterinarians: An Oxymoron?

In 1976 a former chairman of the Royal Netherlands Society of Veterinary Medicine, H. A. van Riessen, stated a very different view from that adopted by veterinarian-philosopher Jerrold Tannenbaum. He said: "If *we* don't do it, who on earth will take the side of the animals? Just about everybody is to blame for the situation in which we have put the domesticated animals. And veterinary science has an inescapable specific responsibility for that state of affairs."[60] According to Van Riessen, veterinarians should play an active role in defending animal welfare. The Dutch Code for Veterinarians (2007) enjoins veterinarians as a professional group to promote the "advancement of the health and welfare of animals" and to assume collective responsibility for advancing the interests of animals.

It is understandable in a way that veterinarians have not taken the lead, given the slack attitude evident in jurisprudence in the Netherlands, and in the rest of the world, where animal welfare is concerned.

Brambell's Five Freedoms

In 1965 the British government commissioned an enquiry, chaired by F. W. R. Brambell, to concern itself with the development of ethical guidelines for farm animals in intensive livestock-raising. The Brambell committee formulated five principles, the so-called Brambell's five freedoms. Farm animals should be free:

1. from thirst, hunger, and an improper diet;
2. from discomfort and physical inconvenience;
3. from pain, injury, and disease;
4. from fear and distress;
5. to express normal behavior appropriate to their kind.

These are splendid ethical principles, but animals on factory farms can scarcely be aware of them. The ethical guidelines exist on paper, but they have fallen on deaf ears.

Symbolic Legislation

Lawyer Dirk Boon has emphasized that there are lots of laws to protect animals, but that they are not enforced. This is a tragic example of "tolerance"—in this case the toleration of matters that are prohibited by law. Boon writes: "I merely observe that the general principle in our jurisprudence that animals may not be abused is tested to a very limited extent by the judiciary. . . . I observe that all attempts to offer active protection to animals, using the animal protection legislation, have failed."[61] Boon claims that this is a case of symbolic legislation. By the same token it could be claimed that the Code for Veterinarians has symbolic value only, in view of the enormous extent of animal suffering to which veterinarians lend their indirect support, by accepting farmers involved in factory farming among their clients, by the failure to take collective action, and, third, by consuming animal products that have been produced in a manner that is in flagrant denial of their own code. Dirk Boon concludes: "This means that in this country you can harm the welfare of animals for your own ends in every possible way without scruples or second thoughts, and although a few questions may be asked and a few eyebrows raised, no one will prevent you from doing what you want."[62] He also states: "Although during the last 25 years every conceivable ethical argument to give protection to animals, made from every conceivable perspective, has been advanced in hundreds of publications, although evolutionary biology, genetic research and ethology . . . have in recent years made ample findings from which it is evident that the differences between the human species and other animal species are gradual rather than essential, that animals' well-being can be harmed, and that well-being is an operational and measurable concept, I feel safe in claiming that so far not a single animal has derived the slightest benefit from all these efforts. We know that animals are harmed by our behavior. But we don't do anything about it. How come?"[63]

What is needed is a cultural change in our conceptions about animals. In the human-animal relationship—and in a wider sense the human-environment relationship—humankind has placed itself on a pedestal. There is a large blind spot where the consequences of human action for animals and for nature in general are concerned. The language sounds good (legislation, codes, intentions), but all these fine words cannot prevent or reduce the harm done to animals.

Whom does a veterinarian work for anyway, animals or human beings? Veterinarians are part of the ruling ideology and practice in which humankind subjugates nature: animals exist for humans, as Tannenbaum asserts, and if it pleases humans to secure help for sick animals a veterinarian is called in. If humans want to get rid of animals, they are put down. Sometimes on an enormous scale, as when poultry is slaughtered. Domestic pets, free-range farm animals, animals in zoos—these are animals that humans are concerned about in one way or another. It looks as if a number of veterinarians suffer from moral and cognitive dissonance: during the day they go to a lot of trouble to keep animals alive and healthy, and in the evening they eat a steak and give their own pets other animals to eat.

The ethical perspective of utilitarianism, putting the suffering and well-being of animals in a central position, can lead to a change in the relations between humankind and animals. Seen from this ethical perspective it is a moral necessity collectively to ban factory farming and individually to stop eating meat. When veterinarians take the side of animal welfare in a serious way, they can play a catalyzing role in the cultural change with respect to animals. In the second half of the twentieth century, a cultural change took place in livestock-raising, from extensive to intensive farming, using mechanization, technology, and, later, automation. Livestock-raising has become an industrial agrarian complex on an enormous scale. The number of farm animals has increased greatly during the last few decades.

What animals do veterinarians treat? They treat animals for which owners call for the help of veterinarians and discuss treatment with them, in which financial arguments play a part. Rich people can request cosmetic procedures for their dogs. Someone who lives on social welfare payments and whose dog is hit by a car and who has no money for an operation can do little but have the animal euthanized. The well-being and health of an animal depend on all kinds of considerations beyond the so-called intrinsic value of the individual animal. Veterinarians are not "physicians for animals" in general, but "physicians for animals to which human beings assign a positive value, whether instrumental or not."

The Netherlands is in many ways an achieved utopia: nowhere else in the world, except in a few other Western countries, is there such a high degree of prosperity and social justice as in the Netherlands. Anyone who looks at the Netherlands with blinders might think that it is a heaven on earth: nobody dies of hunger, women are emancipated, homosexuals are equal and accepted, there is a high degree of individual freedom, and the infrastructure is marvelous. At the same time, however, the Netherlands is a hell for pigs and other farm animals. Just as in the age of Pericles Athens was perhaps a paradise for rich male citizens, and at the same time a hell for slaves, so the Netherlands also has several dimensions. Here, however, the unspeakable animal suffering is invisible to most people. This excuse does not apply to the veterinary profession, however: veterinarians are confronted with intensive livestock-raising, and with slaughterhouses and livestock transports that are monitored by veterinarians.

If veterinarians take as their point of departure "the promotion of the health and well-being of the animal, with regard for the acknowledgment of the intrinsic value of the animal," how can that be squared with the role they play in the industrial agrarian complex?

Article 6 of the Code for Veterinarians (2007) states in part:

In their actions veterinarians are guided by:

- the promotion of the health and well-being of the animal, with regard for the acknowledgment of the intrinsic value of the animal;
- the promotion of public health and environmental hygiene;
- the interests of the owner of the animal and/or the owner of the animal products;
- the place and function of veterinary medicine and its practitioners in society;
- whatever else can reasonably be considered to be of importance.[64]

This raises the question of how the facts about factory farming stated above can be squared with article 6. It looks as if the interests of the owner (the farmer) prevail over the interests of animals. Public health also seems to weigh heavily enough to resort to large-scale slaughter in case of a threatened epidemic.

The philosopher-veterinarian Bernard E. Rollin states in his *Introduction to Veterinary Medical Ethics: Theory and Cases* (2000) that the fundamental question in the ethics of veterinary medicine concerns the duty of the physician to the *individual* animal. Rollin uses these words: "[P]erhaps the most difficult moral problem that confronts veterinarians today concerns the veterinarian's obligation to the animal. Whereas all the other moral tugs—obligations to clients, peers, society, and self—are pretty clearly outlined in social ethics, the question of one's duties toward animals has been virtually ignored by society and by consensus social ethics until very recently. . . . Does the veterinarian have primary allegiance to client or animal?"[65] Rollins answer his question this way: "[Veterinarians] should become proactive and outspoken animal advocates."[66] He is somewhat optimistic about the conversion of intensive livestock-raising into extensive farming and the role that veterinarians can play in it, but he recognizes it will not be easy: "In my view attending to the welfare of agricultural animals in a manner that takes note of economic realities and yet provides the animals with a pain-free (or close to pain-free) and decent life consonant with their natures is the major challenge facing veterinary medicine in the twenty-first century."[67]

There is a long tradition in philosophy of putting humankind on a moral pedestal, elevated above the other animals. Only since the publication of Charles Darwin's *The Descent of Man* (1871), has it been empirically demonstrated that apes and humans are related to each other and have one and the same ancestor, as, in the end, all animals, and further back in time, all organisms have the same ancestor.[68] In his book *Animal Minds and Human Morals* (1995), the classicist Richard Sorabji has researched the arguments that were advanced in classical antiquity to establish a morally relevant difference between humankind and animals that could justify the instrumental approach of humans toward animals.[69]

Animals can suffer. Fortunately, after a debate with behaviorism, a consensus has existed on this subject for several decades. That animals suffer in factory farming is undeniable. If the moral problem becomes greater as the suffering increases (intensity multiplied by duration multiplied by number of individuals) then, because of the huge number of animals on factory farms, the amount of suffering is very large in the Netherlands alone and the moral problem is correspondingly great. Therefore, although veterinarians exist to advance the health and well-being of animals, they are not succeeding in the mission they have set for themselves.

THE PARABLE OF THE SLAVES

How would looking after slaves be for family doctors whose point of departure is "the advancement of the health and well-being of the patient"? Would family doctors be happy if there was a slave caste consisting of people who had to work under the most miserable circumstances? The doctors are called in by the slave owners to heal sick slaves, or to put down ones whose health is failing. The doctors also have to castrate male slaves and artificially inseminate female slaves. What would the role of physicians be in a society in which such a flagrantly unjust system as slavery exists? The physicians may say: "I can't do anything about the system as such; I try to keep the slaves healthy within the unjust system." Or "If I don't do the work, my colleague will." Or "It's the slave owners who are responsible for the living conditions of the slaves." Or "It's the consumers who buy the products made by the slaves." Or "The political system bears the final responsibility for the system of slavery." These possible answers could be called the "Pontius Pilate method": responsibility for the moral problem is sloughed off on others, and the physicians wash their hands of it.[70]

If veterinarians choose, as it states in the Code for Veterinarians, to set "the promotion of the health and well-being of the animal, with regard for the acknowledgment of the intrinsic value of the animal" as their objective, then veterinarians should in practice aim more at taking the interests and well-being of *individual* animals more seriously.

Hopeful Responses from Students

Dear Floris,

The philosophy course has had the effect that we're eating much less meat at home! The meat we're still eating we get from a butcher who guarantees that the animals had a good life and don't come from a factory farm! It is a good deal more expensive, of course. But as the ads say: the consumer is king! Moreover, my view of the world has undergone a major change! I want to thank you for that.

Dear Floris,

Now that I've received my grade, I think it is appropriate to send this. Your lectures have made a big impression on me, and it was very good to learn to think differently for once, at the university and in my daily life. Since seeing the *Meet Your Meat* film I've stopped eating meat. I was already eating little meat, and only organically raised, but it was the push I needed. I try to tell the people around me as much as I can about it and also to read about it myself. I wanted to thank you for this.

Dear Floris,

    Not long ago I was at a family dinner in a very expensive restaurant. I asked the waiter whether I could order something vegetarian, and that was possible. While I was "enjoying" my dish of four kinds of beets, one of my uncles asked why I was eating rabbit food rather than the luscious *wagyu* (marbled beef). I couldn't keep myself from trying out the quote from your book and reacted with: "For my part I can't understand how you can put the tortured corpses of dead animals in your mouth." You're right: it's a huge conversation-stopper.

6. SUPPOSE YOU'RE BORN IN A LOW-INCOME COUNTRY

The number of people on earth suffering from hunger has reached a sad record: one billion. So states a report of the Food and Agriculture Organization (FAO) of the United Nations. The number of hungry people grew by 100 million in 2009 alone. According to the FAO this is a direct consequence of the world-wide recession and of high food prices. The FAO states that the largest number of undernourished people live in developing countries. Some 642 million people in Asia and Oceania suffer from hunger, as do 265 million people in sub-Saharan Africa. The director-general of the FAO, Dr. Jacques Diouf, says that hunger threatens the peace and security of everyone.[71]

THE PARABLE OF THE BUGATTI

One fine day Lucas, an older bon vivant, goes for a ride in his magnificent 1933 Bugatti Royale, an uncommonly beautiful car that is worth a fortune and for that reason uninsurable, and which he regards as an investment for his old age. He parks his car on an abandoned railroad track in an old rail yard in order to take a walk. As he is walking along one of the tracks, to his astonishment he hears a train approaching noisily. Then he hears a cry of help from a boy who has been tied to the track. He quickly realizes that the train is headed for the boy, but he is too far away to allow Lucas to free him. Then he sees the handle of a switch. If he doesn't do something, the train will proceed along its way and kill the boy. But he can also pull the switch so that the train goes onto another track. However, that happens to be the track he parked his Bugatti on. "I don't know this boy," he says to himself. "If I weren't here he would have died anyway. My Bugatti is gorgeous and quite priceless. I'm not prepared to make that big a sacrifice. If only I hadn't parked there!" Lucas turns away and does nothing.

PARABLE OF THE DIRTY POND

A young lawyer named Eric is taking a shortcut through Central Park, dressed in a custom-tailored suit and an expensive topcoat. He suddenly hears a child calling from the nearby pond. He looks up and sees that a boy is in danger of drowning. It is a chilly early-winter morning. Nobody else is nearby. The pond looks filthy. Eric recalls that he is wearing a new suit and good shoes, and that his watch isn't waterproof. Moreover, he is on his way to an important appointment that will have a big impact on his future career. He hurries on and makes it to his appointment in ample time.

PARABLE OF THE TEN SMALL CHILDREN

A group of ten well-dressed lawyers are walking through Central Park early one morning. Suddenly they hear cries from the Pond. They see that there are ten children in it who are in danger of drowning. Seven of the lawyers don't hesitate for a second: they jump into the dirty pond and each saves a child. To their amazement they see that three of their colleagues, among them Eric, have kept on walking. The wet lawyers look at each other in surprise. One of them says: "I'm leaving, I've done my part!" The others follow him. The three remaining children drown.

THE PARABLE OF EARTHLAND

Tariq Banuri, director of the United Nations Division for Sustainable Development, has proposed that we should see the world as one large country, Earthland.[72] In that case Earthland is the country with the greatest social inequality, greater than that of any individual country. This immense country would have the status of a developing country. Why is Earthland no more than a parable, a thought-experiment, a utopia, a fantasy?

What do these four parables teach us? Anyone who is upset by the behavior of Lucas, Eric, and the lawyers, needs to understand what the consequences are. If it is true that you have a great moral duty to save people in distress if you can, even if it asks for great sacrifice, so great that you should even give up your pension for it, then donating money and/or time to save human lives is a grave duty. People go to considerable trouble to escape this moral duty by appealing to the arguments that follow.

Key to the examples is a direct personal interaction with the victim. The stronger the personal link, the greater the moral duty. When a child is in danger of drowning in a pond, it is better if there is only one person nearby rather than a lot of people. When a number of people are witnesses to an emergency, they tend to slough off the responsibility to others. This is so-called bystander behavior.

People most like to give voluntarily to worthwhile objectives and to feel good about it. When it becomes evident that there is a duty involved, giving loses its luster.

The implications for most people's lives are huge. In Peter Singer's view, everything that people spend for things other than necessities cannot be ethically justified so long as that money can save lives by way of food or medical help. Singer notes pragmatically that this probably can't be achieved and therefore establishes a progressive proportionate system: the more you have the more you give. But everyone should give. We are talking about a significant percentage of income: ten percent or more.

Cynics say: "Africa is a lost continent. Why do those people have so many children while they know they don't have the means to feed them and look after them?" What must never be lost from sight is that universal subjectivism and humanism take the individual as their point of departure. And individuals do not determine where they are born. It may sometimes be unwise for parents to have (another) child, but the child should not become the victim. The goal is at the same time to try to reduce the world population and to give maximum opportunities for self-development to the people who already exist, that is: more happiness and less suffering.

Cynics also say: "It doesn't do any good, anyway," and say that foreign aid just props up dictators and maintains poverty. If Eric jumps into the pond to save the child, he can't be sure he will be successful. Suppose the child has already ingested too much water and dies anyway. Should Eric say: "Yes, look here, a child like that can very easily drown; and besides, I could pick up a disease in that water. I can't be sure I'll succeed, so I might as well do nothing." Should we not try to save as many lives as possible? Even if we do know that we won't always be successful. Looking for the best possible solution is part of our moral obligation. If Eric has decided to jump into the water, but goes home first to get his swimming trunks and a towel, everybody will say that he is wasting time. His intentions may be good, but the way he goes about things is stupid. People who realize they have a moral obligation to give also have an obligation to find out whether the project or organization they are giving the money to is effective or not.

With the two methods of applying universal subjectivism, a solution to the problem is simple to determine. But that solution has far-reaching consequences and is not easy to accept. Suppose you yourself were born in Somalia and were racked by hunger, thirst, and disease. Would you not try to optimize your life through accessible health care; a stable, just government; and a sound economic system?

You watch the evening news and you see emaciated children. How would you like to be in their situation? Would you not hope for help? It is too easy to say: "I can't do anything about it anyway," or "It won't do any good." If you don't have faith in organizations, you ought to go there yourself or establish an organization that does meet your requirements.

The more we spend on luxury goods, the more immoral our behavior is. A lot of people could have been saved with that money and the quality of life of a lot of people could have been improved. There are plenty of psychological reasons why people are much more active in offering help if suffering takes place close at hand, and if it affects people we feel close to: the greater the distance, the smaller the compassion. In the case of any disaster in a remote country, we always get to hear whether there are any of our own nationals involved. Countries spare no cost or trouble to protect or care for their citizens abroad, while we often leave the citizens of the remote country to their own devices.

7. SUPPOSE YOU'RE BORN FIVE HUNDRED YEARS FROM NOW

"What's the use of a fine house if you haven't got a tolerable planet to put it on?" Henry David Thoreau asked himself. Suppose that sometime in the future you are born on a barren planet. That means that you have to take account of future generations. The chance that you would occupy the same relatively privileged position you do today is minimal.

If we continue with business as usual, the seas will within a few decades be empty. By empty I mean that there won't be fish in the sea any more. What remains will be plankton and jellyfish. And quite possibly these will disappear, too, as a result of overfishing or pollution.

The tropical rainforest will be radically reduced in size. Gorillas and orangutans will have become extinct. Not just large animals that speak to the imagination will disappear, many species will become extinct. Through human activity, biodiversity will decline on a large scale. Some writers are talking about mass extinction, here and now, right in front of us, through our actions.[73] Even worse: the consequences of modern human behavior are destroying the earth's ecosystem: ecocide.

Many people will now stop reading. Another one of those doom-sayers, they'll say to themselves. Look at what happened to the Club of Rome. In 1972 it published the famous and notorious report *The Limits of Growth*, which outlined a doomsday scenario in which fossil fuels would be exhausted within a few decades and large-scale disasters would occur because of this exhaustion and because of pollution. And just look: the Western world is richer than ever and we're still driving cars, more than we did then, in fact. Everything has turned out much better than predicted.

That's right, the world hasn't gone to hell in a hand basket. Not yet. Two observations can be made about the Club of Rome Report. First of all, it is difficult if not impossible to make exact predictions. The question is whether the Club of Rome was wrong or simply made a mistake in its time scheme. Second, the report did lead to action. It promoted social and political consciousness, and since that time environmental measures have been taken. In this way the report became a self-denying prophecy: because people took it somewhat seriously and measures were taken, the predictions of the report have not (yet) come true.

Apocalyptic visions, i.e., predictions of the end of the world, occur at all times and in many cultures. In the history of life on Earth, five mass extinctions have taken place, approximately one every 100 million years. During the last great mass extinction, some 60 million years ago, the dinosaurs became extinct, probably as the result of a meteorite strike. But that was long before the evolution of human-oids. "Lucy," the oldest human skeleton that has been found, has been dated at between 3.0 and 3.6 million years. The time range of those mass extinctions is so far beyond human time scales that they can't lead to realistic fears. No doubt there are sensible things that can be said to explain why people expand their fear of the vagaries of fate into a fear of the end of everything. What interests me is that there is a difference between irrational fears and rational expectations about the future and about the end of time. Humans seem to be motivated more easily by irrational fears, such as those inspired by religious apocalyptic visions, than by rational prospects.

The alarm bells are ringing. A small but growing number of people are pointing out that it is five minutes to midnight. The documentary film *An Inconvenient Truth* (2006), and the book released with it, were eye-openers for many. Al Gore shows in dramatic fashion the disastrous consequences of the climate change that humans are causing. Sea levels will rise, which threatens millions of people who live in coastal areas. A large part of the Netherlands and Belgium will disappear under water, unless dikes and dunes can be raised substantially. In any case, the situation of the Low Countries will become precarious. But what do people in the Netherlands and Belgium, and in other low-lying coastal areas around the world, think? They confidently expect government to raise the height of the dikes and dunes. Technology will bring a solution.

The Swedish documentary *The Planet* (2006) is unambiguous and shocking. Different aspects of the environmental problem are explained in four installments: humankind is ruining the globe through the destruction of the ecosystem. In the documentary a number of scientists from different disciplines all have their say. All of them make the diagnosis that nature is in rough shape, with major consequences for biodiversity and for humankind itself, because the capacity of the planet to sustain so many people at the current level is limited. To put it crudely: we're screwed! What can we do?

There is a hope for success only if dramatic large-scale changes are achieved. This may be in the form of innovations that ensure that our way of consuming becomes environmentally less burdensome, such as driving hybrid cars that use electricity as well as gasoline, and electric cars. But in that case it is important for electricity to be generated sustainably. Consumption behavior will have to change drastically in other ways: consuming less and consuming sensibly. But there will always be a (large) group who don't care, or who are unwilling to take even small steps. Without compulsion it will be difficult to get people to change their consumption patterns with a view to sustainability. It would help if government agencies consumed sustainably, encouraged sustainable production, and discouraged environmental pollution and waste. Business will not readily be inclined to do the right thing on its own accord. The first objective of a business, after all, is to turn a profit. But government can establish frameworks within which enterprises can and may make a profit in the same way that labor conditions have continued to improve under the influence of labor unions. When they band together, employees can look after their own interests. Nature and animals can't do that. Fortunately there are idealistic organizations and foundations that serve the interests of animals and nature. These groups can lobby governments. It is worthwhile for citizens to support groups like Ecojustice®, Earth First! and Greenpeace®.

THE PARABLE OF THE FROG

When I am honest with myself, I don't believe that the world can be saved. I think we are going into the abyss. One reason is that the consequences of what we are doing are not immediately evident. If a frog is tossed into a pot of hot water, he will immediately jump out, but if he is in water that is slowly being heated he will stay put, even though that means his death. The difference from the unethical frog experiment is that we humans *know* that we are in a pot of water that is slowly being heated, specifically by the greenhouse effect. And we know that this will have disastrous consequences. And yet we don't take real action. How long we have can't be predicted exactly, in part because technological innovation keeps providing "band aids" that postpone the outcome. But the problems are cumulative. The world population is growing, production is growing, and consumption is growing. The climate is warming up.

The misery in a large part of Africa illustrates the future of the rest of the world. I sound like a prophet of doom shouting on New York's Fifth Avenue while the shopping public saunters by without paying the slightest attention. And it is difficult to realize that the game may soon be over. It is just as if you have terminal cancer in a part of your body where it doesn't bother you that much: you know you don't have long to live, but this knowledge doesn't correspond to the way you are feeling. I hope I am wrong.

Would you yourself want to be born in the future even though you know how the world is being mistreated? For most people the foreseeable future is short. People think ahead, for themselves, ego-centrically, in days (what am I going to do this weekend?), weeks, months (where will I spend my holidays?), and years (what's the state of my retirement fund?). But who thinks about what the world will look like in fifty years?

Some people say that they wish that there will be enough left of the world so that their children and grandchildren—and how many generations beyond them?—will be able to live comfortably and even in luxury and will be able to enjoy the natural world. People often take their own children and further descendants as their point of reference; it apparently speaks more to the moral imagination than the fact that "people are all family of each other." Does this mean that so long as your own progeny are doing well, while the great majority of humankind lives in poverty and in an ecologically ruined environment, you can be at peace? And what about people without children: are childless people allowed to have their ecological foot-print become as big as possible without feeling guilty? After all, they don't have to worry that their progeny will fare worse because of their behavior?

THE PARABLE OF THE CAKE

If you are concerned about future generations—not simply about your own descendants but about everybody—the picture changes. In that case the parable of the cake is applicable. You have visitors and you have bought a cake. How should you cut the cake if you want to have as big a piece as possible yourself, even though all the guests get to help themselves before you? If you have cut the cake into bigger and smaller pieces, the chances are good that the guests will choose all the big pieces, leaving a smaller piece for you. If you haven't cut enough pieces, you will get nothing. So you count how many people there are, including yourself, and you cut the cake into equal-sized pieces. If you do that, every guest will take a piece and there will be a piece of the same size left for you. Suppose you know your friend Lars is also coming, but he phoned to tell you he won't be there until later. What do you do when you cut the cake? Do you take account of his planned arrival and save a piece for him? Or do you think: he's not here when the cake is being cut, so he's not part of the group? And does it matter whether he is family, a friend, or your neighbor?

An Economy of Exploitation

The method of reaching a fair and just division is a method of *procedural justice*: the procedure guarantees that the outcome will be just.

The earth is a big cake. But this cake has not been divided fairly. Most people who can manage to get hold of a large piece of the earth cake do exactly that. No one looks after the latecomers, not even if they are expected to show up, like one's own descendants. But is that not terribly stupid and shortsighted, if you know you could be one of them yourself, like in the thought experiment? Yes, it is terribly stupid, shortsighted, and unjust. King Louis XV is supposed to have said: "*Après nous le déluge*" (After us the flood). Decadence means reveling in your own wealth without regard for others or for the future.

In that sense the whole world is decadent, except for a handful of idealists who are pleading for an about-face.

If people are convinced (which they are not) that it is an ethical necessity to take account of the interests of future generations, the life-style of present generations should be sustainable rather than exploitive. That leads to another question: if people take account of those who will live later (*justice across generations*), why should they not have an ethical obligation to take seriously the interests of humans now alive who get only the crumbs of the cake? That is *justice within a generation* of humans.

The parable of the cake demonstrates that there is no ethical difference between the claims of people who are at the party now and those who still have to show up: everyone has a right to a piece of cake of equal size. From a moral point of view, justice among and justice across generations are one and the same thing. It is just as bad that there are people now who are victimized by the lifestyle of others (think of environmental pollution in China and child labor in India), as that people in the future will suffer because of our current pattern of consumption.

The economic system—capitalist as well as communist—does not discount the factor of nature. Nature is seen as something you can use cost-free. When such a system is linked to technological appli-cations in agriculture, mining, the extraction of fossil fuels, etc., a large-scale economy of exploitation becomes possible. This economy began with the Industrial Revolution that began in England in the second half of the eighteenth century. And yet this process is rarely described as exploitive.

Nature has value to humans because humans like to be in nature. But as soon as it costs money to save the natural environment, nature is abused, as when liquid waste is flushed into rivers. In China all the great rivers are heavily polluted, and as a result fish have dis-appeared. Economists tend to see nature as a free good. However, the absorptive capacity of nature, of earth's ecological system, has reached its limits or will soon reach them. A revolution in economic thought is absolutely essential.

Nature is not the only victim of the economic system; there are others. It is said that the capitalist economy works as though an invisible hand regulates affairs, as Adam Smith claimed. In part that is the case. In a free market goods are produced if there is demand for them. The dynamic between demand and supply determines the price. But not all effects and consequences are discounted: nature pays a price. Economic activity benefits some, but others suffer under it, and their suffering is largely ignored. Economists look at the world with blinkers. The invisible hand of the capitalistic system comes up short and tends to cause harm to nature, workers at the bottom of the production chains, future generations, and animals.

Instead of a free economy, should there be a communistic planned economy? Fortunately the history of the twentieth century offers a wise lesson: communism and socialism have failed, and the problems are even greater than in a free-market economy, without the successes of the free-market system. The solution lies in the reform of capitalism, as economists like Jeffrey Sachs have claimed.[74] How to accomplish this is another matter. In the first place it is important to recognize that the current economic system is morally reprehensible, wasteful, and polluting. Only when people come to grips with that can a positive change in the system be attempted. But it needs to be done soon.

In the documentary *We Feed the World* (2005) we get to see how wastefully people in the Western world deal with food. Every day in Vienna enough "stale" bread (two days old!) to feed all of Graz, Austria's second-largest city, is discarded. And this is in just one Austrian city. Think of what supermarkets throw out that is beyond the "best used before" date: dairy products, vegetables, cookies, meat. . . . There is enough food in the world to feed 12 billion people, while there are only 7.1 billion of us. And yet billions live in poverty and hunger. Every day many people succumb to malnourishment. Enough food is produced, but it doesn't reach them. That is tragic, absurd, and unjust.

There are both economic and ecological arguments for veganism. The production of meat for consumption is very inefficient.

Not only is a lot of water needed for producing meat (see the passage about ecological footprint), but the animals also need large quantities of feed (cereal, soy). It is much more efficient if agriculture produces directly for consumption. The lower people eat within the food chain, the more efficient and therefore more sustainable it is. Factory farming also has several bad effects on the environment, such as, the emission of methane, liberated by the digestion of vegetable matter in the stomachs of cattle and pigs, which contributes to the greenhouse effect, or the excess of manure. Although manure can be used to fertilize arable land and meadows, there is a limit to what can be spread. The excess is simply bad for the environment.

Economists are highly regarded. This fact is both strange and worrying. Authors of handbooks for thieves and lecturers to thieves—should they exist—would not be held in high esteem. And yet the economic system as it is taught is a system of exploitation, theft, and the shifting of costs and consequences to the future or to poor countries (e.g., the conveyance of shiploads of garbage or asbestos waste to Africa and India). Economists are ideologues of theft. Students of economics often become thieves themselves.

In dry areas, great forest fires take place every summer. Some of these fires are the result of arson. The police try to track down the arsonists and to have them prosecuted. There is great social disapproval of these pyromaniacs who destroy nature. However, those who use drag nets to fish destroy the sea bottom on a large scale. Yet, except for a small group of environmental activists, there is no social disapproval, and people calmly go to their local fish store or supermarket to buy the cod or sole that is obtained in this way. This reveals them to be hypocrites. Anything that is out of sight can be easily ignored.

At least two great problems threaten the earth's ecosystem. In the first place there is the rapid growth of the number of people.[75] Since the beginning of the twentieth century the world population has grown exponentially, even though it was the bloodiest century ever, with enormous famines and natural disasters thrown in for good measure. The growth of the world population is the consequence of improved agricultural technology. Industrialization is fed by fossil fuels. Fossil fuels are solidified solar energy. For 250 years people have been using this stored solar energy, first in the form of coal, and more recently in the form of petroleum. The entire process of industrialization can be seen as one great fossil-fuel binge.

Starting in the second half of the twentieth century, good contraceptives have become available for the first time, most notably the pill. This has contributed to a drastic decline of family size in the West. Unfortunately, contraceptives are not yet easily available worldwide: cultural, and more specifically, religious taboos constitute an obstacle.

The world population continues to grow. And that is a disaster. It is difficult to say what the absolute maximum number of people that the earth can sustain might be. That also depends on the consumption patterns of humankind. The general rule is: less is more. If there are fewer people, more of them are better off. Quantity leads to a reduction of quality. In the Western welfare states the decline in the number of children per family has led to an improvement of living conditions. Whatever the case, the earth can't accommodate twenty billion people.

To calculate the impact (I) of the human population on the ecosystem Earth, the planet's carrying capacity, the population (P) must be multiplied by the average ecological footprint (F), one human's consumption. Thus:

$$I = P \times F$$

The carrying capacity (C) of planet Earth has to be bigger than the ecological impact (I) on the bio-systems of the earth, thus:

$$C > I \ (= P \times F)$$

If humans want to live in comfort and luxury, i.e., with a fairly large ecological footprint (F), then the size of the world population (P) will need to be small.

Not only is the world population rising, but the average ecological footprint is increasing as well. China and India are experiencing enormous economic growth, accompanied by an enlargement of these countries' ecological footprint. And in the rich countries the average footprint is not decreasing, in spite of burgeoning consumer awareness. For example, more people are flying than ever before, and in warm countries such as Spain water-wasting golf courses are being built. To mention another example, there is not enough copper in the world to construct homes for everyone in China of the kind available in the West, in each of which an average of approximately sixty-five pound of copper has been deployed.

Requiem for the Sea

Dos Winkel's underwater photographs are wonderful, magnificent, fascinating, and breathtakingly beautiful. He is an underwater photographer and "ambassador of the sea" who has captured the beauty below the surface of the oceans all over the world. The result is astonishing. Winkel has an excellent eye for colorful detail and composition. His close-ups of the eyes of fish, for example, are wonderful. His photographic essays, such as *Another World: Colors, Textures, and Patterns of the Deep* (2005), suitable for use as coffee table books, are overwhelmingly beautiful. But Dos Winkel is a prophet of doom. His prophecy is not based on prompting from above, but on his own observations and on scientific research. His 2008 message in *Wat is er mis met vis . . .* (*What's the Catch with Fish . . .*) is unmistakable: if fishing and pollution of the seas proceed as they do now, then the seas will effectively be dead in twenty years and only jellyfish and plankton will survive. Winkel states that it is not five to twelve, but 12:05: it is already too late for a number of species and for the sea bottom in areas where drag nets are used for fishing. It will take about a hundred thousand years for some areas of the sea bottom to recover.

THE PARABLE OF THE JEEPS ON THE SERENGETI

Science journalist Charles Clover offers a gripping analogy with dragnet fishing in his book *The End of the Line: How Overfishing Is Changing the World and What We Eat* (2005): Suppose you install a net of several hundred yards wide between two all-terrain vehicles and you allow those vehicles to drive across the Serengeti along parallel courses. In that net you will find not only big game such as elephants and leopards, but also small animals as well as shrubs and trees. The hunters are only in pursuit of lions, however; the rest is "by-catch."[76] If hunting methods like that were to be used on land, public outrage would be huge, but under water the damage is invisible. What you don't know won't hurt you. In his 2008 book, Winkel shows illustrations of sea bottoms with slow-growing cold-water coral beds before and after a drag net has passed over them.

Empty

Until roughly ten years ago there were still tuna, cod, and herring in the North Sea. No longer: the North Sea is largely empty. The North Sea fishers are fishing elsewhere, ever farther away, ever deeper and with ever larger ships, floating fish factories. Dos Winkel reproaches the wealthy for removing the fish of the poor. The ocean off the Senegal Coast has been emptied by European fishing boats. Even more disturbing: these disastrous fisheries *and* large-scale agriculture are heavily subsidized by the European Union. That is to say, taxpayers also help to finance the destruction of the sea.

There are other books that spread the same message, such as Richard Ellis's *The Empty Ocean* (2004) and Stephen Sloan's *Ocean Bankruptcy: World Fisheries on the Brink of Disaster* (2003). The famous entomologist E. O. Wilson published two books in which he described the extinction of species through human action: *The Future of Life* (2003) and *The Creation: An Appeal to Save Life on Earth* (2007). The fisheries biologist Daniel Pauly, principal investigator of the Sea

Around Us Project, is very outspoken. On the subject of overfishing he has said: "You don't need to worry about these problems, as long as your children like plankton stew."[77] In brief: enough is known about the impending apocalypse, but almost nothing is being done. It is an open question whether the Millennium Development Goals—the eight international development goals, including ensuring environmental sustainability, that were officially established following the Millennium Summit of the United Nations in 2000—are not mere eyewash, a form of symbolic politics. The American economist Jeffrey Sachs is a prophet of doom and an optimist wrapped up in one. In his book *Common Wealth: Economics for a Crowded Planet* (2008) he describes in great detail the critical condition of the earth. But at the same time he is optimistic because he believes that enough knowledge and technology is available to turn the tide (somewhat) and to live on earth in a sustainable way. He believes the disaster scenario can be averted. Sachs urgently stresses the need to achieve the Millennium Development Goals. But what else can we do? The earth is like a patient who has been diagnosed with cancer: you can ignore it and know you will die fairly soon, or you can undergo therapy in the hope of being cured or in any case of slowing the disease down. What are we doing after numerous experts have pointed out the radically destructive way of life that we are collectively leading? Are we going to change our ways or will we leave the earth behind us like a lifeless lump? Our children, who will feel the consequences of our present exploitive economy, will not thank us for our selfish behavior.

But what should we do? If we don't do anything, if we say that we can continue in the same way, then the fish are finished. Who is responsible for that? Fishers, governments, cannery companies, fish merchants, the designers of deplorable fishing methods such as drag nets (with an assist from engineers)? Yes, but in the end, the chief culprits are the consumers: everybody who consumes fish and fish products. Without demand there is no supply. Without demand for fish, there would be no fishing. Without fishing, there would be no problems with fish. This final point is too optimistic, because the pollution of the seas with toxic runoff and waste has a negative influence on ocean life. The seas are all too often seen as a giant garbage can. And that takes a toll: via fish, toxic materials such as heavy metals end up in human beings. For that reason fish is a lot less healthy than the propaganda would have us believe. If nobody ate fish any longer, then the 450 billion pounds of fish that are annually taken from the seas and oceans could simply continue to swim around unmolested. There are several actions that people can undertake. I shall list them here:

- *Stop consuming fish products.* And try to persuade and encourage other people to do the same. Fish from fish farms are not an option because these are fed with wild fish. Fish farms pollute the environment, also because of the antibiotics that are administered to the fish. Animal suffering exists with all methods of fishing and especially those in which drag nets are used: fish can feel pain and do suffer. The method used to kill eel is particularly cruel: to get rid of their slime eels are thrown alive into a bath of ammonia or salt, and it takes around fifteen minutes before they are dead. Declining to eat fish has to be part of a generally sustainable way of life.
- *Take action*, passively as well as actively. Taking action passively means joining an organization that pleads for sustainability, for example Greenpeace. Taking action actively means following large drag nets in small ships and trying to draw media attention to these abuses. One example of taking action was the September 2008 initiative of Greenpeace in dumping basalt blocks into the sea to protect future fish reservations.

    At the European union level agreements have been made concerning sea reservations—small sections of the sea in which fishing is banned—but the implementation is moving slowly through bureaucratic channels. Meanwhile the fishers simply keep on fishing. Greenpeace focused the attention of the public on this distressing issue and the basalt blocks make it impossible to use drag nets and thus protect the fish in that area.

- *Carry out research into and provide information about sustainability.* Or better put, make others conscious of the prospective apocalypse created by humankind. Technological innovations simply deal with the symptoms; what is needed are drastic changes to consumption patterns and the means of production.
- *Look for radical solutions.* One possible solution is the cradle-to-cradle concept of William McDonough and Michael Braungart.[78] Cradle-to-cradle involves the attempt to produce goods that don't make a negative but rather a positive contribution to the next step in the cycle. In this way waste and by-products become material for new products. To close the circle is the important thing.

Dos Winkel's pessimism is part of a far more inclusive scenario of doom: humans are killing the earth, including humankind itself. The world population is growing exponentially, and at the same time consumption is increasing because of growing prosperity. The force of Winkel's disagreeable message is enhanced by the gorgeous images he links to it. The question is whether Winkel's photographic ode to the sea is, in fact, a requiem. To prevent it becoming a requiem, many things will have to change. Here and now. Save the sea, stop eating fish.

Ecological Water Footprint

How can it be explained psychologically that people are aware of the ethical problems associated with their excessive, unethical, unhealthy, and wasteful patterns of consumption, yet rarely do they adjust their behavior to that awareness, except for a few palliatives (bundling newspapers, recycling glass containers).

Winnie Gerbens is an environmental researcher at Twente University who concerns herself with the influence of Dutch consumption on the use of energy, water, and land.[79] She presents a detailed account of information that appears with some regularity in the higher-quality media: the consumption of meat is much more wasteful than that of vegetables because the animals have to be fed. Besides, factory farming has harmful by-products such as manure and ammonia. Twenty percent of household energy use results from food consumption. Although savings within that 20 percent is an ethical duty, greater savings are available within the other 80 percent. This consists of direct energy (electricity, gas, transportation) and indirect energy (all the products people have in their homes). Government campaigns emphasize savings in the use of direct energy, through better insulation, promoting bicycle use, and the like. Yet it would also be intelligent to pay attention to indirect energy use and to buy fewer products, use things so long as they still function, and recycle a lot more than we do now.

Gerbens carries out research into the ecological water footprint, a key aspect of the ecological footprint. The ecological footprint is calculated as the number of acres required to sustain a consumption pattern. In Western countries the ecological footprint is much larger than in poor countries. That won't surprise anybody, but almost nobody does anything to reduce their own ecological footprint, let alone scale it back to a sustainable level. The water footprint is calculated in the number of liters of water needed to produce a certain product. One cup of coffee requires 140 liters (37 gallons). One kilogram (2.2 lbs) of sugar requires no less than 1,500 liters, or almost 400 gallons![80]

What can be done? Gerbens focuses on food consumption. There are a few basic rules: consume less, don't throw stuff away, and use common sense (no strawberries from abroad, as little as possible from greenhouses, eat seasonal local produce), and replace less sustainable with more sustainable products. This requires a lot of research. You have to calculate how sustainable products are in different respects: land use, energy use, water use. So drink beer instead of wine. Drink tea instead of coffee. Eat potatoes instead of rice or pasta. Don't eat meat or in any event eat less of it.

In the case of food, sustainability is only one aspect. Healthfulness is a second. But it is an agreeable coincidence that what is healthful and what is sustainable go together well. Vegetarians and vegans don't consume meat, though they do consume vegetables and fruit. Overweight people tend to consume many products, such as meat, that waste water. The third aspect is ethical: consuming ethically means that you don't want to consume products that are associated with suffering or that have been produced in an unjust way. As a consumer you can hardly manage to avoid buying some unethical, unsustainable, and unhealthy products. But critical consumers strive, on the basis of the knowledge available to them, to develop as responsible (i.e., sustainable, healthy, and ethical) a consumption pattern as possible.

Because I hope that this book will lead to behavior changes, I will summarize the moral of the tale: everyone is able to consume in a more just, more animal-friendly, and greener way. There will always be wasteful people. But to change the world you have to begin with yourself, consuming less and doing so more responsibly. And speak to others about their consumption behavior: "You're planning to fly to New York? It's only a couple of hours by train." Consumers exercise influence through their buying behavior. Be responsible: fly as little as possible, use public transportation, eat as little meat and dairy as possible, buy less food and fewer products, increase your donations to good causes.

The Fable of Intrinsic Value

The preamble of the Universal Declaration of Human Rights begins as follows: "Whereas recognition of the inherent dignity and of the equal and inalienable rights of all members of the human family is the foundation of freedom, justice and peace in the world . . . , etcetera."[81] The Dutch Law for the Health and Well-being of Animals also acknowledges the concept of intrinsic value: "An acknowledgment of the intrinsic value of animals means that animals are accorded an intrinsic value independent of human beings, and that the interests of animals are not automatically subordinated to those of human beings." That's wonderful, but what is "inherent value"? The notions of "intrinsic value" or "inherent worth" also crop up frequently in environmental philosophy. What this means is that there are certain things that have a value in themselves, independent of humankind. Opinions differ as to what these things are. The fundamental problem with this notion is that humans are necessary to assign intrinsic value to something. The intrinsic value derives from humans, not from the thing. How would it be if intrinsic value did not derive from humans but from the object? Then there would be a kind of label on it saying "intrinsic value." It would be up to humans to find that label and act accordingly. Some questions: how did that label get there? Did God put it there? Why doesn't everybody see that label? And, if they do see it, why don't they seem to have much of a clue what to do about it?

Intrinsic value is an absurd notion. It is an example of how philosophy can gum up the works instead of helping to solve the problem. It could be that intrinsic value is nothing more than a label that people apply to certain things as a way of saying: "We think this is very important! Leave it alone!" But it is entirely possible to apply labels without reference to the myth of intrinsic value. The rights discourse offers an example of this. Humans can decide which rights should be assigned to whom. Rights are a means of ordering society sensibly and protecting individuals.

In Switzerland the notion of intrinsic value or worth or dignity (*Würde der Kreatur*) has even been placed in the constitution. It is good, on ecological and esthetic grounds, that an important position is ascribed to nature and that humans don't destroy nature, but the notion of intrinsic value is not apt.

Intrinsic value is a religiously tinted concept, because it is close to the concept of "sanctity." Indeed, it looks like a half-hearted secularization of the concept of "sanctity."

8. SUPPOSE YOU'RE ANNE FRANK

Moral relativism can assume absurd forms: the American philosopher Austin Dacey notes that his students say they doubt that slavery, the Holocaust, and ethnic cleansing were morally wrong because, influenced by postmodern ideas, they do not want to make absolute judgments.[82] According to relativism, morality and justice are always bound to time, place, and cultural context. The rejection of moral relativism is, however, not the same as claiming that the West and, more specifically, the United States are and always have been in the right. A rejection of moral relativism does not equate with a defense of imperialism or neo-imperialism.

Postmodern thinkers as Jean-François Lyotard have announced grandly that "there are no more great narratives," or rather, that the validity of great narratives and the universal claims of ethics has been undermined. Postmodernism tends to lean toward moral relativism. Moral relativism can be very simply and insightfully contradicted by imagining yourself in the situation of a victim. Would you want to be a Jew yourself and be subjected to persecution by the Nazis?

My sons, aged ten and nine, are enrolled in Anne Frank Elementary School. With some trepidation I have tried carefully to tell them who Anne Frank was, but I find it hard to tell them the full story. "Anne was a girl who lived in Amsterdam and kept a diary." So far, so good.

"Anne had to go into hiding with her family; they had to hide because there were people who wanted to capture her and her family."

"Why did those people want to capture Anne, Daddy?"

"Because Anne was Jewish and the Nazis believed that the Jews were very bad, but they really weren't, you know!"

"What happened to Anne, Daddy?"

"She was captured and killed."

Lump in the throat.

Who would want to change places with Anne Frank? Through

her diary, Anne has given a face to one of the six million victims.[83] That number is an abstraction. But Anne Frank offers a clear image. It is deeply depraved to murder six million people. Anyone who puts a question mark after that or seeks to try to relativize it is a moral monster. Most of the Jews who lived in the Netherlands were murdered, often with the complicity of Dutch citizens. Someone betrayed Anne Frank's hiding place. Who is not altogether clear, but in any case it was a Netherlander.

Reading Anne's diary is so poignant because the reader knows how the story ends, but Anne doesn't know she is going to die soon. She is simply fearful and unsure. And yet she is trying to live as normal a life as possible.

It is possible to make moral judgments about the past: nobody would want to trade places with Anne Frank, or with Etty Hillesum, a writer who kept a diary while she was interned in Westerbork transit camp.[84] Hillesum was gassed in Auschwitz in 1943. There are Holocaust survivors who have tried to describe their indescribable suffering, for example, Gerhard Durlacher in *Stripes in the Sky*.[85] This is called "scar literature" or "literature of the wounded." The Italian chemist Primo Levi is one of the best-known authors in this genre. His book *Is This a Man?* and its sequel *The Reawakening* deal with his experiences in Auschwitz and his eventual liberation and return.[86] What he describes is unimaginably gruesome. Levi shows us the darkest side of human existence. The prisoners in Auschwitz are systematically dehumanized. If any literature can have a didactic effect, surely scar literature does. It gives poignant meaning to the phrase "Never again." However, while there may not have been any more gas chambers, since 1945 lots of blood has been spilled and inhumane labor camps have existed on a large scale in Soviet Siberia. And there are still labor camps in China that no one in the outside world pays attention to.

How do you cope with books like these? I was unable to finish reading *Wild Swans* by Jung Chang, a 1991 novel about four generations of women in twentieth-century China, because there was so much cruelty, so much suffering. Every time I come across a book like that I am tremendously happy to have been born in the Netherlands in this era. It is like winning a lottery—a lottery with an awful lot of losers. I am grateful to those who have committed themselves to the achievement of the liberal open society into which by coincidence I happen to have been born. I am grateful to the whole Enlightenment tradition.

In his book *What Is Good?* the British philosopher A. C. Grayling describes the four roots of the open society: (1) the classical world, (2) the Renaissance, (3) the Enlightenment, and (4) the scientific revolution.[87] A milestone is the Universal Declaration of Human Rights (1948).

Judging the Past: The Case of Area Bombing During WWII

"Was area bombing necessary? No.

Was it proportionate? No.

Was it against the humanitarian principles that people have been striving to enunciate as a way of controlling and limiting the war? Yes.

Was it against general moral standards of the kind recognized and agreed upon in Western civilization in the last five centuries, or even two thousand years? Yes.

Was it against what mature national laws provide in the way of outlawing murder, bodily harm, and destruction of property? Yes.

Very wrong? Yes.

Should airmen have refused to carry out area-bombing raids? Yes."[88]

That is the philosopher A. C. Grayling's conclusion after his elaborate historical and moral analysis of the excessive bombing raids that the Allies and especially the British carried out on German cities, i.e., on nonmilitary targets. The topic has been used for impressive works of fiction, rooted in reality, by novelists such as Harry Mulisch, Len Deighton, and, most famously, Kurt Vonnegut.[89] Is it possible to judge the past in a moral sense? That seems like a nonsensical question, because that is precisely what courts do: they judge past actions. Among historians, however, there is a tendency to be reticent in making moral judgments about the past, with the Holocaust as a possible exception. It is possible to understand why bad people do bad things, and we all know that the Nazis committed terrible crimes against humanity. But why do good people do bad things? This is a disturbing question. The question is all the more painful when, as in Afghanistan and Iraq, we are the "good people." We do not only do good things there but also morally reprehensible things, such as torturing prisoners in Abu Ghraib or Guantánamo Bay.

In *Among the Dead Cities: The History and Moral Legacy of the WWII Bombing of Civilians in Germany and Japan* (2007), Grayling offers a moral evaluation of one of the most complicated instances in which the "good guys" committed morally depraved acts: he analyzes Allied strategic bombing during the Second World War. His study of area bombing in Germany and Japan, in which many civilians died and entire cities, including their cultural heritage, were destroyed, differs from most other histories of the Second World War, because Grayling wanted to come to an ethical judgment: "I wished to view the matter solely from the standpoint of someone in one of the victor nations, who inherited the benefits of victory, but hopes that by now there is enough perspective available for a frank acknowledgment of the wrongs done in the course of how it was won."[90] The appendix of the book contains an overview of RAF raids over Germany, with the numbers of civilian deaths and RAF losses. Grayling's book may be characterized as moral history. He approaches history as a case study in ethics. Grayling takes seriously the folk wisdom that "we should be able to learn from the past." His objective is not to establish a new (and posthumous) war tribunal to try those who were responsible for area bombing, but to determine whether there were good arguments that could justify area bombing. Grayling makes an important distinction between *explaining* on the one hand and *justifying* on the other. For example, the decision to bomb Dresden in early 1945 can be explained in the following ways: to help the Russians fighting on the eastern front; to show the Russians what British bombers could do to a city (the alliance with the Soviet Union had deteriorated considerably); there was no longer much German air defense; plenty of British bombers were available. This is the pressure of the technology, or military drift. There are probably additional reasons, but none of these reasons seems able to justify the deaths of tens of thousands and the destruction of a culture-rich city.

Who should decide what constitutes a good reason? Grayling uses many different criteria and strategies to be able to evaluate the morality of area bombing. First of all, he investigates the pre-Second World War international agreements that all condemn the killing of civilians and the destruction of nonmilitary targets. Second, Grayling examines what politicians and senior military men said both before and at the beginning of the war. It is apparent that they were strongly opposed to attacking civilian targets and condemned the Germans because they bombed cities such as Rotterdam in 1940. Third, Grayling looks at what was said about the killing of civilians during the Nuremberg trials. Although the documents condemned the killing of civilians in no uncertain terms, the victorious powers could not be brought to trial because they had exempted themselves from prosecution. Fourth, Grayling examines the international agreements about the conduct of war that were agreed to after the Second World War. These condemn area bombing. Fifth, Grayling studies dissenting voices within public opinion at the time wartime area bombing was taking place. In fact, there were courageous civilians and even military officials who opposed area bombing. As an example Grayling uses the writer Vera Brittain, who protested vigorously against area bombing and in the spring of 1944 published the pamphlet *Seed of Chaos: What Mass Bombing Really Means,* in which she revealed facts about the consequences of area bombing of German cities. Subsequently published in the United States as *Massacre by Bombing: The Facts behind the British-American Attack on Germany,* the pamphlet prompted controversy but found scant acceptance. And sixth, what did the British survivors of German bombing raids think of area bombing on the enemy? The *lex talionis,* or "an eye for an eye, a tooth for a tooth," does not seem to have applied. A majority of the survivors of German bombing raids on English cities opposed the bombing of German cities. On the other hand, people who had not themselves experienced what it is like to be bombed, in the United States, for example, mostly supported area bombing. In this way Grayling uses the criteria of those responsible for area bombing to conclude that they themselves should have found it morally objectionable. Air Marshal Arthur "Bomber" Harris, who oversaw area bombing and championed it fervently, did not receive a peerage after the war, declining the honor when the government refused to create a separate campaign medal for his air crews. After the war there was some criticism of area bombing but no significant condemnation or disapproval. Mostly there was silence. From the safety of a later period, Grayling looks back to make a moral evaluation.

Was area bombing effective? Did it help to win the war or to hasten victory? Grayling painstakingly examines the available evidence. The military leadership, and particularly Harris, claimed that area bombing was a highly effective means of winning the war. But that was in fact not the case, because area bombing had minimal effect on German morale. And carpet bombing had little impact on military operations—the antiaircraft guns were largely operated by older men who could be spared from the front. Precision bombing, on the other hand, did cause problems for the Germans. By the end of the war America's Air Force was capable of carrying out precision bombing raids on specially selected targets, notably oil refineries. These caused problems for German military operations. For example, the Luftwaffe was seriously short of fuel and as a result was barely able to get planes off the ground.

Grayling distinguishes among different phases in the war. During the first phase Germany was winning and Great Britain had to make every effort not to be conquered (the Battle of Britain). In the second phase, once the United States had joined the war and Germany had lost the Battle of Stalingrad, it was clear that Germany would lose. Why then did the RAF orchestrate a huge wave of area bombing of

German cities during the last months of the war? Grayling can't find a good reason, or even an explanation, and comes to the inescapable solution that this was a war crime.

Grayling himself supplies the reason why an analytic philosopher like him has made a detailed historical study: "Only if civilization looks back at itself frankly and accepts what it sees, can it hope to learn from the exercise and progress in the right way and direction thereafter."[91]

CHAPTER 4

THE OPEN SOCIETY

I. PLURALISM

"**C**ultures cannot be of equal value, precisely for the reason that individuals are," thus writes philosopher and humanist Paul Cliteur in his book opposing cultural relativism and multiculturalism.[1] A lot of human behavior is mean, antisocial and unjust, often under the guise of a cultural, ideological, or religious cover. All behavior in which the roles are not morally interchangeable is objectionable. This is the case in many cultural traditions, and the individual is the victim. However, morally the individual takes precedence over the group. After all, you can't want to be in the victim's situation.

All practices involving victims should disappear. They include: female genital mutilation[2] and other involuntary physical mutilation, so-called honor killing, torture, involuntary sexual relations (including forced marriage), discrimination against and social exile of homosexuals, physical punishment and brainwashing, the conscious withholding of knowledge, the enforcement of rules concerning clothing and behavior, irrational social taboos, the torture and consumption of animals, and a lifestyle with an excessive ecological footprint. This is a random summary: it is better for you to think of an example of a social practice and to consider whether it can or cannot be legitimized through the method of universal subjectivism.

Films, documentaries, novels, and reports offer concrete examples of objectionable practices. In world literature the child-rearing practices in cultures strongly influenced by religious orthodoxy are often depicted colorfully. The traumas experienced by children are a source of inspiration for authors in many languages. Strongly religious parenting is distinguished by irrational severity, indoctrination, and lots of irrational taboos that seem designed to spoil children's pleasure, such as bans on music and dancing. The biggest taboo is sexuality.

Cosmopolitan Sampling

During the past few decades, globalization has enriched Western dining culture: the more abundant the supply, the greater the choices available. Anyone can make a culinary world journey according to their tastes. This is a positive aspect of globalization and cosmopolitanism. The taste sensations available today are enormously varied compared with the standard fare of yesteryear. Anyone is free to enjoy this. The important thing is that there are many opportunities for culinary experimentation. This is also possible with all kinds of other cultural expressions. From a humanistic perspective, the ideal is to strive for the greatest possible self-actualization in Abraham Maslow's sense.[3] In other words: try to get as much out of your life as possible. After all, if you have a choice between eating burgers and fries all your life and expanding your taste sensations by means of culinary sampling, it makes sense to go for the second option. There are people who say: "Stick to what you know." That is a personal choice. In an open society in which the possibilities of self-actualization are maximized and knowledge about these possibilities is widely available, everybody is allowed to do what they want. But it should not be the case that the possibility of experimentation is open only to an elite.

Cultural cherry picking, in other words, cosmopolitan cultural sampling combined with individualism and rationality, can be enriching. At issue is cultural and esthetic sampling, which must stay within the framework of human rights. Every person is born within a certain culture. That culture should not be a prison, although in many cases, sad to say, that is the state of affairs. Ethics takes priority over esthetics. Ethics and its social organizational effect in laws and rules provide the framework within which people can live their lives in the greatest possible freedom: a social democratic constitutional state that guarantees individual freedoms.

In the area of esthetic *savoir-vivre* Japanese culture has a great deal to offer. That can be an enrichment for the lives of people from other cultures. Humanists don't believe in fixed national character. For example, it is nonsense to think that only Netherlanders can skate fast. It is also nonsense to believe that traditional Japanese and Chinese arts can only be pursued by the Japanese and Chinese. Anton Geesink and, more recently, Ronda Rousey are just two athletes who have shown that judo is not the preserve of the Japanese, but that by means of lots of training and practice a construction worker from Utrecht or a student from southern California can also reach the top. This applies also to the more esoteric Japanese arts, such as flower arrangement, calligraphy, and tea ceremonies. In these arts Westerners are at an enormous disadvantage relative to the Japanese, because they need to master the Japanese language and handwriting, which is far from easy. But it can be done. I also think it is possible to export these arts to other countries, as has already happened with Japanese martial arts and Zen Buddhism.

Promoting cosmopolitan cultural experimentation does not mean that everything exotic is good. The astronomer and skeptic Carl Sagan once pointedly wrote, "Keep an open mind . . . but not so open that your brains fall out."[4] That has happened and continues to happen to many Westerners in their quest for exotic ways of life. For a large part, New Age and esoterica can't be squared with rationality, secularism, openness, and individualism. In his fascinating *Feet of Clay: A Study of Gurus* (1997), the psychiatrist Anthony Storr describes and exposes a number of popular modern gurus such as Gurdjieff, Bhagwan, Steiner, Jung, and Freud.[5] Storr asks himself how it is that these gurus were and are able to count apparently right-minded people among their followers. Briefly, humanistic cosmopolitan sampling is not consistent with blindly following gurus. The techniques and practices used by some gurus can perhaps be adopted in a humanistic context, e.g., yoga, tantra, meditation, incense, dancing, music, etcetera. On a shopping trip around the world in search for interesting customs people have to maneuver between Scylla and Charybdis: between authoritarian gurus on the one side and spirituality and transcendent temptation on the other; between blind obedience, and the abandonment of rationalism and the scientific world view that often happens with the New Age and spirituality.

Sampling in Japan

"Why did you take up Japanese studies?" people regularly ask me. My answer is: "Why should the culture into which I happen to have been born be the one that suits me best and where I feel most at home?" I wondered whether there was wisdom to be found elsewhere. I chose Japan because China is a communist society, and I have a strong dislike for communism. Japan is a civilized country and yet very different from the West. That attracted me. What also influenced me was that I had been doing Japanese martial arts for years: judo, jujitsu, and karate. Zen as a so-called complement to rational thought, but without God, strongly appealed to me. However, the program in Japanese studies at Leiden University fell short of expectations. Nevertheless I don't feel regret; at most I am disappointed. Japanese culture has enriched my life, in a positive as well as negative sense. The Japanese esthetic was a positive experience but the social repression of individuality and freedom was negative. In my first year at Leiden, searching for the esoteric wisdom of Zen, I read volume one of Heinrich Dumoulin's *Geschichte des Zenbuddhismus: Indien und China [Zen Buddhism*, vol. 1, *India and China].*[6] (Volume two, dealing with Japan, was missing from the library.) That book is a tough read, tedious and dry as dust. *An Introduction to Zen Buddhism* (1934), by D. T. Suzuki, who undertook in old age to popularize Zen Buddhism for Westerners and exported it to the West (particularly the United States), also requires heroic efforts from the reader. I now know I would have done better to read Janwillem van de Wetering's *The Empty Mirror: Experiences in a Zen Monastery* (1999). Van de Wetering had the same idea I did and felt attracted by the Zen monasteries in Kyoto. He was more adventurous than me, however: in 1975 he left for Japan and knocked on the gate of the famous Daitokuji monastery. His account is a great read. And at the same time it is a warning against what Zen is in my view: an egocentric, masochistic way of life that does not lead to deeper insights into existence. "While I was in the monastery I was continually referred back to the daily routine, the simple everyday life. If I wanted to expound some clever theory I was either ignored or ridiculed or curtly told not to talk nonsense. What mattered was 'here and now,' whatever I happened to be doing, whether I was peeling potatoes in the kitchen, washing rice, pulling out weeds, learning Japanese, drinking tea, or meditating. I had to solve my *koan*, the subject of my meditation, and I shouldn't fuss."[7] Although shattered by his experiences in the harsh school of Zen instruction, Van de Wetering did not give in and continued with Zen practice after his return to the United States, describing this in two more books.

A Tinge of Shinto

Two religions are dominant and clearly visible in the cultural landscape of Japan: Shintoism and Buddhism. Shintoism is an affecting, childish religion. I doubt that people actually believe in it. Shintoism is an orthopraxis: what matters is what you do. Because Shinto exists only in Japan, it provides a strong feeling of national unity. The pureness and beauty of rugged nature are central in Shintoism. It is an amoral religion. In contrast with the Abrahamic religions, neither Shintoism nor Buddhism is obsessed about the (sexual) moral behavior of the faithful.

When Annemarieke and I were living in Japan we regularly

visited Shinto shrines. Shinto festivals and rituals are jolly. In a Shinto shrine you pull on a thick bell rope, clap your hands twice, bow down and toss a few coins into a chest. Shintoism is an animistic religion; it is the collective artistic expression, accentuating the beauty of nature. It is curious that Shintoism has survived and has been incorporated into a modernized Japan. The reason for this is, I think, the esthetic attraction of Shintoism. Japan has (or in any case had) a dramatic and beautifully wild natural environment. Shinto shrines are established near exceptionally beautiful rocks or trees: all of nature is animated; beautiful or extraordinary trees, rocks, and mountains become objects of Shintoism. Characteristic of Shinto is the orange gateway to the temple complex. These gates exist in many different kinds and sizes. The orange color blends beautifully with the green of its surroundings. As well, Shintoism is a *quid-pro-quo religion*. There are shrines for special occasions, for passing final exams, for love. Shintoism is about the positive, nice, and frivolous things of life. Buddhism, on the other hand, is about the serious matters. The most important concept in Shintoism is purity. Everything is constantly being ritually purified and renewed. Wooden Shinto shrines are regularly rebuilt. Shintoism has no profundity, no theology, and no metaphysics. The sinister aspect of Shintoism is that it is uniquely Japanese and can be a source of nationalism, as in the 1920s and 1930s. At that time Shintoism was linked to the cult of the emperor, who was seen as Japan's highest deity. Religion, no matter how innocent, can always be used to pour oil on some fire or other. Religion coupled with nationalism makes for a lethally dangerous combination.[8]

Shintoism has had a double influence on Japanese esthetics. First directly: all over Japan there are large and small Shinto shrines that are oases of rest. Properly considered they are public parks. But the Shinto decor gives these spaces an esthetic added value that ordinary parks don't have. A second and even greater influence is the indirect one of purity. The Japanese characteristics of neatness and refinement have a lot to do with Shintoism.

A Tinge of Buddhism

The other great religion of Japan is Buddhism, which was imported from China beginning in the eighth century. Japanese culture has borrowed a lot from Chinese traditions, which developed in a very individual way in Japan. Although Zen Buddhism hails from China, its real flowering took place in Japan. Nowadays Buddhism has hardly any presence in India, the land of its origin, and China, once the most important Buddhist country. But in Japan Buddhism is still substantial and influential. It is interesting to observe that a new wave of expansion of Buddhism and more particularly Zen Buddhism began after 1945, in the form of the export of Zen to the West and especially to the United States. An almost completely autonomous Zen tradition, in which the masters are no longer Japanese, has developed in the West. There are Zen schools and Zen monasteries throughout all of Europe and the United States. There are several dozen Buddhist schools and varieties in Japan. Of these Zen is the best known in the West, probably not without reason. Buddhism is a doctrine of salvation with many different streams and schools. The basic concept of Buddhism[9] is that life is suffering and that, without committing suicide, you can deliver yourself from this suffering by letting go of your desires and relativizing your own deeper self, as it were. Rituals and above all meditation are a means to this end. Buddhism is a way of protecting yourself against the fickleness of fate by mentally establishing distance and detachment. This attitude resembles stoicism. The difference is that stoicism is a cerebral theory, while Buddhism has been institutionalized as a creed with meditation exercises, rituals, monasteries, and etcetera. Above all, Buddhism is an orthopraxis: acting, not thinking, is central. Although the Buddha is not a god but a master who discovered how you can deliver yourself from earthly suffering and taught the way, the Buddha figure has grown to assume superhuman proportions. It is true that images of the Buddha are not worshiped, but these images fulfill a central role in the rituals and practices. However, it is true that no divinity is assigned to the Buddha; he is not a monotheistic god. He is an Indian guru, similar to the diverse group of gurus who still preach their gospels of salvation today.

A World Language: The Esperanto Project

Would it not be wonderful if everybody could understand each other? There are thousands of languages in the world, and although the number of languages is declining, lots of people still can't understand each other. The global language at this moment, the *lingua franca*, is English. It would be nice if everyone would speak English as a second language so that people would understand each other always and everywhere. But big drawbacks adhere to English as the global language. English is the language of the most powerful nation on earth, the United States. For that reason English is not politically neutral; rather, it is very much value-laden. The global language changes in the course of history along with the center of power, which is why it has changed from Latin to French to English. There is a chance that Chinese will be the global language of the future. Then there is the problem of native and non-native speakers. The latter are always at a linguistic disadvantage vis-à-vis native speakers, who have a privileged position as a result. Finally, a natural language is often unclear, ambiguous, and gender-biased. An artificial language does not have to be that way.

Especially at the beginning of the twentieth century, a lot of experimentation with artificial languages took place. Ludwik Zamenhof (1859–1917) thought up the best-known artificial language, Esperanto.[10] Zamenhof was a Jewish-Polish ophthalmologist, polyglot, and philologist. His mother tongues were Russian, Yiddish, and Polish, but he also spoke German fluently. Later in life he learned French, Latin, classical Greek, Hebrew, Italian, Spanish, Lithuanian, and English. Zamenhof seemed to have no trouble in combining Russian, Polish, Lithuanian, and Jewish identities. Today Bialystok, his place of birth, is a Polish city; at that time it was in the

Lithuanian province of the Russian empire. There were ethnic conflicts in the city. Of the 30,000 inhabitants at that time, roughly ten
percent were of Polish, 17 percent of German, 13 percent of Russian,
and 60 percent of Jewish origin. Because of this diversity several different languages were used in Bialystok: German dominated in the
suburbs, Polish was used in intellectual circles, Yiddish was the language of trade and commerce, farmers often spoke Belarusian, and
the official language was Russian. Already at a young age Zamenhof
recognized the problematic character of this multilingual, politically
charged state of affairs. He concluded that miscommunication was
the cause of much misery in his town, and he wanted to create a language that everyone could understand. In 1887 he published the first
manual under the title *International Language: Foreword and Complete
Textbook by Dr. Esperanto.* He used the pseudonym Dr. Esperanto ("he
who hopes") because of his fear that a possible failure would damage
his reputation as an ophthalmologist. The first textbook contained a
summary grammar with sixteen basic rules, 900 etymons, a few trans-
lations, such as the Lord's Prayer, a Bible fragment, several poems,
both translated and original, and a letter. Esperanto is a simple and
yet very rich artificial language. There are only a few grammatical
rules, with no exceptions. The words can be used as building blocks
to create new words. Between the two world wars Esperanto enjoyed
great popularity. There were Esperanto newspapers, magazines, and
radio programs. When the Nazis seized power in Germany, they
banned Esperanto, which reduced enthusiasm for it. Yet the movement has gained new life as a result of the Internet. At present there
are roughly one million people in the world who can use Esperanto.

To someone looking at the world from the outside, an artificial
world language is a fabulous idea. But to people who are historically
grounded there is no direct advantage in learning Esperanto. Unless
people suddenly see the light of reason and begin to learn and use
it. But that depends on the goodwill of individuals. Zamenhof had
thought of something. At a time when no one spoke Esperanto as
yet, how could people be persuaded and tempted to learn an artifi-

cial new language? Zamenhof therefore published a pamphlet with information about Esperanto. Included in it was a form that people could return to him; by completing it they promised that, should a million people be prepared to learn Esperanto, they would undertake to do so. Although this fine plan came to nothing, Esperanto did become the most successful artificial language ever.

What would you come up with as a possible solution to the problem of communication if you yourself could determine the arrangement of societies in their original situation? In the thought experiment, you don't know which country you will turn up in and what you will learn as your first language. (I find the term "mother tongue" to be disagreeably gender-biased: it is, after all, not just the mother who teaches a child to speak, but the entire network of people around the child.) It could happen that you would become part of a group with a language that is spoken by very few people. If you don't learn another language at a young age (preferably a world language such as English, Spanish, or Chinese), you will be at a disadvantage all your life. This problem can be solved with the help of an artificial language such as Esperanto. It doesn't matter if your first language is one that is spoken by many people or not, provided everyone learns Esperanto as a second language, and provided this language is used for intercultural communication.

It would be nice if national governments and international organizations, such as the European Union and the United Nations, used Esperanto as the language of communication. Absurdly high sums of money are spent on translation in the European Union to make all documents and speeches available in all the recognized languages of the EU. English will never become the *lingua franca* because the French would not accept it. If English were to become the official EU language, the French, who generally don't have a very good command of English, would be at a disadvantage. If everyone would learn the simple language of Esperanto, including the English and the French, enormous savings could be made on translation. The money thus saved could be used to propagandize for Esperanto and courses in that language. During the first few years, documents would still have to be translated from Esperanto into the languages of the European Union, to prevent the EU becoming even more remote from its citizens.

The same applies to the United Nations. Cosmopolitanism and Esperanto go hand in hand. Citizens of the world should speak Esperanto.

Fair is fair: I am learning Esperanto only half-heartedly myself. Intellectually it is very satisfying to see that the language is logical and consistent. Its pronunciation is elegant and resembles Italian. It is my hope that this book will be translated into Esperanto.

2. EDUCATION AND PARENTING

Can you *want* to be taught untrue and incomplete knowledge? If, from a meta-perspective, you have a choice of being instructed with lies or empirically founded knowledge, which do you choose? Or are you neutral and don't care? Can you really say of yourself that it doesn't matter to you if you receive no or insufficient knowledge about the world? Is it not the case that everyone would like to have the most unbiased knowledge presented in the educational system? These questions touch the core of universal subjectivism: if there are really a lot of people to whom it makes no difference whether they are in a madrassa, a "Jesus Camp,"[11] or a public school in the Netherlands or the United States, the discussion comes to an end. The problem is that people who have been indoctrinated cannot themselves recognize, or want to recognize, that they are being shortchanged. Only those who are prepared to move up to a higher level of reflection can see where the catch is. Religious instruction is something no one can or will want to choose.

There are three reasons for abolishing religious education throughout the world: organizational, pedagogical, and substantive. The most basic reason is that children have a right to education in which the transmission of knowledge, civics, and individual self-actualization are central. Children have a right to unbiased (scientific) knowledge and, conversely, they have the right to be safeguarded from indoctrination.

Protection of the Freedom of the Child

Government must protect the freedom of children, including their freedom to be safeguarded (at least in school) from the religious views of their parents. Government therefore must be religiously neutral. In the Netherlands this neutrality is interpreted the following way: if there is sufficient demand, people are permitted to establish schools that are rooted in their own ideological convictions and to receive government subsidies for them. By law schools have to fulfill certain requirements, which serve to take the sharp edges off religious education. But problems with a number of Islamic schools, for example, indicate that educational inspection leaves something to be desired.

PARABLE OF AS SIDDIEQ ELEMENTARY SCHOOL

Hennie Metsemaker worked for one year as a teacher in As Siddieq Islamic elementary school in Amsterdam because she very much wanted to become acquainted with other cultures. "The woman teacher was neatly excluded. Non-Muslims had to lunch separately during the break. The greeting *salaam*, peace, did not apply to them, for you wish peace only to Muslims; Muslims befriend other Muslims. No depictions of humans or animals were allowed on the walls, and instrumental music was prohibited. The worst thing, she found, was that she had to teach the children that someday Isa (Jesus) would return to earth and work with pious Muslims to abolish Christianity. Nothing came of education into 'integrated citizenship,' let alone the free expression of opinion."[12]

Government exists for the protection of individual citizens and ought to advocate for the weakest: children. The French model of secularism guarantees a strict separation of religion and the state. What the Dutch government does is to support parents in the religious indoctrination of their children. Children must have the possibility of leaving the ideology of their parents and their environment. Neutral public education in which important ideologies come under discussion facilitates the formation of well-informed opinion, so that children, as they approach adulthood, can choose for themselves whether or not they want to adopt their parents' religion, ideology, or political opinions. It is a kind of indoctrination to describe children as belonging to a religion: a "Jewish/Muslim/Christian child" is a pernicious designation because it includes the child in a certain social-cultural group together with the irrational taboos and untruths that pertain to it, without the child having made a voluntary and well-informed choice.

Religion is like a hobby that you should be able to choose voluntarily and individually. It is important that children be aware of the choices open to them. For this reason, the home schooling of children and the establishment of private schools should not be permitted. Government must make the free formation of opinion possible by means of compulsory secular public education.

Without faith based education, secular public schools will become more multicultural, because students from different cultural, religious, ethnic, social backgrounds will mix and mingle. This stimulates integration because the children of parents who adhere to different religions and ideologies are in school together. That is much more humane and tolerant than separating children on religious grounds. Secular education is therefore multiform and multicolored. Schools could, even more than is now the case, diversify along educational and pedagogical lines, such as Montessori or bilingual/multilingual schools. All education, elementary, secondary, and post-secondary, should be secular. Education and training for religious occupations, it should go without saying, have no place in universities. Theology, which has the existence of a god as its premise, does not belong in scientific institutions. The study of religion as a social, cultural, psychological, and natural phenomenon *does* belong there.

Scientific Worldview and World Citizenship

An important task of education is the unbiased transmission of knowledge about humanity and the world. For that reason all school children need to know something, however rudimentary, about the evolution of humans and other animals. The knowledge that is conveyed in school must be scientific. Stories about heaven or life after death must not be part of education in the natural sciences, but they can be part of education about culture: "There are people who believe in God/heaven/reincarnation etcetera." If pupils ask: "Does God exist?" then the teacher must give the scientific answer: "There are no scientific arguments for the existence of God. In short: no, God does not exist." Education must be secular, that is to say, religion is not allowed to meddle with the content. Secular education is *not* atheistic indoctrination. What matters is that education conveys knowledge as honestly and objectively as possible, about religions in the same way as about other subjects.

When sex education is at issue—it should be part of both primary and secondary education—it must be objective and free from taboos. There should therefore not be any disapproval of homosexuality, for example, as is unfortunately the case in strict religious schools.

Confirmation classes, Bible study, Koran school, and the like are morally reprehensible because you cannot of your own volition choose to be sold a bill of goods, to be taught untruths. In a liberal society, however, the situation is paradoxical. Although it is morally reprehensible for parents to indoctrinate their children with a certain religion, as long as this does not happen in school, there are few if any liberal ways of counteracting it.

History education should outline the course of world history as objectively as possible. It is important that thorny issues like slavery, the Holocaust, the Armenian genocide, and the history of the state of Israel be presented as objectively as possible. The value of the study of history is to draw lessons as to how things can go better without the same mistakes happening again and again. A major problem of human cohabitation is the conflicts between human groups. Instead of living together peacefully they make war. Nationalism and religion have turned out to be catalysts of violence and intolerance. We have to realize that we are all in the same boat, planet Earth, and that it would be better to make the most of it together. And a good way of accomplishing that would be using universal subjectivism to improve the worst possible situations.

Knowledge about religion is part of knowledge about art and culture. It is important that people become aware of the great diversity of religions. Religions that exercise a great influence on the culture around us will get more attention than the religions of remote regions.

It is of the greatest importance that school children develop an insight into and an understanding of the open society and the rule of law. Social studies should not be a minor but a major subject. Human rights, constitutional democracy, individual freedom, equality among people, citizenship, and the open society are subjects that need to get their place in the sun.

Education in the Scientific Worldview

"Big History" is a fairly recent concept that is used in looking at the past. History generally begins with the written word, at the time of the Sumerians about 6,000 years ago. Archaeologists dig a little deeper. Art historians are thrilled by the marvelous 17,000-year-old cave paintings of Lascaux and Altamira. Paleontologists search for fossilized bones and puzzle humanoids together. And so we can go ever further back in time. Evolutionary biologists have created an overview of the origins of species. Geologists study the history of the earth. Chemists experiment in their laboratories with primordial soup in order to explore the step from the inorganic to the organic (the birth of life from inert matter). Astronomers carry out research on the origins of the planets, stars, and galaxies; and cosmogonists occupy themselves with the origin of the universe, with the very fraction of time when all the atoms came into being, *ex nihilo*, out of nothing as it now seems. Big History combines the major developments and cross-links among different learned fields into a running story. Christopher Lloyd has succeeded in writing an accessible work of popular science, *What on Earth Happened?* in which he explains Big History.[13] It can be fleshed out at different levels, in greater or less detail.

The Universal Declaration of Human Rights

There are lots of fine documents, such as the Universal Declaration of Human Rights (1948) and the Convention on the Rights of the Child (1989). The tragedy lies in the abyss between the words and the reality.

Convention on the Rights of the Child, Article 13

> The child shall have the right to freedom of expression; this right shall include freedom to seek, receive and impart information and ideas of all kinds, regardless of frontiers, either orally, in writing or in print, in the form of art, or through any other media of the child's choice.[14]

Individual freedom is the highest value in an open society. Stronger yet: individual freedom is the ultimate human value. Non-open societies do not have the ideal of individual freedom as an objective to strive toward, while open societies do. The job of government is to safeguard that freedom (negative freedom) and to facilitate it through the creation of self-actualization possibilities such as education, culture, and sports (positive freedom). In an open society, government should interfere as little as possible in the private lives of citizens. Friction results when citizens themselves try to limit the individual freedom of others. Not only must government refrain from limiting the freedom of citizens (vertical freedom relationship) but it must also make sure that citizens accept each other's freedom (horizontal freedom relationship). The latter can occasionally be problematic. The police must try to prevent violence and to arrest law breakers. That seems unproblematic, but nevertheless there are problems with violence, especially within the family: so-called honor violence, genital mutilation of girls (and, although much less serious, the circumcision of boys is also a form of irreversible mutilation and should—if not medically indicated—be punishable if performed on minors), violence against women, rape within marriage (and that may take getting used to), indoctrination in untruth, and lack of freedom. Are children their parents' property, and are these allowed to do almost everything to their children, including circumcision, forced marriage, and emotional torture? An upbringing that involves indoctrination is an upbringing rooted in denial of freedom and falsehood. An objection often made to this argument is that secularists, atheists, liberals, devotees of the Enlightenment, humanists, and freethinkers are themselves intolerant and fundamentalist and subject those who disagree with them, including their own children, to indoctrination. At issue here is the difference between an open and a closed upbringing. Philosopher Herman Philipse shows in his essay *Enlightenment Fundamentalism?* (2005) that it is a contradiction in terms to label Enlightenment thought as fundamentalist.[15] But it is indeed true that liberals—I use the term to include all the categories of people named above—are intolerant, that is, intolerant of intolerance. Let me clarify this point with a short piece of dialogue:

Liberal: It is intolerant to marry your daughter to someone against her will.

Fundamentalist: No, you are intolerant yourself to meddle in my affairs. You want everybody to do what you do and think what you think!

Liberal: Not at all: you can do and think what you want, just as long as you don't coerce others, your daughter included!

Fundamentalist: You see how intolerant you are. I don't interfere with the way you allow your daughter to walk around looking like a slut! I am tolerant; you're intolerant!

If government takes individual freedom seriously, it cannot stop at the front door of homes when dealing with abuses of that freedom. But it should not place surveillance cameras in homes. A problem for liberals is how to protect the freedom of individuals without unnecessarily limiting it. A comparison with the war on terrorism is appropriate. Government can take draconian measures and expel anyone with even vague connections with Islam from the country or lock them up in internment camps. But if a government takes measures like that, the country ceases to be an open society in which individual freedom assumes a central place. A liberal open society has fewer means of coercion at its disposal than a dictatorship, and we should cherish that. It is up to the political system and the policy makers to find a precarious balance between freedom and security.

The relationship between government and individual freedom is most uncomfortable in the areas of education and child-rearing. The state is stuck with legal privileges granted to religious bodies and with social views that hold that it is absolutely all right if parents raise their children in an atmosphere of falsehood and lack of freedom. Fortunately, many religions in the West have become less restrictive during the last few decades. In the educational system as in child-rearing practices, religion often doesn't mean much anymore, at least where the mainstream Christian denominations are concerned. Parenting and education are often closely connected. Parents who indoctrinate their children generally look for schools that will reinforce the process. It is deplorable that an open society tolerates this possibility and in some jurisdictions even provides financial support for it. Because it is much more difficult for a liberal government to monitor children within their own homes (although the regular medical examination of girls from high-risk families in order to prevent genital mutilation, as proposed by Ayaan Hirsi Ali,[16] is to be welcomed), it is fundamentally important for primary and secondary education to be public and compulsory, so that even children who come from a strongly religious milieu will have an opportunity of escape. As a matter of course the state should do everything to guarantee the freedom of individuals to withdraw from any group without fear of repercussions.

A former teacher in a Catholic elementary school writes to me: "Neutral points of view don't exist: a public school, with its secular environment, has such an effect on children that little or nothing goes right with their receptiveness to a philosophy of life." Yes, exactly, not a lot of people will freely opt for religion after pursuing a secular education in which the scientific transmission of knowledge assumes a central place, and which pays attention to world religions and democratic citizenship.[17] The goal of secular education is to equip children with the soundest knowledge available and with a bundle of possibilities for leading a good life. In practice this will have the consequence that not many people freely choose to adhere to a religion.

A self-proclaimed "right-thinking liberal" writes: "After all, is it not up to each individual to desire the best kind of education for the child and to make it possible?" Yes, indeed, the standard liberal view is that parents have the right to choose how to raise their child and what kind of education to offer to him or her. Still, that is not a defensible liberal position. After all, if liberalism stands for individualism, why should parents then be entitled to indoctrinate their children? Why should parents be entitled to raise their children in falsehood and lack of freedom? Government therefore has to offer a strictly secular education. The possibilities for choice should be restricted to the kind of secular school they want. Schools may differentiate on pedagogical grounds. Parents are very much allowed to choose what they believe to be best for their child, but within government-mandated limits established to protect the freedom of children. The "right-thinking liberal" comments that parents with sufficient money are free to pay for a private religiously based school. But that means that you can use your money to buy the right to have your children indoctrinated. I therefore oppose private schools—all schools should be public.

As a final point, the "right-thinking liberal" notes that, "as far as he is concerned, religious universities should be allowed to continue to exist, because university students are adults who can choose for themselves a university that suits them." Indeed, adults are free to choose their own institutions of higher learning. And I am also of the opinion that religiously inspired institutions of higher learning should be permitted to exist, but they should not receive public funds and should not be academically accredited. Religion and science constitute separate worlds. The state should subsidize and accredit only scholarly research and education based on that research.

In reality, in many cases religious universities show no evidence of their religious origins. That is good, because it means that the universities can keep on going in the same way without a religious identity. Scholars and scientists are allowed to draw their inspiration from their religion or some hobby or other. That is their personal choice. But a scholarly and scientific bulwark subsidized by the state cannot and should not be inspired by religion.

Reading Ethically

Learning to read is an important task of education. The most important reason to stimulate reading, it seems to me, is, as has been said, that reading literature can contribute to ethical development. Literature can be an *éducation sentimentale*, a development of the emotions, because the range of your emotions is expanded beyond your own experience. A novel enables you to see the world through the perspective of the protagonist(s). You learn to see the world through the eyes of the other sex, from the point of view of people from other cultures, other ages, other social settings, in other conditions, with other possibilities. I am not concerned about moralizing novels. On the contrary, reading ethically is not about the author's message but about the reader's empathy. Good literature can lead people into the world of the story the author tells. A fair amount of literature deals with adolescents who are curbed in their development by their parents through the imposition of all kinds of prohibitions and taboos. The novels of Maarten 't Hart and Jan Wolkers come to mind.[18] When I read them my hair stands on end: why are these children treated so harshly? In 't Hart's novel *A Flight of Curlews* a boy ('t Hart's fictional alter ego) is not allowed to listen to classical music, although he would rather do that than anything else. This is an ethical situation: the parents impose an absolute prohibition under which the child suffers. The ethical question is: is this prohibition reasonable? How would I like it if I were no longer allowed to do something I really like, reading, for example? Would I as a parent inflict something like that on my children?

Literature can also carry you along to another culture entirely, which can lead to reflection. Take *The Innocent Anthropologist* (1986) by Nigel Barley. He goes to work with a tribe in Northern Cameroon.[19] One of the customs is the circumcision of boys in which the penis is completely flayed. Sometimes the victim does not survive this, and in any case he has to hide himself as a pariah for nine months. The absurdity of this custom prompts reflection. If this custom is pernicious, it leads also to questions about male circumcision among Jews, Muslims, and Americans.

Cultural relativism is dangerous: if a group approves of something, then it is all right, for example, to circumcise women. That is nihilism, of which many cultural anthropologists continue to be guilty. Who would voluntarily allow his penis to be flayed? As I see it, you cannot rationally, being in your right mind, want to be abused or mutilated. This very simple universal finding is a strong argument for the rejection of relativism. Some cultures are superior to others. You can take yourself as criterion in the situation of the weakest, the way literature does.

The ethical element of a novel does not reside in the author's intention but in the reader's attitude. A good method is talking and reflecting about stories. Reading ethically expands one's moral horizon. You can imagine how others feel. Reading ethically does not, in my opinion, need to lead to greater altruism, but it does lead to something that in practice looks a lot like it. If you can empathize with other perspectives and genuinely do so, then you will arrange your norms and values in such a way, choosing them instead of accepting them thoughtlessly, that they are reconcilable with as many individual points of view as possible. This will lead to universal values, such as the ones summarized in the Universal Declaration of Human Rights.

Active Discouragement

The attitude of the state to religion should be the same as to smoking: active discouragement. A liberal government cannot and should not ban things that are bad for the individual's health. But government should make sure that others are not bothered or hurt by it. In the case of smoking these are the passive smokers. Parents should not smoke in the presence of their children, whether in their own home or in the car. In the case of religion, children of believers are exposed to indoctrination in untruth and lack of freedom. The state cannot and should not ban religion, but it can discourage it and in any case should take steps to ensure that other people, including the believers' children, suffer as little from it as possible.

Going back to the previously cited Article 13 of the Convention of the Rights of the Child, adopted by the General Assembly of the United Nations in 1989, does strict religious education conform to these rights? In some religious schools, taboos exist with respect to certain images in books, to honest information about sex, and to homosexuality. Article 14 makes clear that children have a right to freedom of thought, conscience, and religion—children are allowed to express their views without being punished for them. Article 29 states that education should be directed toward "the development of the child's personality, talents and mental and physical abilities to their fullest potential."[20] I deny that strict religious education meets this requirement.

3. FREEDOM OF EXPRESSION

Insults—though perhaps not polite—are permitted, threats are not. Freedom of expression is the basis of the open society. An open society is about people with different ideas and from different cultures living peacefully side-by-side and tolerating the opinions and culture of others. People don't need to have respect for each other's views or culture. Tolerance is enough. In the same way, you don't need to find all clothes or fashions attractive. The sociologist Erik van Ree writes, "Tolerance is the acceptance of the absence of respect." And, conversely: "To demand respect is the essence of intolerance."[21]

THE PARABLE OF TINKEBELL

In 2004 the artist Tinkebell (Katinka Simonse) made her pet cat into a handbag. She claimed her cat was ill. She wrung the animal's neck, skinned it, and turned it into a handbag. Her objective was to raise the question why it is socially acceptable to kill animals like cows and pigs for consumption but not a household pet. Her action unleashed a storm of publicity and criticism, including hate mail and death threats from all over the world. Tinkebell then made a masterly move. She collected and organized the hate mails, and with the help of artist and designer Coralie Vogelaar she searched all over the Internet for personal information about the senders. To her amazement, many personal details are easy to find in blogs and on websites such as Hyves, the largest Dutch social networking site. The book *Dearest Tinkebell* (2008) contains about a thousand hate mails as well as the personal details of those who sent them.[22] Vogelaar carried out the search for personal details in what she calls "the armpit of the Internet," i.e., personal weblogs and social media. The hate mails have been reproduced in their entirety, including one fifty-nine-page e-mail with just one word, "motherfucker," repeated over and over. The e-mail turned out to be from Davide, aged twenty-one, in Rome. The three photos of him make him look like a normal, friendly lad. The book is full of photos of normal-looking men and above all a lot of women, with cats.

With Annoyance

There should be as few restrictions on freedom of expression as possible. Only when there is an issue of "clear and present danger," with humans being threatened physically, or where there is an issue of physical violence, should the state curb freedom of expression. As in the case of yelling "FIRE!" in a crowded theater, when there is no fire. An open society is based on tolerance. Tolerance means the acceptance—if need be with annoyance—of others' opinions, even though you happen to have no respect for them at all.

It sounds paradoxical, but the freedom to insult and to ridicule is a sign of civilization. This means the state does not have to take the values and sensibilities of religious groups into account. Insults and ridicule are permissible. The problem with insults, whether in the context of mockery and humor or not, is that they are *subjective*. Insults are in the eye, or the mind, of the beholder. A believer may *feel* insulted by well-founded criticism, whether in the form of humor or not, or may feel offended by, say, a Gay Pride parade. Politicians may feel insulted by nightclub comedians, cartoons, or columnists. Jews may feel insulted by Islamic utterances, and so on and so forth. In a closed society such as a totalitarian state, there are no nightclub comedians, polemical columnists, nonconforming thinkers, demonstrators, or Gay Pride parades. Insults and ridicule may hurt, but as long as there is no issue of direct danger of physical violence, they come under the rubric of freedom of expression.

Accepting that insults are a part of civilization requires a Gestalt switch. When government starts to use punishment or censorship to protect individuals or groups who feel insulted, it is the beginning of a police state and the end of the open society. Civilization includes being able to insult individuals, situations, and opinions in speech and writing, to dump on works of art, and to vent contrary opinions about appearance and behavior, opinions and religions. Without this freedom there can be no cabaret, no polemics, no *The End of America*, no Paul Krugman or P. J. O'Rourke, no secularization, no liberal democracy. Invective, insults, unvarnished or subtly nuanced criticism form part of an open society; indeed, they are its essence. *Submission* (2004),[23] the short film by Ayaan Hirsi Ali and Theo van Gogh, criticizes in an artistic way the treatment of women in the Koran and Islam and should be freely available in the media. That some people are offended by it is irrelevant. Religious rules apply to those people who believe that such rules apply to them; the rules and taboos have no authority outside their own circle. To be concrete: nobody is going to force Muslims to hang pictures of the prophet or even of humans or animals in their mosques or their homes. But that Islamic taboo has no validity in public spaces. If people are confronted with an image or an utterance that they find insulting, they can simply avert their eyes or stay away. The photos of Sooreh Hera, which depict Muslim homosexuals with masks of Mohammed, were bound to be offensive,[24] and people who find them insulting would have been well advised not to visit the Municipal Museum in The Hague or the Gouda Museum. But no one was forcing them to go there. The notorious and famous Mohammed cartoon is easy to find on the Internet. No one is forcing Muslims to display it in their homes. The heated and violent reactions to the cartoon's republication in Danish newspapers—as a reaction to the foiled attempt to murder the cartoonist—are in flagrant contradiction to freedom of expression and the ideal of an open society.

Under the rule of law in a liberal state the rights of citizens are protected. The state has to stand behind its monopoly of force and has to protect its citizens against threats and attacks. Ayaan Hirsi Ali is a Dutch citizen, and the Dutch government should therefore protect her against attack, irrespective of where she is domiciled. Words and drawings can't kill, but words and drawings can prompt threats of violence. That is absolutely not allowed. Freedom of speech can cause hurt. Freedom of expression involves criticism and commentary that can be hurtful to those affected by it, but it serves the good of society. Freedom of speech and a free and independent press are pillars of the search for truth and justice. In that search, we cannot preemptively exclude certain subjects or people from comment. When persons or subjects are immunized from discussion, the truth can never emerge. Left-wing politically correct opinion makers sometimes say that criticism is acceptable as long as it is applied subtly. In other words, whoever expresses criticism has to take the *potential feelings* of those who are criticized into account. Anybody who starts out on this course closes not only the door to criticism, but also the doors of theaters. Anybody who goes to a nightclub performance knows that comedians play with the limits of the seemly. Ridicule and insults are their stock in trade. The nice thing about an open society is that a comedian, too, gets criticism in the form of reviews. If no one wants to listen to a stand-up comedian, the theater will be empty.

Article 10, section 1 of the European Convention for the Protection of Human Rights and Fundamental Freedoms (1950) states:

1. Everyone has the right to freedom of expression. This right shall include the freedom to hold opinions and to receive and impart information and ideas without interference by public authority and regardless of frontiers.

Section 2 of the article lists several grounds for limiting freedom of expression in the interests of national or public safety.

2. The exercise of these freedoms, since it carries with it duties and responsibilities, may be subject to such formalities, conditions, restrictions or penalties as are prescribed by law and are necessary in a democratic society, in the interests of national security,

territorial integrity or public safety, for the prevention of dis-
order or crime, for the protection of health or morals, for the
protection of the reputation or rights of others, for preventing
the disclosure of information received in confidence, or for
maintaining the authority and impartiality of the judiciary.[25]

The convention contains no limiting clauses about insults. On paper
the European Union is an open society.

By way of contrast, the astonishing Article 137c of the Criminal
Code of the Netherlands provides that anyone who makes a deliber-
ately insulting statement, orally, in writing, or in depiction, about a
group of people on the grounds of their race, their religion or philosophy of life or their hetero- or homosexual orientation, may be
punished by a prison term of up to one year as well as a fine. Should
anyone make a profession or habit of such an action, or should it be
committed by two or more people, the prison term may be as high as
two years and the fine may be greater.[26]

I am not a lawyer, and I don't know the origins of this article. I
do know the law is fortunately a dead letter, at least until now. The
call from some sections of society to punish insults can, it seems,
be validated by an appeal to the criminal code. The question is:
who decides what is insulting? Is it the party who feels insulted or
the judge, or does it depend on the intention of the person whose
comment is at issue?

Article 137c is a dangerous obstacle to an open society. The
same could be said of Section 319 of the Canadian Criminal Code,
which imposes penalties on "public incitement of hatred."[27] In the
United States, however, the First Amendment to the Constitution
does protect freedom of expression, in principle if not invariably
in practice. The Dutch Article 137c offers a clear case for improvement. Inspiration for how it should be rewritten can be derived
from the European Convention for the Protection of Human Rights
and Fundamental Freedoms, which can be traced back to the 1948
Universal Declaration of Human Rights.

Nothing in the European Convention or the Universal Declaration, or in the Dutch Constitution for that matter, states that freedom of expression should be limited by prohibition. Everything that is not explicitly forbidden is implicitly permitted. It should therefore be permissible to insult people, to offend them or be disrespectful to them, in contradiction to Article 137. Threats or the use of physical violence are prohibited, just as libel and slander are, as well as discrimination, that is, treating people differentially on the basis of their race or gender.

Even more than the media, art is preeminently a sanctuary where the ideal of freedom of expression should be allowed to test the frontiers of the legally permissible, in the process offending against social conventions and taboos, cutting people to the quick and stepping on their toes. The essence of stand-up comedy is playing with taboos and social conventions: lack of respect, breaking taboos, offending and insulting people are part the profession. The same applies to political cartoons. Open societies enjoy a high measure of freedom of expression. The broadcasting of the pornographic film *Deep Throat* (1972) on Dutch television in 2008 aroused protests from orthodox Christian circles, but they found little resonance. *Deep Throat* apparently breaks fewer taboos than the twelve-minute film *Submission* (2004), which criticized the subjection of women in Islam.

Because groups of Muslims react heatedly to any criticism of their religion, whether justified or not, and to satirical treatment of their beliefs, and because this overstrung reaction is coupled with threats of violence, which have been shown not always to be empty, people censor themselves. In an open society you don't need to have respect for the opinions and beliefs of others. To emphasize the point: in an open society there is a minimum of rules that facilitate a maximum of individual freedom. In practice this leads to a great diversity of opinions and philosophies of life that do not need to have mutual respect. It is important that there be minimal social conventions to govern the contact between people who have totally different views of life. In the Western world, shaking hands is among these social conventions.

The Utopia of a Moral Esperanto

The Leiden University philosopher Paul Cliteur pleads for a moral Esperanto, that is, a universal minimum set of rules, conventions, and norms that are needed to enable people living completely different lives to coexist.[28] The Universal Declaration of Human Rights is a clear example of moral Esperanto: it consists of rules established by human beings, independent of belief and applicable to all people. A distinction can be made between moral Esperanto as, on the one hand, outcome, i.e., minimal consensus about the rules of social life, and, on the other, a method of achieving consensus, the language in which sensible negotiation can take place and in which there is a possibility for consensus that does not exist when incommensurable languages are employed. Universal subjectivism seeks to be a moral Esperanto, as a method (the thought experiment) as well as an outcome (see the eco-humanistic manifesto).

The Dangerous Argument for Censorship and Self-Censorship

In an open society you run the risk of being confronted with insulting, offensive, indecent, or disrespectful utterances. What can you do when you feel insulted or offended? Let it first be clear what you must not do: you may not threaten violence, use violence, or call on others to use it.

Suppose there is a group within a democratic society that is systematically shut out and at a disadvantage. That can lead to frustration, exclusion, and a feeling of powerlessness. There are people who believe that this has happened to Islam and Muslims in the Netherlands, where there is vigorous public criticism of Islam, Muslims, and Islamic traditions. Can this kind of exclusion ever legitimize violence or the threat of violence? What matters in an open society is that individuals must have the largest possible measure of freedom. For that reason racism and discrimination must be prevented.

Is it true that Muslims are outcasts in the Netherlands? Is it true that they are not listened to and never get to speak? Are they excluded from the media? I regularly see Muslims and imams on television, read commentary about and against criticism of Islam. There is a Muslim broadcasting service. There are mosques, Islamic schools, and cultural organizations. It is therefore not true that Muslims are never listened to. The danger of adopting censorship and self-censorship is that intolerance is tolerated and abuses are obscured.

What to Do When You Feel Insulted

There is no such thing as a limited amount of freedom of speech. It can hurt. People can feel offended or insulted. In a free society, in which individual freedom is at the center, what can you do when you feel insulted? There are at least seven strategies of dealing with indignation.

1. Enter into *dialogue* with whomever insulted you.
2. Make a *rejoinder*: write about it, discuss it, send a letter to the editor, etcetera.
3. *Insult or offend right back*, within the limits of the law. This is not very nice and not very constructive, but it is a legally permissible option.
4. *Register a complaint* with the authorities. If you believe there has been incitement to hatred or violence, or if discrimination is involved, a complaint can be made to the police.
5. *Grow a thick skin.* It is of fundamental importance that citizens in an open society possess a certain resilience and react with a shrug of their shoulders to possibly offensive utterances. You can also try to avoid situations you find offensive: don't watch *Deep Throat* on television, avoid certain exhibitions, don't go to cabarets.
6. *Satire.* Poke fun at your opponents, the way Bill Maher does so marvelously in his TV shows and most notably in his film

Religulous (2008). The Smokers' Church founded by Michiel Eijsbouts is a great way of showing up the ridiculous side of belief.[29] He has created a completely ludicrous religion. And believers recognize this at once, but the problem is that they can't respond to him, because their own belief is very similar except that it is institutionalized and therefore widely accepted.

7. Most difficult of all: engage in *reflection*, look inward. You can take others' arguments seriously. Is their criticism justified? If it is, should you adjust your opinions?

THE PARABLE OF THE SMOKERS' CHURCH

Religions are not by definition old. The Church of Scientology, for example, dates from 1952, and the One and Universal Smokers' Church of God was founded by Michiel Eijsbouts in 2001. "The Smokers' Church is a religious denomination that unites believers in their appreciation of and accompanying fear of God. The daily religious observances are based on the Divine Trinity of Smoke, Fire and Ashes."[30] Church members come together to "to pray to God through the use of smoking materials." Its officials wear comic articles of clothing such as fool's caps. On the basis of divine revelation the Smokers' Church prescribes smoking as a sign of honor to God and bans the consumption of pork before 10 a.m. on Sunday. Bars and cafes can, under strict conditions, adhere to the Smokers' Church, upon which the enterprise can display a certificate indicating that only church members may smoke. According to its own publicity, the church had more than 4000 registered members in 2009 and five approved locations. Eijsbouts appeared on a religious television program in 2008, and his deadpan explanations clearly disconcerted his two Christian hosts. (In the United States, the Church of the Flying Spaghetti Monster has some similarities with the Smokers' Church.)[31]

4. THE GOOD LIFE

How should we live? In the end, everybody has to decide this for themselves within the possibilities available. Acting ethically is making choices, as the French existentialist thinkers, Albert Camus, Jean-Paul Sartre, and Simone de Beauvoir have emphasized. In the end all individuals decide how they should act: giving in to group pressure is a choice, too. Making ethically sound decisions is not always easy.

Radical Simplicity: Joop Boer

Joop Boer has arranged his life in such a way that he fills no more than two garbage bags a year. He has minimized his ecological footprint to two-and-a-half acres. He eats organic food and is a vegan, so he doesn't need a refrigerator. That means he doesn't get to drink chilled beer, but he does drink an organic wine. He has an orchard and a large vegetable garden, works part time for his solar panel business, gets around everywhere on his bicycle, and is in perfect health. "Many people find my way of life strange. But the way I see it I don't deny myself anything. Because I don't need to earn a lot of money, I have lots of spare time." A near-fatal accident when he was twenty-three gave his life a dramatic turn: "I realized how unbelievably beautiful the world is and decided henceforth to treat myself and other people as well as I could, and to do as little as possible to harm the earth. As a human being you get free air, free beauty, the whole world, the universe, every day. That is so much! Why then would you want to mess up our planet in return? Since that event I have arranged my life in order to exist as frugally as possible."[32]

What Is to Be Done?

People should not take the earth's wealthy as their role models, but citizens like Joop Boer. It is sometimes said that there are no more wise people nowadays. But Joop Boer is wise in the traditional meaning of the word. He preaches his wisdom actively through lecturing, writing articles, and via his website. He makes a lot of effort to be as small a burden to others as possible. And yet Joop is no ascetic; he lives soberly, but he does enjoy life.[33] He has a lot of time and freedom, few money worries, and he does what he wants to. He is also independent: he does not allow others to upset him but goes his own way and does what he thinks is necessary. He does not follow fashion trends and has no materialistic urges.

It is reassuring that researchers from different disciplines have all found that happiness depends only in part on riches and prosperity. Above a certain level, the added value of more wealth declines rapidly. If you are a millionaire you can probably live worry-free, but an added million does not increase the happiness level by much. On the other hand, if someone is very poor and is able to secure a small income, this will mean an enormous increase in happiness.

Why do people not act accordingly? If we know that greater riches, more property, a more luxurious car, a bigger or a second house, or more holidays don't contribute to happiness, why do people strive to get hold of these things? In the United States people work on average 20 percent more hours annually than Europeans. Americans are entitled to less vacation time, however, and since the real income of many Americans has stagnated during the last forty years, they are forced to work harder. In Europe there is more room for freedom. What is the use of money if you don't have time to spend it? Conventional wisdom expresses it this way: do you live to work, or do you work to live? In Japan it is clearly the first: you live to work. Most Japanese earn a good living. But they don't have much holiday time. When they are at liberty, they travel at breakneck speed through Europe, passing through ten countries and twenty cities in two weeks. There is even a word in Japan for people (men) who literally work themselves to death: *karoshi*. Aside from materialism of the kind that also exists in the United States, there is Japanese group culture. An employee goes home only when his boss does. And the boss goes only when *his* boss does. You build your career by being at work a lot of the time. Performance is secondary to conforming to the culture of the group. Japan is not a meritocracy, where people are rewarded on the basis of performance, but a neo-Confucian group culture. Individual happiness is not rated highly. Strange to say, Americans are more engaged in arranging their own lives, but they do not do this in a rational way.

Universal subjectivism is a liberal political and ethical theory about justice as fairness. It is not about happiness, or in any case not directly. In liberal theories, individuals get to decide for themselves how they want to live their lives. But it would not be accurate to say that happiness is unimportant. In life, happiness is what it is all about. But freedom is very nearly a precondition of happiness. A conclusion of Ruut Veenhoven's sociological research into happiness is: the more freedom people have, the happier they are.[34] Look, you are born and you will die. During the time in between, you can be happy to a greater or lesser degree. Looking back you can say, "Well, life really was an agreeable adventure that I enjoyed," but it is also possible that you will say, "What a dreadful ordeal this vale of tears was!" What matters is that for a while you find things to your liking here on earth. Unfortunately it is impossible to strive for happiness directly. Just as it is impossible to strive for beauty directly, there must always be a beautiful object. Only drugs can briefly impart a euphoric feeling. The ubiquitous use of coffee and alcohol also prompts a temporary improvement in the feeling of well-being.

It is advisable for people to ask themselves what is important to them in life and what makes them happy. Life is a rapidly running river that pulls you along, but you can climb up the side and, from that vantage point, observe life and make fundamental choices, just as Joop Boer did when he was twenty-three and decided to become an eco-vegan.

In any case, universal subjectivism provides insight into why you should live in such a way that you cause as little as possible harm to others. Joop Boer is not some strange freak. It is not Joop who is weird, but the rest of us who don't live the way he does. We are the ones who are antisocial, the criminals who shift the costs of our consumption pattern to people in poor countries and to future generations. It is not only people who storm into banks and shops with drawn revolvers who are criminals. Even people who lead exemplary lives by conventional middle-class standards fall into in the criminal segment of the moral spectrum if we take into account that they are accessories to animal suffering and to exploitation of workers, including children, and that they have a large ecological footprint. It is quite likely that readers will notice that, by these criteria, they, too, belong in the criminal segment of the spectrum.

Doing-Thinking

While reading this book you have probably felt a tendency to say with a sigh: "You can't do the right thing, anyway," or "Nothing does any good, so I might as well do nothing," or "I'll just keep on living the life I live." And, "How do you like that, reading a book whose possible conclusion is that you're a criminal who is leading a deplorable and morally substandard life! But I make charitable contributions, don't I? I'm a member of the Sierra Club, I contribute to the World Wildlife Fund, and I volunteer for the American Heart Association, don't I? I'm in the Parent-Teacher Association executive of my children's school, and I'm active in the local residents' association, right?"

It is wonderful and ethically desirable for people to get involved in activities of that kind. It is just that these good deeds don't cancel out the bad ones. Imagine a mafia capo or a *yakuza* boss: he, too, may be a solicitous husband and father, concerned about his family, courteous to his neighbors, a contributor to good causes and possibly to his church. Suppose that a mafia capo donates a million dollars to Greenpeace®. Is that a good deed? Greenpeace can certainly use the money. Suppose this extra million dollars contributes to a successful campaign against whaling, as a result of which it is banned: does this make the capo a good person or not? It is a good thing for someone to give money to worthy causes, but the precondition is that this money has been obtained honestly. If I generously give each of my friends a thousand dollars, they will be grateful, but if they learn that I raided my mother's savings account, then, I suspect, they will appreciate it less and may even return the money, even if they intended to donate it to a good cause.

My point is that, in general, good deeds cannot be used to offset bad ones. Even if a child molester gives a million dollars to the New York City Department of Parks and Recreation, to be spent on beautiful children's playgrounds, he will still have to face the music for his crimes. Good people can do good and bad people can do good, but the good does not erase the bad.

It is not easy to live a morally neutral life. The average Westerner causes and is responsible for an untold amount of animal suffering, the transfer of burdens onto poor countries, and mortgaging the future. Yet not a few of them are actively engaged in volunteer work with a host of organizations. When people like that think about the lives they are living, they will probably tend to value their own good deeds. Again: it does not compensate for the morally objectionable things. In the Catholic tradition it was customary to do penance for a moral fault or sin by means of prayer or money. After the penance you could start again with a clean slate. It looks as if this Catholic practice has come into more general use.

Suppose that everybody lived in as ecologically neutral a way as Joop Boer, but without performing voluntary work or other altruistic acts; would that be better or worse than living like the average Westerner today? What is preferable: a hermit in a hut in the woods, or a contractor who lives expansively and who at the same time supports the community with large sums of money (something the hermit doesn't do)? Perhaps moral intuitions differ about this, but I am inclined to select the hermit over the contractor. Someone who lives in an ecologically neutral way causes no harm, not to animals, not to nature, not to other people, not to future generations.

The philosopher James Garvey writes in his spectacular, life-changing book *The Ethics of Climate Change* (2008) that his readers must change their lives, even radically, depending on the kind of lives they are living.[35] It is asking an awful lot to expect people to become ethical saints, eco-vegans who devote themselves full time to good causes and give a large proportion of their incomes to those causes. But it is the ethical ideal toward which we should strive. It is good to have heroes. And better that Joop Boer should be a hero than a highly paid sports figure like Tiger Woods, who is sponsored by Nike®, a corporation that uses or used child labor[36] and underpaid workers in sweat shops. Tiger Woods may well be a great example of how to play golf, but his is not a way of life to be emulated, because as a general rule the richer people are, the larger their ecological footprint is. When people become rich they buy more cars, boats, even airplanes. Rich people don't have to worry about high fuel prices. Let us hope it is an urban legend, but it is said that Saudi princes leave the air conditioning on in their palaces even when they aren't there. The more money people have, the more they waste.

THE PARABLE OF LA-LA LAND

Chantal and Ethan have two jobs, one full- and one part-time, two children, a nice car, and a large new house in the inner suburbs. They decide to have a third child. Their neighbors, Ashley and Blair, actually have four, but they can easily afford it. Blair drives a BMW X5® and of course they have a second car. They enjoy overseas holidays, skiing trips, and home renovations when the spirit moves them. Perhaps they are saving up for a sailboat. Welcome to la-la land, where life is good. It's a place that does not seem to be located on Planet Earth but instead is a dream world, a cocoon inhabited by la-la landers.

When I pick up my children at school I am surrounded by la-la landers. I'm an alien in la-la land. Most of them are pleasant, friendly, and helpful people, but at the same time they are cruel omnivores who are largely unconcerned about their ecological footprint. Even people who are members of organizations like the Sierra Club and the World Wildlife Fund eat meat, drive cars, fly when they want to, and sometimes have more than two children. What is necessary not just to raise the consciousness of la-la landers, but to get them to change their lifestyle?

The Scale of Ethical Actions

You can place ethical actions on a scale. At one end the negative ("the Devil"), at the other end the good ("the saint"). The benchmark on this scale is the ecologically neutral footprint. Everyone who exceeds it (virtually everyone) is in a negative position. You can put every individual action on this scale, and you can put the sum of your actions on it. I suspect that the saintly ideal is unreachable, but you can try by means of ethical reflection to move your own actions as far as possible in the direction of the good. You have to be flexible and ready to adjust your actions in the light of ethical arguments. In this way I became a vegetarian approximately fifteen years ago, and I am moving ever farther toward veganism (I'm almost there).

What you have to do is constantly assess your life and adjust it so that you are moving in the right direction. Universal subjectivism can work as a guiding principle. You can try to constantly reduce the harm your behavior causes, to people in other countries, animals, the environment, and future generations. Aside from this you can also actively do positive things, such as fighting against injustice and trying to reduce or prevent suffering. In our consumer society it is very hard to move in the right direction, because the entire society is organized to have people move in the other direction. Today's growing consciousness of the environment and animal suffering leads to a pilgrimage to the rear, two steps forward and three steps back.

Animal Activism: Henry Spira

The life motto of Henry Spira (1927–1998) was, "Droplets turn into streams than can finally turn into tidal waves of change."[37] He also said, "I guess basically one wants to feel that one's life has amounted

In that case it seems as if this identity is not *in* the shopping cart as an item but is the cart itself. When you look at all the things in your identity cart, you can see whether they are in harmony or not. The label "astrologist" would flagrantly contradict labels such as "rationalist" and "skeptic." Once I had "Roman Catholic" in my shopping cart—my parents took me along to church from time to time, was baptized and confirmed, went to communion—but I threw that out and replaced it with atheism and humanism.

Religious people often refer to their religion as their identity. But why? Why would you call yourself Christian or Muslim when your identity is at issue? Bridge, skating, or ballroom dancing are normally not named in that context. Is your identity not the totality of labels you apply to yourself or others apply to you? Identity is the totality of the labels in your shopping cart.

In the debate about a multicultural society, a lot of attention is paid to identity. What this means in practice is that a *religious* identity is held to be important. Translated into policy this has the effect that more money is given to the stimulation of religious identities. If you define yourself as belonging to a certain religion you close yourself off from a lot of others. Religion is an excluding identity. It is better to define yourself not as religious but as cosmopolitan. Instead of identifying yourself on the basis of contingent facts such as your parents' religion, your gender, sexual orientation, or ethnic origins, it would be better to assume an identity on the basis of accomplishments, such as sportsperson, artist, musician, volunteer, and the whole of these parts. One problem is that others attach an identity to you in the form of a label. Identity, understood as a distinctive label, is a myth that gets in the way of opportunities for self-actualization. On the one hand because people allow it to limit them, on the other because people attach labels to people in order to discriminate against them. In order to move toward a pluralistic, meritocratic redefinition, identity has to be separated from the mythic origin of people and fatherland and freed from contingent facts.

Philosophy is the search for inconsistencies in your views.

The shopping-cart metaphor is a means of tracking down those inconsistencies.

The Freedom of Nudism

"Nudism, also called naturism, [is] the practice of going without clothes, generally for reasons of health or comfort. Nudism is a social practice in which the sexes interact freely but commonly without engaging in sexual activities. The origin of the practice in Germany in the early 20th century coincided with a rebellion against the rigid moral attitudes of the late 19th century. The first known nudist club, Freilichtpark ("Free Light Park"), appeared about 1903 near Hamburg and was soon followed by Richard Ungewitter's seminal work *Die Nacktheit* (*Nakedness*, 1906), which went through several printings. Nudism spread through Europe after World War I and became established in North America during the 1930s."[39] There is no necessary connection between humanism and nudism, but it is a likely combination. Humanism is a good fit with nudism, just as esperantism, atheism, veganism, and liberalism are other isms that form a good fit with humanism. Humanism is an empty shopping cart that accommodates countless isms and some not at all. For theism, fascism, sexism, and speciesism there is no room in the humanistic range of thought. My life is an accumulation of isms; I keep running into new isms that appeal to me. Humanism in itself is naked and can be dressed with the help of any number of isms, including, paradoxically, nudism. Humanism in itself is a naked combination of individualism and rationality.

Just as with many other isms, such as veganism, you've heard about it and distantly you kind of agree with it, but you have never really considered it. For example, about fifteen years ago I had that experience with veganism, and more recently with nudism. It is customary to wear swimming trunks on the beach, but when you think of it, why? When I could not think of any reason for wearing trunks other than convention, and I could think of various reasons for wearing nothing (no tanning line, no wet trunks after going swimming, and a feeling of freedom) I finally stopped wearing trunks. I asked myself whether nudists have other things in common other than a preference for naked recreation—using a sauna, possibly. But are nudists also vegans, for example, or libertines, or leftists, or is nudism represented among all social and ethnic groups in the Netherlands? I tend to doubt it, because it strikes me as unlikely that there are nudists among the Muslims in the Netherlands. In fact, nudism is not a topic that often comes up in conversation, but that may be due to my circle of acquaintances. Although a lot of people frequent mixed saunas,[40] among my acquaintances I know of only one nudist. And he is also a fervent humanist, but not a vegetarian.

Taboos are usually obstacles that keep people from enjoying life—with the liberal humanistic proviso that everything is permitted as long as there are no victims. Why are nude beaches always hidden away and why are the textile beaches (where people wear suits) so prominent? In Denmark nude recreation is permitted on all beaches. What is more normal: a piece of (wet) textile on your body on a warm day, or simply nice and naked? Actually, I also find it odd that you have to wear a swimsuit in a swimming pool. In Sweden topless feminists were expelled from a pool—they argued that if men were allowed to swim wearing just trunks, women should be allowed to do it, too.

The existence of a flourishing subculture of nudism in Europe in the form of nude beaches, nude camping grounds, wellness centers, body-painting festivals, and so on, is an indication of a measure of openness. In an open society lots of subcultures should flower, from Goth to nudist. In a closed or less open society you won't readily find nude beaches or nude camping grounds. France, a secular and open society, is the epicenter of nude recreation. In Saudi Arabia, a nude beach would be unimaginable. Where more public nakedness is found the more liberal, tolerant, and humanist the society is likely to be.

CHAPTER 5
TOWARD A
BETTER WORLD

ECOSOPHY: TOWARD A MINIMUM
ECOLOGICAL CONSENSUS

We urgently need a global rescue plan to avert the global ecological crisis. It is necessary to reach an ecological synthesis, a more holistic perception of the relationship between humans and the environment. Many scientists and nongovernmental organizations (NGOs) tend to focus on and limit themselves to fragments of the total problem. We need a worldview based on scientific knowledge in which sustainability, global justice, and a response to animal suffering come together. The most fundamental questions are: What kind of world do we want to live in? And what can we do to get to that world? Is it possible to reach a consensus on a minimal worldview that is essential to a sustainable and socially just world, even though the world is divided into conflicting worldviews? "Ecosophy" is this minimal worldview. Within that framework there is room for as much pluralism as can be reconciled with the most fundamental values. Pluralism and multiculturalism ought not to tolerate intolerance.

A debate exists among scientists about the details of the damage that has been done to the environment and the climate, but there is a consensus that human actions are having a destructive effect on the planet, such as, worldwide deforestation, depletion of fish stocks in the oceans, water and air pollution, wholesale extinction of species, increase of CO_2 and other greenhouse gases that are warming the earth, rapid growth of the world population, and the exhaustion of fossil fuels and natural resources. Humans use more raw materials than the planet makes available in sustainable form. We are facing a broad spectrum of ecological crises. Our ecological footprint is too big. This is particularly true of those of us who live in the Western world. Humans are using up the natural capital of our world instead of living off the interest that that capital provides.

Tragedy of the Commons

At the core of the human-caused environmental crisis is the tragedy of the commons: what may be good for individuals is not good for all of us. "The worldview underlying conventional economics is that an economy is a system that is essentially isolated from the natural world and involves a circular exchange of goods and services between businesses and households. This model ignores the origin of natural resources flowing into the system and the fate of the wastes flowing out of the system. It is as if a biologist had a model of an animal that contained a circulatory system but had no digestive system that tied it firmly to the environment at both ends. The steady-state economic view recognizes that economic systems are not isolated from the natural world but are fully dependent on ecosystems for the natural goods and services they provide," writes James Garvey.[1]

Overfishing will lead to empty seas. Every fisher will try to catch as much fish as possible, without worrying about sustainability. The same is true of (illegal) logging, which causes deforestation and erosion, which in turn cause an increase in CO_2 and other greenhouse gases and a decrease in biodiversity. What may be good for an individual at a particular moment is not always good for the group as a whole. The tragedy of the commons can be resolved by regulating how common property can be used sustainably and justly. "One main purpose of social institutions, especially legal institutions, is to internalize externalities, preventing people from shifting the cost of their activities on to others. . . . Institutional frameworks can be judged according to whether they put people in a position, first, to recognize when they face a commons problem, and, second, to respond to that problem in a measured, effective, peaceful way."[2] Lasting results depend on good international agreements. "Science alone cannot help us with the answers we need," the environmental philosopher James Garvey writes.[3] And the Intergovernmental Panel on Climate Change (IPCC), which consists entirely of scientists, says about the science of climate change: "Natural, technical, and social sciences can provide essential information and evidence needed for decisions on what constitutes 'dangerous anthropogenic interference with the climate system.' At the same time, such decisions are value judgments determined through socio-political processes, taking into account considerations such as development, equity, and sustainability, as well as uncertainties and risk."[4] Values and norms supplement science, as in the question: what kind of world do we want to live in? By itself science cannot generate an answer to that. We need values that *harmonize with* science. Values that will lead us to eliminate consumerism that is based on the emission of CO_2, because our planet does not have the capacity to deal with it. Values that are in harmony with environmental science can be the basis of a worldview.

Biologist Marc van Roosmalen, a specialist on the biodiversity of the Amazon basin, is pessimistic about the relationship between humans and the environment: "Our species seems to want to do nothing other than use its technical achievements to destroy its own natural environment as quickly and completely as possible. All forms of life originate in the oceans and, more recently, in the rain forests. The destruction of the rain forest will have catastrophic consequences, comparable to a meteorite impact. The earth will certainly need another 50 million years to once more develop a type of rain forest."[5]

THE TRAVEL PARABLE

Bill and Mary are planning to visit Mexico in their RV. When they have covered a fair distance Mary notices that she has been holding the map upside down and that they are driving north, to Canada, instead. Bill has the solution: he will drive more slowly. Mary thinks this is a great idea and compliments Bill on his problem-solving ability.

We, humanity as a whole, are Bill and Mary. We have known for decades that we are to blame for an environmental crisis that will end up in catastrophe. We have been warned. We have received wake-up calls. And indeed, we're doing something about it. All kinds of environmental measures are being taken. And yet, when we look at humankind as a whole, its pressure on the environment continues to mount because of a growing population and an increasing average ecological footprint. In other words, we know we are headed in the wrong direction, and as a remedy we have opted to drive a bit more slowly, but still in the wrong direction. What is needed is a U-turn, a radical reversal. Not on the part of a few ecologically aware people, but on the part of humankind as a whole. Although in principle a reversal of this kind is possible, it is extremely unrealistic to hope for it. Bill and Mary will never arrive at their intended destination.

The Ecosophy of Arne Naess

The Norwegian philosopher, mountaineer, and activist Arne Naess (1912–2009) developed the idea of *ecosophy* (environmental philosophy). It is an attempt to create an ecological worldview through the combination of philosophy, science, and an attitude of life that can serve as a motivation for individual and collective action. Since Naess introduced the concept of ecosophy in 1972, many changes have taken place in environmental philosophy and environmental knowledge, but his holistic vision is still inspirational and gives us a beacon to move toward in the dark times of the environmental crisis. Naess distinguishes between shallow and deep ecology. According to Naess, shallow ecology is a movement dedicated to the struggle against pollution and opposed to the exhaustion of natural resources. Deep ecology is a relational, holistic, nonanthropocentric approach to nature. The difference is between the battle against symptoms, as in shallow ecology, and the attempt to find the origins of environmental destruction, which is the mission of deep ecology.

Shallow ecology is like a smoker who, upon learning he has lung cancer, tries to smoke fewer cigarettes per day while switching to a low-tar brand, begins to work out regularly, and starts eating a lot of fruit. This may help a bit. It would be better to quit smoking altogether, however, and it would have been even better never to start in the first place. Even quitting is no guarantee of a cure and subsequent good health, but under the circumstances it is the best option. Environmental scientists have made a detailed analysis of the health of the earth's ecosystems, and a broad consensus exists that, as a result of human action, these ecosystems are in rapid decline. Shallow ecology, the most dominant form, tries to find a cure for the worst symptoms of ecological decline. I am thinking of acid rain, the hole in the ozone layer, or the disastrous effects of the use of DDT, as described by Rachel Carson in *Silent Spring* (1962). A lot of energy today is devoted to the fight against global warming. We should put the best scientific knowledge and technology to work in order to restore the natural world and at the same time to guarantee the well-being of all humans. Every product should be produced sustainably, that is to say without exhausting nonrenewable resources and without producing dangerous toxic waste that pollutes the environment. Science and technology must be applied responsibly, i.e., according to the principle of "first, do no harm."

Arne Naess's concept of ecosophy combines environmental science and the values of social justice, now and in the future. "In general, however, people do not question deeply enough to explicate or make clear a total view. If they did, most would agree with saving the planet from the destruction that's in progress. A total view, such as deep ecology, can provide a single motivating force for all the activities and movements aimed at saving the planet from human exploitation and domination."[6] Shallow ecology is directed more toward short-term solutions; deep ecology is more concerned with long-term solutions.

In contrast with a scientist who specializes in the fields that are relevant to the analysis of climate change, a philosopher depends on the best available scientific knowledge, such as the findings of the Intergovernmental Panel on Climate Change (IPCC), in order to make a well-considered judgment. Although the popular media may make it seem that there is skepticism among scientists about the role played by CO_2 and other greenhouse gases in global warming, in fact there is overwhelming evidence that people are treating the earth in a way that is not sustainable in the long run. "By now it is an intellectual fraud to continue spreading the notion that global warming is one more theory that may or may not prove true."[7]

The problems of resource exhaustion, pollution, deforestation, fresh water shortages, rising sea levels, population growth, and a rapid growth of the ecological footprint in countries such as China and India, are very alarming. Skepticism about the environmental crisis is like continuing to smoke, and even smoking more, after getting a diagnosis of lung cancer.

Shallow ecology is roughly about the following strategies: looking for alternative, renewable sources of energy, such as wind and solar energy; switching to organic fuels and the use of different kinds of biomass, such as palm oil and chicken manure; the underground storage of CO_2; and the raising of dikes to cope with higher sea levels. Deep ecology, as the term suggests, probes more deeply into the origins of the problem of the human impact on nature. Deep ecology pleads for measures that will radically change society, the economy, agriculture, and consumption. As a result of technology, population growth, and globalization, the impact of human action on the world's ecosystems is greater than ever before in history.

It seems very unlikely that shallow ecology will succeed in finding a balance between nature and a sustainable lifestyle. Deep ecology searches for the origins of the rapid, human-caused decline of nature. For example, Bill McKibben writes in his book *The End of Nature* (1989) that the impact of humankind on nature is such that nothing in nature, from the deepest oceans to the highest mountains, has remained untouched by human hands. "The essence of deep ecology is to ask deeper questions," write Bill Devall and George Sessions, who introduced the philosophy and practice of deep ecology as developed by Norwegian philosopher Arne Naess to the North American public. "The adjective 'deep' stresses that we ask why and how, where others do not. For instance, ecology as a science does not ask what kind of society would be the best for maintaining a particular ecosystem—that is considered a question for value theory, for politics, for ethics. As long as scientists keep narrowly to their science, they do not ask such questions. What we need today is a tremendous expansion of ecological thinking in what we call ecosophy. *Sophy* comes from the Greek term *sophia*, or 'wisdom,' which relates to ethics, norms, rules, and practice. Ecosophy, or deep ecology, then, involves a shift from science to wisdom. For example, we need to ask questions like, why do we think that economic growth and high levels of consumption are so important? The conventional answer would be to point to the economic consequences of not having economic growth. But in deep ecology, we ask whether the present society fulfills basic human needs like love and security and access to nature, and, in so doing, we question our society's underlying assumptions. We ask which society, which education, which form of religion, is beneficial for all life on the planet as a whole, and then we ask further what we need to do in order to make the necessary changes. We are not limited to a scientific approach; we have an obligation to verbalize a total view.'"[8]

Adherents of deep ecology are more attached to nature than the average person. They apply the concept of intrinsic value to nature as a whole. However, nature in itself has no value or, better said, it is value-free. There are no intrinsic values in nature. Without a supernatural justification, a reasoned debate is needed to determine what we attach value to and why.[9]

A problem for biocentrists and adherents of deep ecology like Paul Taylor,[10] who assigns intrinsic value to all living organisms, or to nature as a whole, is to resolve the conflicts between human needs and the intrinsic value of the rest of nature. When this train of thought is followed to the furthest extreme, deep ecology ought to lead to suicide: after all, we are part of the problem.[11] Indeed, deep ecology has adherents of this kind, such as the Finnish philosopher and radical environmental activist Pentti Linkola. He asserts that it would be best for nature (and therefore morally good) if the majority of humankind were to perish. Linkola is a misanthrope who accuses humans of destroying the environment. He has promoted the idea of genocide as a method of saving the environment by reducing the population. He is a fervent champion of deindustrialization. These ideas are known as *ecofascism*. The problem is that ecofascism implies that people who need help should not get it, and that wars and deadly pandemics are beneficial. Ecofascists do make an important point: the *number* of people is in itself a serious problem. But if we take the eradication of individual suffering as a moral axiom, then we need to try to reduce the suffering of those who are alive. The reduction of the number of people should not be the result of suffering and sorrow, but rather of family planning and contraception.

Education, emancipation, and the empowerment of women are of great importance in reducing the number of children born per woman. According to Arne Naess, "We have the goal not only of stabilizing human population but also of reducing it to a sustainable minimum without revolution or dictatorship."[12] The economist Herman Daly also emphasizes the importance of population control and a steady-state economy, stating that we need "an institution for maintaining a constant population size within the limits of available resources. For example, economic incentives can be used to encourage each woman or couples to have no more than a certain number of children."[13]

THE PARABLE OF TARZAN

Tarzan is a deep ecologist before the term was even known. Tarzan, thinker of the jungle, was the brainchild of Edgar Rice Burroughs (1875–1950); *Tarzan of the Apes* (1914) was the first of a long series of bestsellers with Tarzan as the hero. Best known are the *Tarzan* films, particularly those with Olympic swimming champion Johnny Weissmuller in the starring role (1932–48). My grandfather and I watched the black-and-white films with bated breath, although my grandfather often dozed off. Tarzan is just like us: he has Western parents, but they have died in an airplane crash. Tarzan is raised by a chimpanzee, and he lives in the jungle in harmony with nature. He takes no more than he requires for his immediate and simple needs. In addition, he emerges as lord of the jungle in order to protect the animals and the unspoiled jungle from Western interlopers who want to conquer it by hunting animals, cutting down trees, and exploring for mineral resources, particularly diamonds. In this way, the Tarzan films and books can contribute to a reappraisal of the way we see the tropical forests.

However, while viewers of the Tarzan films identify with the hero, all of us are, in fact, the brutes from the cities who plunder the jungle. The time has come not just to lose ourselves in the Tarzan legend but to become Tarzan ourselves. The most important lesson taught by Tarzan is that we Westerners have to deal with nature more circumspectly. All of us, even when we think ourselves to be green, are despots. Our entire modern industrial society is based on the short-term exploitation of nature, the consumption of the natural capital. Our economy operates on nonrenewable fossil fuels and on eating into the earth's natural capital by extracting the finite supply of mineral resources, fishing out the oceans, and cutting down the forests.

One intriguing Tarzan film is *Tarzan in New York* (1942), in which he goes to that city to free his imprisoned chimpanzee friends. The contrast between the way Tarzan behaves in the city and the way

Westerners behave in the jungle is striking. He doesn't shoot the city dwellers. He harms nobody. But the city has nothing to offer him. He finds urban life strange, alienating, and superficial. He doesn't steal anything, as Westerners do in the jungle. Who is actually civilized and what is civilization? Who is living authentically? When we talk about civilization we mean, in fact, the extent to which a group of humans succeeds in wrecking nature. With his attitude to life and his relationship with nature, Tarzan makes a more sensible contribution to the solution of the problematic human-nature relationship than ninety-nine percent of philosophy. Tarzan always fought against the despots and, as in so many Hollywood films, he overcame evil. But Tarzan is dead. Who will stand up to defend the jungle today?

The Synthesis: Ecosophy in the Manner of Universal Subjectivism

Deep ecology is an ideology that places humans *in* nature, not *against* or *over* nature. It emphasizes that the earth as a whole is a harmonious and ecological system that is disordered by human action.

Deep ecology attaches more value to nature than many other ideologies do. But it has significant disadvantages. The notion of inherent or intrinsic value, which occupies a crucial place in deep ecology, is vague and cannot be substantiated. Adherents generally believe that nature has intrinsic value, apart from the instrumental value it has for humans. But what things or entities have intrinsic value, and how can we know it? What arguments can be made for intrinsic value? And if there are things with intrinsic value—nature, let us say—then how should we live?

Adherents of deep ecology try to find inspiration in religious and spiritual traditions. The problem is that a conflict results with science, common sense, and other religious traditions and spiritual practices.

Within deep ecology, there is no clear criterion for establishing priorities when there is a conflict of interest between humans and other species. After all, if all species (animals, plants, bacteria) have inherent value, what criterion can be used to resolve this conflict?

Bill Devall and George Sessions have elaborated deep ecology into a well-argued world- view, based on the ideas of Arne Naess. In their study, Devall and Sessions pay a lot of attention to what they regard as the sources of deep ecology, including the religious and philosophical insights of aboriginal peoples. They may be right, but it leads to philosophical confusion, because religious and spiritual traditions postulate tales about the world and about reality that are often in conflict with science. If deep ecology is a part of scientific ecology, there cannot be a blending with spiritual and religious world-views. Furthermore, if deep ecology is also about social justice, it has to keep in mind that there are great differences among religious and spiritual traditions concerning social justice. Many religious convictions, for example, ones that call for the subjection of women and the exclusion of homosexuals, are inconsistent with human rights and with the results of universal subjectivism.[14]

A revised version of ecosophy, which I am calling "ecosophy, universal subjectivism style" or ecosophy US for short, is based on Naess's idea to regard the planet as a whole and to appreciate nature. Ecosophy US takes science seriously (scientific naturalism); it scraps the concept of intrinsic value, and in order to resolve conflicts of interest, it implements the three ethical principles listed below. This revised version could serve as a minimum set of shared values for all humans, that is to say, a scientific, enduring worldview, and a beacon for ethical action.

To solve the problem of conflicting views about how we ought to deal with nature, including animals, it is possible to borrow concepts from ethics and political philosophy: Peter Singer's utilitarian equality principle, John Stuart Mill's concept of individual freedom, and John Rawls's concept of a hypothetical social contract.

First of all, we have Singer's moral axiom: equal assessment of equal interests. "The essence of the principle of equal consideration of interests is that we give equal weight in our moral deliberations to the like interests of all those affected by our actions."[15] Kicking a dog for no reason is just as bad as kicking a human being for no reason. Both the dog and the human feel pain when they are kicked. It is morally irrelevant which species gets kicked as long as it is capable of feeling pain. However, it makes no sense to say it is wrong to kick a stone, because the stone is lifeless and cannot experience pain.

Second, John Stuart Mill puts the emphasis on the individual: what matters is individual freedom. The primary task of the state is to protect the freedom of the individual. Political or social curbs on that freedom may be imposed only when its exercise infringes on the freedom of others. Recall Mill's famous quote from *On Liberty*: "The sole end for which mankind are warranted, individually or collectively, in interfering with the liberty of action of any of their number, is self-protection. That only purpose for which power can be rightfully exercised over any member of a civilised community, against his will, is to prevent harm to others. His own good, either physical or moral, is not a sufficient warrant. . . . Over himself, over his own body and mind, the individual is sovereign."[16]

James Garvey reformulates Mill's perspective, applying it to climate change: "How a person lives is always up to him, unless how a person lives has bad effects on others." He continues: "Irresponsible lives of high consumption have consequences beyond the short-term gratification of individual people."[17] The application of Mill's liberalism, also called individualism, implies that people ought not, by destroying nature, to harm the options of future generations. On the positive side this means that people can bequeath art and culture to future generations that will enrich the lives of those generations. Mill's liberalism can be applied to (social) justice between generations (intergenerational justice), with an additional advantage that the earth's ecosystem remains as it is, and (social) justice among people who are now living (intergenerational justice). We should not allow our lifestyle and consumption patterns to harm the quality of life of others, both humans and other animals. Westerners have a lifestyle with an ecological footprint that is too big and unsustainable.[18]

According to deep ecology, citizens have a moral responsibility to live ethically and maintain a sustainable ecological footprint. Eating lower in the food chain, by eating cereals and vegetables, instead of feeding these to animals as feed and eating the animals, is much more efficient in the use of water, food, and energy. This transition will be difficult, and there will be plenty of psychological and sociological barriers and pressure from lobby groups. However, voluntary reduction of the ecological footprint (voluntary simplicity) is a moral duty, not a nonobligatory choice. The good news is that sociological research shows that people who live according to the principles of voluntary simplicity are generally more satisfied and happier than they were when they followed their old way of life.

Third, the political philosophy of John Rawls is about optimizing the conditions of those who are in the worst possible situations. This seems to be a fairly general principle and its application to environmental problems and animal welfare is not immediately obvious.

However, when we expand the notion of the individual in a utilitarian fashion, with the help of Bentham and Singer, then it does not seem just that people should cause farm animals[19] to suffer on an immense scale, as happens in factory farming all over the world. When a utilitarian calculus is made, we have the serious and prolonged suffering of millions of animals on one side and the gratification of the taste of millions of humans on the other.[20] Humans, at any rate in the developed countries, do not need meat and dairy for a healthy and tasty diet. Why should people be able to ignore the right of animals to be free from suffering caused by humans? As for applying the principle to environmental problems, if human beings (because only humans are capable of acting morally) are trying to minimize their impact on the liberty of other creatures, it seems reasonable to involve future generations in this as well.

The Problem of Pluralism

Can there be a minimum consensus about the environment? Can we apply an ethical Esperanto to the environmental problem? Ecosophy, with sustainability as the core, can be seen as such a consensus. This ecosophic worldview incorporates the basic rules whereby we should be able to live on this planet ethically and sustainably. In my eco-humanistic manifesto (see chapter 6), I shall expound what, with the help of universal subjectivism such an ethical Esperanto would look like.

Pluralism means a diversity of worldviews. It will make matters clearer if we distinguish between deep pluralism and superficial pluralism.[21] Deep pluralism means that there is fundamental disagreement is (what could also be called a "collision") over what the values are and about how we should live. Superficial pluralism means that there is consensus about fundamental values, but that within that framework there is diversity. Within a democratic, constitutional state, for example, people enjoy a great measure of individual liberty. A society like that is an open society in which diversity can flourish, within the limits of the law. Intolerance is not tolerated, because it breaks the law.

THE CAMPING PARABLE

Bill and Mary are driving through a national park in their Jeep Defender. They pull up beside a beautiful lake. In order to start the biggest campfire possible, Bill uses his chainsaw to fell several trees. To get rid of those annoying mosquitoes, Bill sprays chemicals that make the bugs disappear and also kill the nearby birds. Then he goes fishing to get something for the barbecue. A couple of sticks of dynamite make things easier. The following morning Bill and Mary pack up, leaving behind their garbage—cans, aerosol containers, plastic, paper, and glass bottles. Life is great in the wild! They get into their Jeep and drive to the next campground; they still have a good two weeks ahead of them. The next day, Alice and John, who go backpacking through the park every year, arrive at Bill and Mary's spot after a hard day's hike.

Is it ethically justified to camp the way Bill and Mary do? It seems as if it is ethically justified, because this is how most Westerners live and how our economy works. We just never think about it. Bill and Mary are us!

Leave No Trace as a Guide to Hiking and Living

Leave No Trace[22] is a national and international program designed to assist outdoor enthusiasts in reducing their impact when they undertake activities in the outdoors. The program seeks to educate all those who enjoy the outdoors about the nature of their recreational impact as well as about techniques to prevent and minimize it. Leave No Trace is best understood as an educational and ethical program, not as a set of rules and regulations. The program helps visitors to public lands understand and practice minimum impact skills and environmental ethics.

The Leave No Trace program is a combination of science and common sense for enjoying the outdoors responsibly. It consists of seven principles:

1. Plan Ahead and Prepare
2. Travel and Camp on Durable Surfaces
3. Dispose of Waste Properly
4. Leave What You Find
5. Minimize Campfire Impacts
6. Respect Wildlife
7. Be Considerate of Other Visitors[23]

Trail ethics is a miniature version of environmental ethics. "Leave things the way you find them" can be expanded to "Do not use up nonrenewable resources and create waste and pollution." "Respect wildlife" can be expanded to "Respect animal life." "Be considerate of other visitors" can be expanded to "Be considerate of all humans and of future generations." Leave No Trace is thus a comprehensive philosophy of life, providing answers to long-asked questions.

There are six stages of ecological change: diagnosis, research into causes, consciousness-raising, developing solutions, implementation, and evaluation. First there has to be a detailed diagnosis of the condition of the environment (the ecosystems of the earth). At issue is an ecological checkup of "patient Earth." Since the 1970s it has become clear that the environment has suffered seriously as a result of human action. After the diagnosis, research has to take place into the causes of the decline in environmental quality. If physicians know how lung cancer can be diagnosed, research goes in two directions: toward cure or treatment, and into the causes, such as smoking. Environmental scientists are constantly checking the earth's various ecosystems. Crisis reports appear regularly, such as by marine biologist Daniel Pauly, professor and the project leader of the Sea Around Us Project at the Fisheries Centre at the University of British Columbia who warns that the seas will soon be empty if we continue with current fishing methods.[24] And when the diagnosis has been made and further research has been done, policy makers and the public must become aware of the problem, or be made aware of it. If people are unaware of the seriousness of problems, they will not vote for green politicians who will undertake thoroughgoing action, nor will they change their lifestyle or world-view. Once there is a broad social *awareness*, policy and behavior change are required on all levels: government, agriculture, the economy, and, of key importance, consumption (shopping involves ethical choices). When ecological awareness has penetrated, green policies and technology must be implemented. And finally, constant evaluation of the results achieved must take place by means of a feedback loop.

The environmental crisis is getting worse. The positive and negative effects of economic growth, world markets, and consumerism are not in balance. Environmental injustice means that the rich get the advantages and the poor the disadvantages. The rich have opportunities to ensure that waste products and pollution stay out of sight. The strongest shoulders bear the lightest burdens. Today's neoconservative capitalism is based on economic growth and consumerism, and factors in neither the environmental costs nor the social injustice they cause and implicitly support. We need a planetary ethic that takes into account the environmental costs as well as social justice. But how are we to implement this new planetary ethic? Before we can think about concrete measures, a paradigm shift has to occur, from explicit short-term anthropocentrism and a preoccupation with growth and consumerism to sustainability and global justice. This paradigm shift will have at least the following aspects. The environmental costs are taken into account. This can be done by creating a sustainable, green economy: the creation of a steady-state economy, in combination with the moderation of consumerism. Small subcultures already exist in which consumerism does not play a central role, such as "voluntary simplicity"[25] and the "enough is enough" movement.[26] We need to strive toward global justice, away from national egotism, and toward worldwide social justice. We must take seriously the suffering of animals caused by factory farming, as well as the enormous pollution, greenhouse gases, and inefficient land use. Veganism appears to be a logical part of ecosophy as a sustainable worldview.

Nine Principles of Ecosophy in the Manner of Universal Subjectivism

With the help of universal subjectivism, the principles of deep ecology can be reexamined in order to incorporate the pathocentric perspective, in which suffering is central.

1. Today's human interference with the nonhuman world is excessive, and the situation is rapidly getting worse.
2. Equal interests deserve equal ethical appraisal. Suffering must be diminished and happiness promoted.

3. Humanity is not outside nature (dualism) but is part of nature. Humans are animals among the other animals (ecological perspective).

4. Humans should not reduce the richness and variety of nature, except to satisfy vital human needs and then only in such a way that ecosystems are not disrupted and no suffering, or as little as possible, is caused to other beings, including the interests of future generations.

5. A reduction of the human population is necessary for ecological balance.

6. Cultural diversity is possible, and desirable, within the guidelines established by human rights legislation and the "do-no-harm" principle (application of universal subjectivism).

7. Policy influences economic, technological, and ideological structures. Policy therefore must be changed. This will result in a fundamentally different socioeconomic order than the one that now exists.

8. The key change in ideology lies in the acknowledgment of the quality of life rather than the pursuit of a ceaselessly improving living standard.

9. Those who endorse the preceding points have an obligation to try to implement the necessary changes.

Arne Naess made a plea for what he called an ecological Enlightenment: "A realistic appreciation of the drastic reduction in life quality, an increased influence of deep ecological attitude, [and] a slow decrease of the sum total of unsustainability."[27] Ecosophy is a worldview that combines sustainability, science, and social justice. My version of ecosophy combines the input of environmental science and scientific naturalism with three basic principles from ethics and political philosophy: the principles of "equal treatment of equal interests" (Singer), the "do-no-harm" principle of Mill, and the "maximization of the worst possible situation" (Rawls). One problem with a worldview of that kind is that it diverges from the great majority's worldview. The vague and unscientific concept of intrinsic or inherent value, central for most ecological thinkers, is discarded without deep ecology losing the power to protect nature from destruction by humans. This revised ecosophy can function as a beacon for scientists, politicians, economists, activists, and consumers. It is neither unreasonable nor unrealistic to propose a minimal ecosophy as a worldview that can be shared by all the world's inhabitants. This new ecosophy is a dynamic worldview based on environmental science and three basic ethical axioms. Ecosophy promotes a lifestyle that is of equal value to all humans, species, and generations. Political scientist and pioneer in environmental social science Lester W. Milbrath offers this observation: "Our species has a special gift: the ability to recall the past and foresee the future. Once we have a vision of the future, every decision becomes a moral decision. Even the decision not to act becomes a moral judgment. Those who understand what is happening to the only home for us and other species are not free to shrink from the responsibility to help make the transitions to a more sustainable society."[28]

CHAPTER 6

ECO-HUMANIST MANIFESTO

T his eco-humanist manifesto is the result of applying the thought experiment of universal subjectivism. Most of the articles have already been mentioned earlier. This chapter adds a few more.

Universal subjectivism is a procedure of generating ethical rules and agreements so that humans may live together in the best possible way, making the most of this world and optimizing even the worst possible situations. This is a procedure you can carry out on your own, but you also can and should discuss it with others. I have listed a number of possible outcomes of the procedure of universal subjectivism, with an emphasis on animal welfare, sustainability, and nature. This eco-humanist manifesto is my proposal for an ethical Esperanto. In my view, the 1948 Universal Declaration of Human Rights can be justified by universal subjectivism. However, universal subjectivism goes further because it is a method of identifying blind spots in our morality. No matter how marvelous the Universal Declaration may be, it is not perfect. Therefore the possible outcomes of universal subjectivism need to be enumerated.[1]

TOWARD A SUSTAINABLE FUTURE

This manifesto is based on the concept of a sustainable planetary social contract: we have to share this planet with each other, and it would be useful to do our best to make the most of our situation for ourselves, here and now; and for humans elsewhere; and for the generations that will come after us. The manifesto applies universal subjectivism to the human-caused climate and environmental crisis: ecocide.

Dancing on a Volcano

Humans and other animals depend on a healthy planet in order to live and enjoy life. It is a tragic paradox that just at the moment prosperity is increasing at the global level and the world population is growing rapidly, the consequences of human action are destroying the planet. There is debate among scientists about details and about just how bad the situation is, but there is consensus that our human activities are having a bad influence on the earth's ecosystems: for example, through worldwide deforestation, the overfishing of the seas, water and air pollution, mass extinction of species, an increase in CO_2 and other greenhouse gases that cause global warming and climate change, rapid growth of the world populations, exhaustion of fossil fuels, and the nonreplaceable natural resources. People use more resources than the earth can provide in a sustainable way. We face a large array of ecological crises. Humans, notably in the Western world, have much too large an ecological footprint. People are using up the natural capital instead of living off the interest. No treasurer would approve of this, but who is the world's treasurer? As a result of this irresponsible, unethical lifestyle, future generations will suffer from the consequences of our behavior. The philosopher James Garvey puts it this way: "There is going to be a lot of death in the future, a lot of death which wouldn't have happened had we and those before us acted otherwise. There will be a lot of extra suffering, disease, thirst, hunger, violence and the like, horrors which wouldn't have happened had we and those before us acted otherwise. What we do now and in the next few years is going to matter—what this generation does is going to matter a lot."[2]

Tragedy of the Commons

In essence, the human-caused environmental crisis is a planetary version of the "tragedy of the commons" and the "prisoner's dilemma": what is good for each individual separately is not good for the collective. What is good for an individual at a particular moment is not always good for the whole, or in the long run. The tragedy of the commons can be resolved by making rules about how common resources, including the seas, are to be used. Sustainability depends on good international agreements.

1. Future Generations

Today's generation of humans uses nonrenewable sources of energy and the planet's natural capital. Future generations will suffer because of today's lifestyle. Therefore the current (Western) lifestyle is deeply unjust to future generations. The German social psychologist Harald Welzer states in his 2008 book *Klimakriege* (*Climate Wars*) that climate change will lead to wars. In his view the war in Darfur is the first climate war, since drought has led to a conflict, caused by scarcity, over water and fertile lands. The conflicts are fought along ethnic and/or religious divisions. "Climate warming, the result of the insatiable hunger for fossil fuel in the old industrial countries, hits the world's poorest areas hardest: a bitter irony that contradicts the expectation that life should be fair." Welzer concludes ominously: "Violence has a great future in this century." Therefore we "have to escape from the deadly logic of continuing growth and unlimited consumption."[3]

2. Steady-State Economy

The concept of an ever-growing economy on a finite planet is suicidal. Natural resources, including fossil fuels, are scarce, and the capacity of the aerial ocean[4] to absorb greenhouse and other gases is limited. When a reasonable, comfortable level of welfare has been reached, it is enough to maintain equilibrium. The economy does not then need to keep growing. Capitalism is about the maximization of profit and the reinvestment of part of it in the enterprise so that it may grow and make more profit. If there is growth, it should only be sustainable development. According to the 1987 Brundtland Commission of the United Nations, "humanity has the ability to make development sustainable to ensure that it meets the needs of the present without compromising the ability of future generations to meet their own needs."[5] In the case of sustainable development there is an optimal balance between ecological, economic, and social interests. The ecological economist Herman Daly defines a steady-state economy this way: "A steady-state economic system is characterized by balanced, opposing forces that maintain a constant stock of physical wealth and people through a system of dynamic interactions and feedback loops. A low rate of flow or throughput of matter and energy resources maintains this wealth and population size at some desirable and sustainable level. In such systems, emphasis is on increasing the quality of goods and services without depleting or degrading natural resources to unsustainable levels for current and future generations."[6]

Business schools and economics programs require a green and ethical revision. A healthy steady-state economy does not live off natural capital. A large-scale cultural and economic change is inescapable.

3. Fresh Water Scarcity: Planetary Blue Revolution

We are facing the threat of world-wide water shortages, notably in developing countries, as a consequence of climate change and intensive agriculture. Global warming is causing droughts and desertification. All over the world aquifers are being drained to irrigate crops. To prevent a crisis, many countries will have to conserve fresh water, pollute less, regulate supply and demand, and limit population growth. A "blue revolution" is needed to deal with water shortages on a local, national, and international level. Water management comprises water purification; policies to counteract the wasteful use of fresh water, such as watering lawns and especially golf courses; the improvement of methods of irrigation; the recycling of municipal waste water; and, most important, the conservation of water used for industrial purposes.[7]

4. Sustainable Oceans

In 1997 the American yachtsman Charles Moore discovered a "plastic island" in a gyre, a place in the ocean where various sea currents come together in a gigantic circular movement. This is where floating plastic waste comes together.[8] Plastic is not biodegradable. When exposed to sunlight, it breaks up into ever-smaller parts. Larger pieces such as bottle tops are eaten by birds, among them albatrosses, and can kill them. The smaller pieces are eaten by fish and thereby enter the food chain, of which humans are a part. Moore calculated that a quarter of the Pacific Ocean is affected, an area of 3.32 million square miles in which close to a hundred million pounds of garbage are floating around, or roughly thirty pounds per square mile.[9] What can be done about this? Cleaning the oceans is an almost impossible task. It would be best to stop polluting. But the entire society and economy of the modern West are based on a throwaway culture. It is difficult and inconvenient to change this way of life, but there is no choice. I read the following on an environmental website: "I worked on cruise ships in the 1980s and at night we dumped all the ship's trash through a hatch into the sea. Thousands of black garbage bags during the months I worked there. At that time nobody thought about the problems."

The plastic islands are only *one* problem, along with the dumping of toxic and nuclear waste, crude-oil pollution, and the overfishing that together result in empty and polluted oceans. For too long we have regarded the oceans as a place to dump our trash while at the same time catching as much fish as possible. As a consequence of these two contradictory attitudes toward salt water the oceans are becoming increasingly polluted and empty. Instead of searching for a structural solution, fishers are trying, in every corner of the earth, to catch the last fish. A simple solution would be to stop eating fish (an added advantage of this is that we would be avoiding fish that, as the result of plastic and other pollution, contains a lot of contaminants) and to stop using the ocean as a vast garbage disposal unit. Absent a demand for fish, the commercial fishing industry will stop fishing. The second best solution would be creating large sea reservations and combining strict fish quotas with sustainable and "animal-friendly" methods of fishing. Such methods exclude drag nets. An "animal-friendly" method of fishing means no great nets in which fish are pressed together and undergo a slow and painful death, but a quick and painless method.

5. Climate Change: Stop Greenhouse Gas Emissions

Climate change will cause great disasters around the world, in coastal areas where flooding is likely as a result of rising sea levels, and in still fertile agricultural areas as a result of drought. Only a drastic reduction of greenhouse gas emissions, especially CO_2 and methane, can counteract a continuing warming of the earth. But even drastic measures cannot negate the damage already done; they can only prevent further damage. A large-scale redesign and makeover of our CO_2-emitting economies is essential. However, this change is unlikely. And yet, in the past there have been rapid large-scale changes in the economic industrial complex, such as the mega-project of "landing a man on the moon, and returning him home safely," initiated by President Kennedy. If politicians and citizens see the need for drastic and dramatic change, it can happen. There may be hope that the leadership of President Obama can change the tide. Besides, because of Obama's presence in the White House, Al Gore is no longer a voice calling in the wilderness. We have no choice, we have no time.

Let's get moving: we recognize that our ship is sinking so let's get off the sundeck and get to work to stop the leak. There is no choice. A cancer patient has no guarantee that chemotherapy will be effective, but he must try it all the same because doing nothing will irrevocably lead to death.

6. Population Balance

How many people living a comfortable life can our planet support? The number depends on two variables: the average ecological footprint and the number of people. What matters is the quality of life, not the quantity. People around the world should become aware that more than one child per person will contribute to world population growth. There should be a global information service about population growth as well as contraception and its free availability. The education, emancipation, and empowerment of women are of great importance in reducing the number of children per woman. The higher the education level of women, the lower the average number of children and the higher the age at which women have their first child. The result of this is population growth will be slowed down.

7. Sustainable Energy Use

Instead of using nonrenewable sources of energy that produce greenhouse gases or, in the case of nuclear energy, dangerous waste, we must give top priority to the development of new forms of sustainable energy such as wind and solar energy.

8. New Sustainable Technology

In order to win back nature and at the same time guarantee the well-being of all people, we have to apply the best scientific knowledge and technology. We need a transition from nonsustainable to sustainable technology and production. A lot of knowledge is already available; the problem rests in the implementation of the innovation process. All products should be manufactured sustainably, that is, without using nonrenewable resources and without toxic, dangerous waste or by-products that harm the environment. All new technology should be sustainable. It is unacceptable for nonsustainable technology to be developed or applied. Science and technology should be applied and put into service responsibly and sustainably.

9. Biodiversity: Large Nature Reserves All Around the World

The extinction of species has increased dramatically in recent decades.[10] This mass extinction seems to be the sixth of its kind. The previous five mass extinctions were caused by natural phenomena such as volcanic eruptions and asteroid impacts. The sixth mass extinction is entirely due to human action. We are at risk of ourselves being one of the species that may become extinct, because we are making our habitat, the earth, unlivable. To temper the extinction rates, large nature reservations must be set aside, including coral reefs[11] and the Amazon rain forest. The World Wildlife Federation list of protected animal species should serve as a policy guide. Whale fishing should be entirely banned, including for (so-called) scientific purposes.

10. Wilderness

The beauty of unspoiled nature should be protected as much as possible. Nature should not be regarded only from an economic perspective. For example, instead of building (yet) another ski resort that ruins the mountain landscape, people should be able to use nature sustainably. Around the world large stretches of wilderness should be preserved, with a view to biodiversity, to maintenance of the balance of Earth's ecosystem ("the lungs of the earth"), for the sake of the beauty of nature (the esthetic argument), because of the possibility of finding new botanical medicines or edible plants, and for the benefit of future generations. We ought to leave the world intact for those who will come after us.

11. Farewell to Speciesism

We acknowledge the moral implications of the capacity for experiencing pain. It is not limited to the human species but extends in differing degrees to a range of living beings. Due to the development of factory farming during the second half of the twentieth century the number of farm animals living under pitiable conditions has increased exponentially. For example, there are almost 17 million people in the Netherlands and 450 million farm animals. Some problems have simple solutions. Animal suffering in factory farming, the large-scale water use, the deforestation that opens up land for fodder (including soy), and the emission of greenhouse gases by the animals (methane) can be solved quite simply if lots of people consume less meat or none at all. Eating meat is, to put it mildly, ethically and ecologically problematic. We should therefore work toward an immediate world-wide ban on factory farming, including fish farms, and take the welfare of farm animals more seriously.

Scientific and medical experiments using animals should be limited as much as possible and we should invest in the development of alternative experimental methods in which animals are not used. Cosmetics should not be tested on animals. After all, there are enough shampoos on the market already. The policy with respect to animal experimentation should be one of "only if," that is, that animal experimentation is permitted only if there are very weighty interests and reasons at issue, and everything possible is done to limit animal suffering.

12. Higher Primates and Dolphins

We must expand the notion of human rights to cover at least the great primates (bonobos, chimpanzees, gorillas, and orangutans) and dolphins.[12] In evolutionary and therefore genetic terms the great primates are closely related to us and so their mental capacities, including the capacity for suffering, are considerably greater than those of most other animals. Dolphins have highly developed cognitive, social, and emotional powers on the basis of which it is reasonable to accord them rights. The habitat of the great primates is threatened, such as in the Borneo jungle, where the orangutans live, and in the mountains of the Congo, where the gorillas live. We should have strict laws that stipulate under what conditions great primates may be imprisoned (including in zoos). Experimentation on the great primates should be banned altogether.

Drawing on the Great Ape Project[13] and the World Declaration on Great Primates, we can accord them the following rights: the right to life, the protection of individual freedom, and the prohibition of torture and maltreatment. This applies also to dolphins. Fishing must be carried out in a dolphin-friendly manner. The killing of dolphins that still takes place in Taiji, Japan, must be banned.[14]

13. A Green Revolution in Agriculture: Organic, Sustainable, and Animal-Friendly

Intensive methods of farming have increased the yield of agrarian products enormously, but these methods have disastrous side-effects for the environment and for animal welfare. The focus has rested and still rests one-dimensionally on production increases and profit maximization. Pollution, deforestation, fresh-water shortages, large-scale monoculture, and animal suffering in factory farming are examples of the side-effects of intensive agriculture. Mechanized agriculture, dependent on oil,[15] chemical fertilizers and pesticides,[16] is not sustainable. We must therefore introduce ecological innovations into the entire process of agriculture and food production. This does not mean that we have to go back to preindustrial times, but that sustainable technology has to be deployed in a sustainable, steady-state economy. This will result in lower average yields. In sustainable agriculture, crops are grown and farm animals are raised on the basis of organic fertilization, the preservation of fertile land, frugal water use, biological methods of combating diseases, and the minimization of the use of nonrenewable fossil fuels.

14. Ecological Justice

Rich consumers and powerful companies succeed in getting rid of their garbage, unwanted by-products, and waste by using cheap labor in developing countries.[17] A lot of discarded electronic items end up in Africa, where they are dumped. The people who suffer most from environmental pollution and climate change are not the ones who have a comfortable Western lifestyle but the ones who are already in the worst situations.

The moral and legal concepts of responsibility for the by-products, waste, and other consequences of production and consumption need to be reviewed: both the producer and the consumer should assume responsibility.

15. Lifestyle Change: Voluntary Simplicity

People with a Western lifestyle have a large, non-sustainable ecological footprint. Websites, such as www.myfootprint.org, allow you to calculate your ecological footprint. Individual world citizens ought to live in an ethically responsible way and to have a small, sustainable footprint. Eating lower in the food chain, by eating plants rather than feeding them to animals and then eating those animals, is much more efficient from the point of view of food production and the use of land, water, and energy. This transition may be difficult and inconvenient because of psychological and social pressure. Automobile use, flying (especially holiday travel), eating meat, air conditioning, and consumerism in general are problematic. Voluntary simplicity is a moral duty. It is not noble, worthy of emulation, or a nice hobby; no, it is a moral duty. The good news is that sociological research has established that people who adopt a simpler life are generally happier and more satisfied than they were before.[18]

16. A New Ideal of the Good Life: Leaving Consumerism Behind

Perhaps it is difficult to understand and accept, but a major social, economic, and technological reversal is needed; in fact, there is a strong moral imperative for it. A paradigm shift has to occur from a non-sustainable to a sustainable socioeconomic system. Changes must take place at all levels: global (United Nations), European (EU), national, local, for NGOs, businesses, organizations, and individuals.

The more people earn, the more expansive their consumption pattern and the larger their ecological footprint becomes, and the more morally objectionable their way of life becomes. Rich pop stars and sports stars tend to live reprehensibly from an environmental point of view. The media, especially the fan magazines, propagandize this morally reprehensible lifestyle.

Eco-quota

It is possible that government will establish a quota on consumption. Everyone gets the right to an annual ecological footprint of a size that is within the earth's carrying capacity, so if everyone on earth abides by their maximum quota, total consumption will be sustainable. How people spend their quotas would be a matter of individual choice. Just as you now complete a tax return, you would have to complete a form on the basis of which your ecological footprint is calculated.

Reduce, Reuse, Recycle, and Reconsider

The slogan "reduce, reuse, recycle" is helpful as a rule of thumb. But it should be preceded by "reconsider." Think before you buy or do something: perhaps that purchase or action is unnecessary. This will require a great cultural change, leaving consumerism behind, and it will be a departure from the fashion and shopping culture in which people buy things they don't really need. Marketing is intended to make people buy as much as possible, regardless of whether they really need it. The vicious circle of consumerism, marketing, and the pressure for more must be broken. That may seem to be Mission Impossible, but we don't have a choice.

World Improvement for Beginners

You want to make the world a better place, but how? Where do you begin? What do you have to do? To live is to consume, to make choices. You can try to live an actively ethical life by not making victims through what you do and consume. As a result—inconveniently as it might appear—veganism is a moral base line. And you can actively try to make the world a better place by reducing suffering, for example, by becoming active in a human rights association like Amnesty International® or an environmental organization like Greenpeace®. Ethical self-help for beginners: there is only one person responsible for yourself, and that is you.[19]

17. Think Globally, Act Locally

The other day, when I came home on my bicycle via the beautiful green route, I was startled to come across a large metal container in which I spotted pieces of the beloved fir tree that had previously embellished the garden of our neighbors to the rear. It was this tree that gave our townhouses a touch of class. Now the tree is gone. Spring has sprung, and the great saw-fest has begun. From a legal point of view people may have the right to cut trees in their yards, but doing so affects the quality of their neighbors' residential environment. It pains me to look outside and see the great emptiness. It rather seems as if the current esthetic garden ideal is a paved, treeless space. Would it not be a lot more beautiful if there were more trees and shrubs, if nature returned to the city? Without trees and shrubs there are no birds and hedgehogs. Wouldn't it be nice to live in a forest or park? Nowadays it seems as if trees and vegetation are considered a decorative trim. Should we not give a more prominent place to vegetation and to nature? The stroll through the neighborhood would become a stroll in a park. The community should not be shaped from the driver's perspective but from the pedestrian's. We are in the midst of a great, worldwide ecological crisis. Nature hardly exists any longer. We should therefore do our best, in a small way, to come to a new relationship to nature by bringing the forest into our towns and cities. The slogan "think globally, act locally" applies here. Below, I will make a number of suggestions for how the residential environment can become greener, more attractive, more agreeable, more sustainable, and because of all these, can at the same time become a closer social community. Who wouldn't want to live in a beautiful, more pleasant neighborhood?

Ideas for a Greener, More Attractive Residential Environment

- More green: There should be trees along every street along with parks and parkettes with shrubs, so that hedgehogs and other animals get some habitat. Nature must get space in the neighborhood. The stringent division between city and nature must yield to a harmonious relationship between humans and nature in the residential environment.
- Fewer cars: Encourage cycling, walking, and public transportation by making better than merely adequate provision for them. Discourage auto use while at the same time stimulating the use of shared automobiles, such as Zipcars, and of small,

energy-efficient automobiles. Streets can be narrowed—one car wide, with areas for passing. The policy should be "cars are guests."

- Separate pedestrian paths and bicycle and walking routes.
- Arboretum: The variety of trees and shrubs can turn towns and cities into instructive arboretums.
- Orchards: Trees that are not alongside roads can be fruit trees. Harvesting can be done by volunteers.
- Fair trade Towns: These are towns in which people and organizations use their everyday choices to increase sales of Fair trade products and bring about positive change for farmers and workers in developing countries. "Becoming a Fairtrade Town is a shared achievement and an opportunity for local government, schools, businesses, community organizations and activists to work together."[20]
- Twinning with a green community in another country: This strengthens the idea of world citizenship.
- Encouragement of green energy by subsidies and other methods.
- Solar panels on streetlight (charging the battery for the night): These new solar-energy lights could have an attractive design.
- Green all around: Meadows and undeveloped lots could become part of a green zone, part relaxation and part recreation area (forest/park).
- No pesticides and herbicides to be used.
- Encouragement and subsidizing of organic farming.[21]
- Discouragement of traditional intensive agricultural and livestock-raising.
- Green schools with green schoolyards and solar panels: New schools should be green and sustainable.
- Green industrial parks with walkways: In industrial parks a lot of attention should be paid to vegetation—a collective park garden with paths for pedestrians between and around the buildings, complete with and garden furniture.

- Benches and picnic tables.
- Jogging circuit: Public spaces should encourage outdoor recreation that causes as little damage as possible to humans, animals, and the environment. Fitness exercises, jogging, running, cycling, and roller-blading are suitable activities.
- Volunteer labor (a park commission): This could be used to harvest fruit from fruit trees, among other tasks.
- Green noise barriers along highways: These would not only contain noise but also serve as a habitat for plants, insects, and birds.

What Can I Do?

In the preceding pages I have identified a number of changes that could lead us to a better, more just, and more sustainable world. But what can the reader do with it? Universal subjectivism is meant to be a means for getting to a better world—not in the abstract, but concretely. This book is not only an ethical and politico-philosophical treatise about the justification of morality and about the nature of a just society, but also an appeal to act ethically and to live the good life while on the way to a better world. As a result, this book has something of a preachy tone. But experience teaches that people can read, see, or hear deeply affecting arguments and then do nothing with them. There is, alas, a difference between being persuaded and acting on the basis of that persuasion. To provide assistance and by way of conclusion, I shall offer suggestions as to what you as readers can do to live the good life and to work toward a better world. These concrete pointers are derived from the model of universal subjectivism, and readers should also be able to derive them for themselves.

Asking Too Much?

My students sometimes wonder if it is not asking too much to confront people all at once with so many ethical issues and to expect them to change their lives drastically in the light of this moral reflection. My answer is that as a philosopher I follow the logic of the argument. And it cannot be the case that the only objection against an argument is that you don't like the conclusion (the First Law of Philosophy).

THE PARABLE OF THE ETHICALLY TROUBLED SLAVE OWNER

Henrico has a cotton plantation with a hundred slaves. One day he reads a pamphlet that states that slaves, too, are people who can suffer and therefore have rights. Henrico thinks about this at his leisure and is convinced by the arguments. He therefore makes an ethical decision. He frees ten slaves. When people ask him why he does not give all his slaves their freedom, he answers that it would be difficult to operate a cotton plantation without slaves. Surely you can't expect him to abandon his entire plantation?

TO A BETTER WORLD IN ELEVEN STEPS

To paraphrase Arne Naess, the direction itself may be revolutionary but not the steps in that direction. Here are eleven steps that, taken together, can produce a peaceful but nevertheless revolutionary ecological change.

1. Apply universal subjectivism in your own daily life. So, test for exchangeability of situations.
2. Observe ethically: enlarge the morality. Look for blind spots by focusing on victims.
3. Stop eating meat and fish. Adopt a plant-based diet and become a vegan.

4. Decrease your ecological footprint. Become ecologically neutral. This can have major consequences for your lifestyle. (Reconsider, reduce, reuse, recycle.)

5. Stop population growth. No more than one child per person. If you do want more than one per person, adopt a child.[22]

6. Spread ethical consciousness, in your immediate environment to begin with.

7. Give money (not just minor amounts, but substantial ones); apply knowledge, material goods, time, care; donate blood. Allow your organs to be transplanted after you die. Work toward a better world with less suffering and more happiness.

8. Become active in Nongovernmental Organizations (NGOs): human rights (e.g., Amnesty International), overseas help (e.g., Oxfam®), the environment (e.g., Ecojustice®, Greenpeace), animal welfare (e.g., PETA®, World Society for the Protection of Animals®).

9. Promote political change by getting involved in a green, animal-friendly, socially just political party.

10. Be tolerant and combat intolerance.

11. Enjoy the good life without causing harm to others. Activism and altruism don't have to lead to a sour, ascetic way of living. You can enjoy life to the full without wrecking the environment or harming other people. Besides, committing yourself to the achievement of a better world is a meaningful use of your life.

HUMANISM: THINKING FOR YOURSELF, LIVING TOGETHER

I am a secular humanist and an atheist. Humanism is a worldview that is based on science (and therefore is dynamic) and is directed toward the individual.[23] Organizations exist that give a presence to humanism in society, help people with their self-determination and self-actualization, and help make society more humane. I am involved in several humanist organizations and serve as director of the secular-humanist think tank Center for Inquiry Low Countries, which is part of Center for Inquiry Transnational. There are a host of humanist organizations in the world, among them the American Humanist Association.[24] Humanism is naturalistic and individualistic. Its point of departure is that humans have to make the most of things in this life, on this earth, and with each other. Self-determination is a central value of humanism.

Humanist philosopher Paul Kurtz speaks of *secular* humanism to make clear that it is about nonreligious humanism. Kurtz has systematized and characterized secular humanism by means of six elements.

1. Humanism is a method of knowledge. This method is critical and rational and conforms to scientific criteria.
2. Humanism consists of a scientific, naturalistic worldview. It is the synthesis of the results of scientific inquiry into the cosmos. Thus this worldview is dynamic and can be adjusted on the basis of new or improved knowledge.
3. Secular humanism is nontheistic. Humanists don't believe in god, gods, gnomes or "something out there." This is the negative part of humanism and indicates what humanists are not, namely, religious believers. The next three points are positive: they say what humanism does stand for. Humanism is more than atheism.
4. In a humanist ethic, individual freedom, self-determination, and self-actualization are central, along with John Stuart Mill's "do-no-harm" principle.
5. Secular humanism offers a socio-political perspective, that is, an open society in which the freedom of the individual occupies a central place and is safeguarded in a social-liberal constitutional state with a sharp division between religion and the state.
6. Secular humanism has universal, global pretensions, and

rises above national, religious and ethnic identities. Secular humanism offers a perspective on the world as *one* great society: the world as Earthland.[25]

Universal subjectivism is a positive, humanist philosophy, an ethical system, a social-political philosophy, and a global green vision. The core values and concerns of organized humanism are coming under discussion, and universal subjectivism can provide a coherent solution for issues such as abortion, euthanasia, homosexuality, education, and multiculturalism. What is new is that universal subjectivism also makes animals, future generations, and nature part of the discussion.

Humanism has to stand up for the core values of the Enlightenment: freedom of the individual and freedom of expression. Under no circumstances should humanists, whether under pressure or not, trade away these core values. An easy-going approach by means of a dialogue about fundamental values leads to the possibility of tolerating intolerance, and, in the area of the scientific and rational standards of humanism, to the acceptance of irrationality. Humanism cannot go together with faith. This may be a statement not all humanists would agree to. It is the opinion of *secular* humanists and freethinkers that faith/superstition,[26] religion, worship, and spirituality on the one hand, and humanism and science on the other, are like water and fire. The philosopher W. K. Clifford does not pull his punches when he argues: "It has been judged wrong to believe on insufficient evidence, or to nourish belief by suppressing doubts and avoiding investigation."[27] Clifford claims that there is a *moral duty* to accept no assertions as true on the basis of insufficient evidence.

Because humanism stands for selected values it also excludes a lot: superstition and the oppression of individuals. Some humanists have respect for religion—wrongly so, in my view. Religions don't deserve respect, but they are tolerated in an open society, provided they, like every other organization, observe the law. How can you have respect for religion, which is based on unverifiable dogmas and irrationality and almost always leads to oppression? Religions should not enjoy privileged positions compared with other clubs.

Morality has priority over rationality; if people believe all sorts of nonsense[28] and nevertheless live within the normative framework of human rights while showing tolerance toward dissidents, apostates, gays, lesbians, bi- and transsexuals, etcetera, there is no problem. Everybody is entitled to their own delusions, provided that they do not hinder others (including their own children)[29] in their free development and do not indoctrinate others, including children. But that is not how it is with religion in our world.

In recent decades many Christians have become more liberal and humanist in their beliefs. Many are religious humanists: they attend church because they find comfort there, but they no longer believe many of the dogmas and, in the case of Catholics, no longer unquestioningly accept the moral authority of the pope. Many other Christians still believe in the basic dogmas of their faith, however, and religion is far from dead. From a global point of view there is, sad to say, little evidence of secularization. I take a very inclusive view of religion as the belief in propositions on the basis of insufficient evidence: including ideologies that are not based on a belief in god but do have definite dogmas that do not square with a scientific worldview. I regard Hinduism, Taoism, Maoism, New Age spirituality, and Confucianism as religions. As Bertrand Russell writes in the introduction to his *Sceptical Essays*, "It is undesirable to believe a proposition when there is no ground whatever for supposing it true."[30]

Why do freethinkers and atheists such as Richard Dawkins, Daniel Dennett, Sam Harris, and the late Christopher Hitchens get so worked up about religion?[31] *Because religion, by and large, leads to the oppression of individuals.* Even if religion has an enormously positive influence (something for which, as far as I know, there is no sociological or psychological evidence), even then there is no reason for ignoring the suffering caused to people in the name of religion. The criticism of religion is therefore a pillar of humanism and freethought.

Humanism is a universalistic way of looking at life and the world. It is a cosmopolitan worldview. It is therefore desirable for organized humanism to look across national borders, as the Netherlands-based Humanist Institute for Development Cooperation (HIVOS), does.[32] In his *Dictionary of Atheism, Skepticism, & Humanism,* Bill Cooke devotes a relatively large amount of attention to humanist, atheist, skeptical, and rationalist thinkers and currents of thought in non-Western countries.[33] It was an eye-opener for me to see that such thinkers and currents also exist outside the Western tradition. In two ways, however, the Western tradition differs fundamentally. First of all, because of the scientific method and the technological spinoffs that have developed in the West. It hardly needs saying that science is universal and not bound to a culture or region. Unfortunately, the increased influence of science in a society does not always lead to secularization and the growth of humanism. The second point of difference is that "the discovery of the individual" and a polity in which the interests of the individual are central first took shape in the West. Individual interests are universal and therefore also valid outside the Western world. The moral and political ideology that puts the individual at the center is superior to ideologies in which the interests of a certain group prevail. The reason is simple: can you wish, of your own accord, to be one whose interests are being subordinated to those of the group?

Aspects of Enlightenment thought, such as criticism of authority, of kinds of oppression, and of religious claims to truth and authority, are present in non-Western cultures, but not the whole bundle. It is good to realize that humanism is a consistent aggregation of norms and values. Humanism is an outlook on life that fits seamlessly with a scientific worldview. An outlook on life is not the same thing as a worldview, because an outlook on life requires you to make normative choices, which in the case of humanism means putting the individual and rationality at the center.

Humanism, like science, is fallible and open. The humanistic bundle of norms and values can be adjusted on the basis of good arguments. In the course of time that has happened. The task of freethinkers and humanists is to stay on the ball, to take criticism seriously and where necessary to adjust the bundle of norms and values. The humanist bundle comprises the scientific worldview and the humanist morality, art of living, and political philosophy. Humanists have the habit of codifying their bundle of norms and values in manifestos and statements, such as the *Humanist Manifesto 2000* of the secular humanists drafted by Paul Kurtz,[34] and the 2007 Brussels Declaration put together by a number of humanist associations.[35]

It astonishes me that so far the humanist movement pays almost no attention to animal suffering. Animals constitute a big blind spot for humanists. This may partly be reflected by the word: humanist, namely, that humans are central. That is why I prefer to identify myself as a freethinker, which leaves everything open, rather than as a humanist, where a position has been staked out in which the human being is at the center. As far back as 1975 the Australian philosopher Peter Singer published the trail-blazing book *Animal Liberation*, in which he argued that it is arbitrary to discriminate on the basis of belonging to a certain species of animal.[36] In the eco-humanist manifesto (above), animals are included within the circle of morality.

Humanism should stand foursquare for the core values of rationality and individual freedom. Criticism of religion continues to be a pillar of humanism. Humanists and freethinkers need to look actively for moral blind spots. Two of these have been discussed: animal welfare as well as tolerating intolerance.

The Transnational Roots of Humanism

According to humanist thinker Bill Cooke, "the Universal Declaration of Human Rights is the most significant humanist vision ever created."[37] And rightly so. Humanism—the term was coined by the German thinker Friedrich Niethammer (1746–1848)—"is one of the most foundational words relating to our current understanding of the world."[38] Humanism is a manmade concept, like religion.

Unlike believers, humanists are aware of this fact and appreciate it. Humanism is therefore a dynamic concept, or as historian of ideas Bill Cooke writes; it's "a movable feast."[39] In his book *A Wealth of Insights. Humanist Thought since the Enlightenment* (2011) Cooke shows that humanistic ideas can be found in many different cultures, also before the term was coined. He makes it clear that humanism is not just a Western idea. Cooke's well-written book is unique in the history of ideas, and especially the history of humanism, to significantly incorporate non-Western thinkers. Humanism is a cosmopolitan endeavor, but most of what is written about humanism has been about humanism in the West. Cooke expands the horizon of humanism beyond the boundaries of the Western world. In the introduction he writes enthusiastically, "Humanism . . . is the most transcultural mode of thought ever conceived."[40] And by showing that there are humanist or at least humanistic thinkers even in the Islamic world it becomes clear that humanism is a cosmopolitan and universal life stance and worldview. Cooke takes a broad definition of humanism so as to be able to include liberal believers. After a long journey in the global history of ideas, Cooke ends with what he calls "a summary of attitudes that seem common to most of the people we have studied":

- Life is intrinsically worth living
- A sufficient grounding in humility
- Not against or beyond nature, but within it
- Learning from and valuing the past
- Grounded in our culture, yet beyond nations
- Placing a high value on learning

Religion and superstition along with authoritarianism are two widely spread curses that haunt humankind. In most cultures there have been partial humanistic traditions that oppose (some aspects of) religion, superstition, and the repressive rule by undemocratically justified government. These humanistic traditions have tried to live a meaningful life here and now. Cooke gives examples of thinkers who have criticized religion and authoritarian rule. He points out that Chinese Confucianism is mainly a form of humanism, because there is no supernaturalism involved. Confucianism is an ethical and political code about how we should live. But, and this is one of my main points of critique, Confucianism does not recognize the freedom of the individual, but stresses that humans have a fixed place within a social network in which women are subjected to men, the ruled by the ruler. The problem is what one considers to be essential to humanism in order to be included in the humanistic traditions. It is very good to expand the narrow-mindedness of Western-focused intellectual history, but I find it hard to agree when Cooke writes, "Chinese civilization is essentially humanist." Just think of the inequality of women, the lack of democracy, no human rights tradition, the unhelpful Chinese medicine, all the weird superstition, and the like. Maybe there is a humanistic tradition, but it is an exaggeration to call Chinese civilization basically humanist. If Cooke would have begun with a strict definition of what humanism is—for example, the secular humanism of Paul Kurtz, which is naturalistic (it excludes the paranormal/supernatural) and which attributes a central role to the freedom of the individual—Cooke's book would have been much thinner. Also, if (scientific) naturalism is seen as an essential element of humanism (as it is according to humanists such as A. C. Grayling, Paul Kurtz, Richard Dawkins), then Christian humanism is a contradiction in terms. Well, that is also the conclusion, which can be easily drawn from the chapter on Christian humanists, when one sees how hard it is to keep something of religion when a rational train of thought gets started. Cooke quotes Kauffman on the humanistic theologian Paul Tillich: "Tillich wants to have his Nietzsche and eat his bread at communion, too."[41] Cooke has chosen to include all those who call themselves humanists and then to examine their thought. And he includes humanistic thinkers who did not call themselves humanist but who were humanists nevertheless, according to Cooke.

A precondition for a flourishing of humanism is an open society, which is a liberal democracy that guarantees individual liberty: "It is hard for humanism, of whichever variety, to prosper outside of democracies. It can't breathe in an atmosphere where questioning is frowned upon or carries with it social and even physical dangers."[42] Cooke argues at the end of the book for a planetary humanism, a word coined by philosopher Paul Kurtz, because "no major problems can be solved on anything less than a planetary scale. Climate change, population pressure, technological change, globalization— these are all planet-wide problems that cannot be solved by this or that legislature working in isolation. Any proper understanding of planet-wide interdependence means that *Homo sapiens* aren't the only species to be taken into account. All species on the planet are inextricably interwoven in complex webs of interdependence."[43] Cooke elaborates on webs of interdependence and the importance of protecting the ecosystems that sustain us: "any commitment to a principle of humanity involves a sense of commitment to all the other species we share it with."[44]

It seems that the best in all traditions from all over the globe are humanist and humanistic ideas. That might seem like a fallacy, calling all the good ideas humanistic. But humanism is dynamic and open to reason. Bill Cooke's book plays an important role in defining and creating humanism. Too often humanism is considered to be too vague, and people shy away from it. But it is important to have a name for this bundle of ideas that is both a life stance, a worldview and, foremost, a method of inquiry based on reason and science. Humanism might not be easy, because one has to think for oneself and take responsibility. Humanism seems to be a glimmer of hope in, as philosopher John Passmore has said, "the light of humanity's ongoing capacity for wickedness and stupidity."[45]

A Wealth of Insights gives an enlightening view of the history of humanism and humanistic ideas all over the world. The topics overlap with the history of philosophy and it would be good if students interested in philosophy would also read this book. Cooke discusses philosophers and thinkers who didn't make it to the canon of philosophy, some of whom turn out to be more interesting and more humane. The history of philosophy contains a lot of nonsense and dangerous ideas, like Plato's totalitarianism. The history of humanism has a much better record.

Reading this transnational history of humanism makes me proud to be a humanist. Can anybody read this book and not consider him/herself to be a humanist?

THE MORAL OF THE STORY: LESS SUFFERING, MORE HAPPINESS

The thought experiment of universal subjectivism is a method for tracking down injustice and bringing about justice. By imagining yourself into the worst possible situations, the so-called victim situations, you can try to optimize them (the maximin strategy). With the help of universal subjectivism, moral blind spots can be tracked down. Today those blind spots are: future generations, animals, and the environment (though only indirectly). Universal subjectivism puts suffering at the center. The objective is to minimize suffering and to optimize enjoyment or happiness. The ability to suffer occurs, to differing degrees, among all animals, humans included. It is important to take account of the ability to suffer. This is therefore a pathocentric theory. Those who use universal subjectivism as a guide to ethical action will reflect on their lives and try to minimize the harm that their lifestyles cause to others (including animals and future generations), and try also to make a positive contribution toward achieving a better world. The theory of universal subjectivism is not just a theory but also and above all an appeal to work at building a better, more just, more animal-friendly, peaceful, sustainable, pleasant world.

POSTSCRIPT: A GAZE INTO
THE CRYSTAL BALL

I find it hard to stay on topic. I live a prosperous, carefree life, with satisfying employment and growing children. I take piano lessons; buy books; read and write; watch DVDs; and enjoy holidays, travel, museums, saunas, yoga, running, and thousands of other things. In short, mine is a happy and worry-free life with my great love and our two children. It seems as if nothing is the matter. The environmental crisis seems far off and abstract. I don't see anything at all of global warming, overfishing, deforestation, desertification, plastic floating in the oceans, polluted rivers, or hungry people. I don't notice that millions are living in shanty-towns; women are oppressed; hundreds of millions of animals are being tortured on factory farms; that there are wars; or that there are shortages of fresh water, medicine, care, education, and good infrastructure. I know that these problems exist and I also know that my lifestyle contributes to them, but in the world immediately around me entirely different matters are at issue. We live in Utopia. But information about the misery in the broader world is widely available—I have included a selection in the mediagraphy. I live in two worlds. In one I busy myself with my career as writer, philosopher, university lecturer, and with the development of our sons; about where to spend our vacation, whether to improve our garden or our house. In the other world, the mega-perspective, I see misery and the threat of environmental disasters looming in the near future. But it is just like the people who live on the San Andreas Fault in California: they know about it, but mostly they manage to push it to the back of their minds. And it is a reassuring feeling that millions of others are doing the same thing. One day things will go wrong, and then they will go wrong on an enormous scale. San Francisco and Los Angeles will have to deal with huge earthquakes that will very probably result in a lot of victims. People know this but suppress the thought, or tell themselves that buildings and infrastructure are proof against earthquakes, that technology will protect them. In the same way people believe that the environmental problems won't be all that bad because technology will help us cope with them. Let us hope that this is true, but it is not a very rational hope. It is better to dare to face reality and then to act accordingly, however difficult that may be, because it requires a drastic change in lifestyles.

Am I pessimistic or, after all, optimistic because I have written a book with the title *Philosophy for a Better World* instead of *Philosophy of Our Downfall?* Pessimistic, I fear. When I contemplate all the information available about our numerous environmental problems, when I see the number of people is increasing and the average ecological footprint is also increasing, it is impossible for me to be positive about the future. That makes me sad. When I look at the future through a crystal ball, I see untold suffering. I have two sons and it grieves me that they are probably facing a difficult future. Or will technology provide a postponement? But then it will be their children, my grandchildren, who will suffer and go down. And *we* are guilty of the suffering in the future. We know it, and yet we don't act accordingly. The theory of universal subjectivism shows that it really is possible to live ethically and establish a socially just, sustainable society.

NOTES

CHAPTER I: INTRODUCTION TO A BETTER WORLD

1. In his book *Darwin's Dangerous Idea: Evolution and the Meanings of Life* (New York: Simon & Schuster, 1995) the philosopher Daniel Dennett speaks about "design space" that contains all possible forms of existence that could come about through the process of evolution (potential) and the part of them that is realized. By analogy, Dennett applies the concept of design space to the field of memetics: there is a universe of ideas that are potentially possible and a part of it that has been realized. On the one hand, philosophers are looking for the unknown, for new ideas in design space; on the other hand, they apply an ethical and epistemological evaluation to ideas that have been realized. Philosophers are, or should be, the examiners of ideas, testing whether ideas are good or bad (and for whom), and whether ideas are true or false.

2. Jeremy Bentham, *An Introduction to the Principles of Morals and Legislation*, ed. J. H. Burns and H. L. A. Hart (London: The Athlone Press, University of London, 1970 [1780]), p. 283. The reference to French policy relates to a code issued in March 1685, regulating the status of slaves in the French West Indies, which "forbade the killing of slaves by their masters, and gave the royal authorities the power to protect slaves from maltreatment." *See* p. 283n.

3. A. C. Grayling, *What Is Good? The Search for the Best Way to Live* (London: Weidenfeld & Nicolson. 2003).

4. Paul Kurtz, *Toward a New Enlightenment: The Philosophy of Paul Kurtz*, ed. Vern L. Bullough and Timothy J. Madigan (New Brunswick, NJ: Transaction Publishers, 1994).

5. Jonathan Israel *A Revolution of the Mind: Radical Enlightenment and the Intellectual Origins of Modern Democracy* (Princeton, NJ: Princeton University Press, 2009), pp. viii–viii.

6. Jonathan Israel makes the illuminating distinction between radical and moderate Enlightenment in his book *A Revolution of the Mind.*

7. A comparable parable provides the basis for the wonderful book *Good and Evil* by Richard Taylor (Amherst, NY: Prometheus Books, 2000), which uses the uninhabited-island parable to show that morality is dependent on what people want. The idea of malleability, "working together to try to make the best of things," is the central idea of Taylor's book, as it also is of mine.

8. *See* Bill Bryson, *Bill Bryson's African Diary* (New York: Broadway Books, 2002).

9. For an extensive list of utopian literature, see *The Utopia Reader*, ed. Gregory Claeys and Lyman Sargent (New York: New York University Press, 1999).

10. Thomas More, *Utopia*, trans. Paul Turner (London: Penguin Books, 1965 [1516], p. 80.

11. Ibid., p. 79.

12. Ibid., pp. 47 and 48. On the tragedy of the commons *see*, for example, David Schmidtz and Elizabeth Willott, "The Tragedy of the Commons," *A Companion to Applied Ethics*, ed. R. G. Frey (Malden, MA: Blackwell, 2003). "Commons problems are ubiquitous in human history, but not every problem is a commons problem. Moreover, just as history is replete with commons problems, so too is history replete with people who figured out how to solve, or at least survive, commons problems," p. 672. Thomas More fits into this tradition as well. Schmidtz and Willott suggest a different solution than More: " Institutional frameworks can be judged according to whether they put people in a position, first, to recognize when they face a commons problem, and second, to respond to that problem in a measured, effective, peaceful way," p. 672.

13. Bertrand Russell, *History of Western Philosophy* (London: Routledge, 1993 [1946]), p. 508.

14. More, *Utopia*, p. 49.

15. *A History of the Modern World*, 9th ed. by R. R. Palmer, Joel Colton, and Lloyd Kramer (New York: Knopf, 2002), depicts the depressing consequences of collectivist and totalitarian ideologies. The twentieth century was the bloodiest century ever.

16. More, *Utopia*, p. 75. *See* Frederic Rouvillois, "Utopia and Totalitarianism," *Utopia: The Search for the Ideal Society in the Western World*, ed. Roland Schaer, Gregory Claeys, and Lyman Tower Sargent (New York: The New York Public Library/Oxford University Press, 2000).

17. More, *Utopia*, p. 75.

18. Ibid., p. 71.

19. Ibid., p. 76.

20. Hans Crombag and Frank van Dun, *De utopische verleiding [The Utopian Temptation]* (Amsterdam: Contact, 1997).

21. Karl R. Popper, *The Open Society and Its Enemies*, vol. 1, *The Spell of Plato* (Princeton, NJ: Princeton University Press, 1971 [1943]), p. 165.

22. More, *Utopia*, p. 84.

23. John Stuart Mill, *On Liberty*, ed. Gertrude Himmelfarb (London: Penguin Books, 1985), p. 28.

24. More, *Utopia*, p. 80.

25. Ibid., p. 104.

26. Ibid., p. 103.

27. Almost two centuries after More, John Locke, champion of tolerance and liberalism, also exempted atheists from the scope of political toleration: "Lastly, those are not at all to be tolerated who deny the being of a God. Promises, covenants, and oaths, which are the bonds of human society, can have no hold upon an atheist. The taking away of God, though but even in thought, dissolves all; besides also, those that by their atheism undermine and destroy all religion, can have no pretense of religion whereupon to challenge the privilege of a toleration. As for other practical opinions, though not absolutely free from all error, if they do not tend to establish domination over others, or civil impunity to the Church in which they are taught, there can be no reason why they should not be tolerated." John Locke, *A Letter Concerning Toleration* (1689), http://www.constitution.org/jl/tolerati.htm.

28. More, *Utopia*, p. 120.

29. Ibid., p. 123.

30. Popper, *The Open Society and Its Enemies*, vol. 1, p. 168.

31. Crombag and Van Dun, *De utopische verleiding [The Utopian Temptation]*, p. 138.

32. This is an important qualification. If this is interpreted broadly and also includes respect for animals, the environment, future generations, labor conditions in poor countries, and human rights, it places restrictions on economic activity.

33. This was not always the case. The journalist Nic Paton noted early in 2010 that before the financial crisis of 2008–2009, business schools were less concerned about ethical issues than afterwards: "As the bodies responsible for teaching so many of the 'masters of the universe' who did so much to cause last year's meltdown, it is perhaps not surprising that business schools have spent the past year doing some serious soul-searching about their culpability for the recession. Go back to the 1980s and 1990s, when many of today's corporate leaders were studying for their MBAs, and business ethics and sustainability—in other words, issues around corporate governance, social responsibility and long-term decision-making, played little part in business school curricula." Nic Paton, "Business Schools Put Ethics High on MBA Agenda," *The Guardian*, January 23, 2010. http://www.guardian.co.uk/search?q=Nic+Paton&date=date%2F2010

34. Robert Philips, "Stakeholder Theory and a Principle of Fairness," *Business Ethics Quarterly* 7 (1997): 51–66.

35. A. C. Grayling, "Business Ethics," *Ideas that Matter: The Concepts that Shape the 21st Century* (London: Weidenfeld & Nicolson, 2009), p. 63.

36. Bertrand Russell, *History of Western Philosophy*, p. 622.

CHAPTER 2: LEARNING TO THINK PHILOSOPHICALLY

1. Michel Onfray, *Contre-histoire de la philosophie*, 6 vols. (Paris: Bernard Grasset, 2006–).

2. Stephen Jay Gould, "Nonoverlapping Magisteria," *Natural History* 106 (March 1997): 16–22.

3. *See* Hans Crombag and Frank van Dun, *De utopische verleiding [The Utopian Temptation].* (Amsterdam: Contact, 1997).

4. Etienne Vermeersch and Johan Braeckman, *De rivier van Herakleitos [The River of Heraclitus]* (Antwerp/Amsterdam: Houtekiet, 2008), p. 13.

5. *See* Adam Hochschild, *Bury the Chains: Prophets and Rebels in the Fight to Free an Empire's Slaves* (Boston: Houghton Mifflin, 2005). In 1838 the British Empire abolished slavery. It is estimated that at that time more than 1,500,000 slaves were working in the mines and on the plantations of Brazil, roughly 400,000 were working in Cuba, and more than two million in the United States. However, the Brazilian and Cuban slaves had to wait another fifty years for freedom. The end of slavery did not mean the end of injustice, but that in international law it is now a crime against humanity to enslave people is unquestionably *one* measure of human progress. Hochschild notes that the abolitionists based their hopes not on holy writings but on human empathy.

6. Vermeersch and Braeckman, *De rivier van Herakleitos [The River of Heraclitus]*, p. 85. It should be noted that Philo was a Jew.

7. Ibid., p. 15.

8. Ibid.

9. Ibid., p. 43.

10. Ibid.

11. Robert Todd Carroll, *Becoming a Critical Thinker: A Guide for the New Millennium*, 2nd ed. (New York: Pearson, 2004).

12. Vermeersch and Braeckman, *De rivier van Herakleitos [The River of Heraclitus]*, p. 372.

13. Ibid., p. 378.

14. Ibid., p. 381.

15. Kelly designed a poster for Earth Day in 1970: http://www.igopogo.com/we_have_met.htm.

16. "I believe that this nation should commit itself to achieving the goal, before this decade is out, of landing a man on the moon and returning him safely to the earth. No single space project in this period will be more impressive to mankind, or more important for the long-range exploration of space; and none will be so difficult or expensive to accomplish." John F. Kennedy, May 25, 1961. http://miller center.org/scripps/archive/speeches/detail/3368.

17. Immanuel Kant, "What Is Enlightenment?" trans. Peter Gay, *The Enlightenment: A Comprehensive Anthology,* ed. Peter Gay (New York: Simon and Schuster, 1973), p. 384.

18. Journals of information, opinion, and review worth considering include, among others, *Atlantic Monthly, Free Inquiry, Harper's, Guardian Weekly, History Today, New Humanist, New Yorker, New York Review of Books, Philosophy Now, Skeptical Inquirer, New Republic,* and *Times Literary Supplement.*

19. Tony Buzan, *How to Mind Map: The Ultimate Thinking Tool that Will Change Your Life* (London: Thorsons, 2002).

20. It is, in fact, a contradiction in terms to link fundamentalism to the ideas of the Enlightenment. The Enlightenment stands for a fallible and open method of knowledge, while religions are distinguished by a closed and infallible canon. If what is meant is "convinced of the superiority of method of knowledge and/or ethical principles" (that is, a certain measure of consistency), then the word "fundamentalism" could be used. But, as I said, it is a sobriquet.

21. Philosophy of law tries, to the best of its ability, to structure and arrange the rules of society, and to determine what can or should and cannot or should not be regulated by laws.

22. Genesis 22:2–3, 10–12, New Revised Standard Version.

23. *See* Luke 10:29–37.

24. http://verlichtingshumanisten.web-log.nl/museum_kwetsende_kunst/.

25. *See* the American movie *Act Naturally* (2011) about by J. P. Riley in the USA.

CHAPTER 3: UNIVERSAL SUBJECTIVISM AS THOUGHT EXPERIMENT

1. A lot of books have been written about Rawls and his work. Two good and readable introductions are by Paul Graham, *Rawls* (Oxford: Oneworld, 2007), and Percy B. Lehning, *John Rawls: An Introduction* (Cambridge and New York: Cambridge University Press, 2009). More extensive is Samuel Freeman, *Rawls* (London and New York: Routledge, 2007). *See also* Samuel Freeman, ed., *The Cambridge Companion to Rawls* (Cambridge and New York: Cambridge University Press, 2003).

2. Peter Singer writes very accessibly and the best introduction to his thought is through his own books. A brief overview of his philosophy can be found in a book by Hyun Höchsmann, *On Peter Singer* (Belmont, CA: Wadsworth/Thomson Learning, 2002).

3. Peter Singer, quoted in Thomas Mautner, *A Dictionary of Philosophy* (Cambridge, MA: Blackwell Publishers, 1996), p. 572.

4. Peter Singer, *Animal Liberation* (New York: Avon, 1991).

5. Singer, quoted in Mautner, *A Dictionary of Philosophy*, p. 572.

6. Peter Singer, *One World: The Ethics of Globalization* (New Haven and London: Yale University Press, 2002).

7. Peter Singer, *The Life You Can Save: Acting Now to End World Poverty* (New York: Random House, 2009).

8. Peter Singer, "The Singer Solution to World Poverty," *New York Times Magazine*, September 5, 1999, p. 63.

9. Peter Singer, "Famine, Affluence, and Morality," *Philosophy and Public Affairs* 1 (1972), p. 231.

10. Ibid., pp. 242–43.

11. Jan Verplaetse has done original research into the intuitive sense of justice of people. There seems to be a gap between rationally optimal and intuitively just. As philosopher, should you cling to what is best from a rational point of view, or do you sometimes have to calculate the human psyche into it? Jan Verplaetse, *Localising the Moral Sense: Neuroscience and the Search for the Cerebral Seat of Morality, 1800–1930* (Dordrecht and New York: Springer, 2009).

12. In his fine work of cultural history, *Toward the Light of Liberty: The Struggles for Freedom and the Rights that Made the Modern Western World* (New York: Walker, 2007), A. C. Grayling devotes a lot of attention to the Universal Declaration of Human Rights as being for now the high point of the expanding circle of morality. Unfortunately, Grayling has some blind spots: animals, future generations, and the environment. Grayling mainly looks to the past; he should have done more to look to the future.

A lucid introduction to the concept of human rights is Andrew Clapham, *Human Rights: A Very Short Introduction* (Oxford and New York: Oxford University Press, 2007). A more philosophical introduction and a defense of the universality of human rights is Jack Donnelly, *Universal Human Rights in Theory and Practice* (Ithaca, NY: Cornell University Press, 2003). In his books *Filosofie van den mensenrechten [Philosophy of Human Rights]* (1999) and *Darwin, dier en recht [Darwin, Animals, and the Law]* (2001), Paul Cliteur pays attention to the importance of according rights to animals, but future generations and the environment escape his purview. Singer shows how important it is to look actively for blind spots in morality.

13. Tom Regan, *The Case for Animal Rights* (Berkeley: University of California Press, 2004).

14. *See* G. Tyler Miller, *Living in the Environment: Principles, Connections, and Solutions*, 15th ed. (Belmont, CA: Thomson Books/Cole, 2007); Joseph R. DesJardins, *Environmental Ethics: An Introduction to Environmental Philosophy*, 4th ed. (Belmont, CA, and London: Wadsworth and Thomson Learning, 2006); Dale Jamieson, *Ethics and the Environment: An Introduction* (Cambridge: Cambridge University Press, 2008).

15. *See* "Living in Fear: Tanzania's Albinos," http://news.bbc.co.uk/2/hi/africa/7518049.stm.

16. Rob Vreeken, "Zo gaat het nu eenmaal: Vrouwenonderdrukking in Afghanistan" ["That's Just the Way It Goes: The Oppression of Women in Afghanistan"], *De Volkskrant*, July 4, 2009.

17. Phyllis Chesler, *The Death of Feminism: What's Next in the Struggle for Women's Freedom* (New York: Palgrave Macmillan, 2005).

18. *Baekjeong* in Korea; *dalits* in India, Pakistan, Bangladesh, and Nepal; *khademn* in Yemen; *osu* in Nigeria; gypsies and Roma in Europe, especially Rumania.

19. "The Global Reporting Initiative (GRI) is a network-based organization that pioneered the world's most widely used sustainability reporting framework. GRI is committed to the Framework's continuous improvement and application world-wide. GRIs core goals include the mainstreaming of disclosure on environmental, social and governance performance." http://www.globalreporting.org/AboutGRI/WhatIsGRI/.

20. WPSA's goal is "to build a global animal welfare movement." PETA is currently the largest animal rights organization in the world.

21. http://video.google.com/videoplay?docid=-513747926833909134#.

22. http://video.google.com/videoplay?docid=6361872964130308142#.

23. I hesitated in showing the trailer to my students at Utrecht University in my lecture on Peter Singer. I asked them if they wanted to watch it. And they did. I warned them once more and offered them the possibility of leaving the lecture hall. Two female students availed themselves of it. But why should we avert our eyes from reality, especially if we share in the guilt by consuming animal products and failing to resist it? Only those who are vegetarians or vegans and who are actively engaged in the campaign for animal welfare can reasonably refuse to watch this film. Someone who finds this film to be disgusting, but nevertheless uses animal products, is a hypocrite. Averting our eyes doesn't help to improve the animals' welfare. Everyone who consumes animal products should be obligated to watch this film, all 95 minutes of it.

24. *See* http://www.animalfreedom.org/english/; *see also* the animated short films available on http://www.themeatrix.com/.

25. School excursions should take children to water filtration plants, sewage treatment plants, landfills, factory farms, slaughterhouses, and prisons. The point

is to show children that lots of things are hidden from public view. A society whose prisons are humane is a well-run society. In an open society it is important that children get a liberal education and honest information about what society looks like and particularly how the less attractive aspects of society have been organized. Children must not be raised in a fairytale world in which they get to see only a part of reality. On open society must be a transparent society. There should be no "no-go zones."

26. Marian Stamp Dawkins, *Animal Suffering: The Science of Animal Welfare* (London and New York: Chapman and Hall, 1980), p. 8.

27. Natalie Angier, "The Cute Factor," *New York Times*, January 3, 2006. http://www.nytimes.com/2006/01/03/science/03cute.html?_r=1.

28. Ian McEwan, *Saturday* (Toronto: Alfred A. Knopf, Canada, 2005), p. 127.

29. A. Stolba and D. G. M. Wood-Gush, "The Behaviour of Pigs in a Semi-Natural Environment," quoted in Bernard E. Rollin, *Farm Animal Welfare: Social, Bioethical, and Research Issues* (Ames: Iowa State University Press, 1995), p. 75.

30. "Australia suspends cattle export to Indonesian abattoirs," *Guardian*, May 31, 2011, http://www.guardian.co.uk/world/2011/may/31/australia-suspends-cattle-export-indonesia. There was little comment on the apparent absurdity of shipping Australian cattle to Indonesia for slaughter.

31. J. M. Coetzee, *The Lives of Animals*, ed. and introduced by Amy Gutmann (Princeton, NJ: Princeton University Press, 2001), p. 38. The quotation from Plutarch appears in *Animal Rights and Human Obligations*, ed. Tom Regan and Peter Singer (Englewood Cliffs, NJ: Prentice-Hall, 1976).

32. *See* Bernard E. Rollin, *Farm Animal Welfare: Social, Bioethical, and Research Issues* (Ames: Iowa State University Press, 1995).

33. The concern about potential lack of protein intake for vegans/vegetarians seems to a nonproblem, since it appears that consumers tend to take much more protein than is healthy for them. A balanced vegan diet which includes for example oatmeal, soymilk, brown rice, vegetables, and nuts provides enough proteins and other essential nourishment, including for athletes. *See* the Vegetarian Resource Group: http://www.vrg.org/nutrition/protein.htm.

34. Watch this interview with Carl Lewis: http://www.youtube.com/watch?v=bOTETXwfIaY.

35. http://www.veganstore.com/.

36. http://www.exploreveg.org/issues/videos/meet-your-meat-video.

37. If you already have an eiderdown duvet don't get rid of it, of course. Just don't buy a new one.

38. *See* Michael Allen Fox, *Deep Vegetarianism* (Philadelphia: Temple University Press, 1999).

39. If there should be a god (which there isn't) he would have to appear before the International Court of Justice in The Hague for crimes against humanity. After all, god had the choice of making a world or not. If this one is the best he could do, god is a bungler or, if it could have been done otherwise, he is a sadistic monster.

40. For Marcel Dicke's talk, *see* http://www.youtube.com/watch?v=O6GimGZz 6a8. *See also* Josie Glausiusz, "Want to Help the Environment? Eat Insects." http://discovermagazine.com/2008/may/07-want-to-help-the-environment-eat-insects.

41. David DeGrazia, *Animal Rights: A Very Short Introduction* (New York: Oxford University Press, 2001), p. 42.

42. From my own experience in addressing the annual congress of the Royal Netherlands Society of Veterinary Medicine in 2008, it seems that younger practitioners are more sympathetic to my views than older ones, a number of who walked out on me. I confronted the veterinarians with the contradiction between their own code of ethics and their role in factory farming. Are they blind to the contradiction? After the address there was a dinner featuring dead animals, of which I did not partake. The ideas of Bernard Rollins are getting a hearing from academic veterinarians, but Peter Singer, Tom Regan, and other animal rights philosophers are still out of the picture. Still, the fact that I was invited to speak to the congress suggests that a change in the human-animal relationship may be in the offing.

43. Jerrold Tannenbaum, *Veterinary Ethics: Animal Welfare, Client Relations, Competition and Collegiality,* (St. Louis: Mosby-Year Book, 1995), p. 408.

44. L. J. E. Rutgers, *Het wel en wee der dieren: ethiek en diergeneeskundig handelen [The Weal and Woe of Animals: Ethics of Veterinary Practice]* (Utrecht University: published PhD dissertation, 1993), p. 43.

45. This seems to me to be a gross understatement.

46. An argument that is based on an appeal to "yes, but that's what we always do" is fallacious.

47. Tannenbaum, *Veterinary Ethics*, p. 409. This, too, is a fallacious argument: the fact that the majority believes something is no guarantee of its correctness. A majority of humankind believes, or in any case believed, that women are inferior to men, and that homosexuality is wrong. A majority of humankind also wrongly believe in a supernatural power.

48. *See* Tom Regan. *The Case for Animal Rights. Updated and with a New Preface.* (Berkeley: University of California Press, 2004 [1983]).

49. By using the word "us" Tannenbaum employs a rhetorical device, putting the reader on his side and against the animal-welfare activists, the absolutists. Tannenbaum, *Veterinary Ethics*, p. 409.

50. The historian and Holocaust specialist Charles Patterson compares factory farming to the Holocaust in his book *Eternal Treblinka: Our Treatment of Animals and*

the Holocaust (New York: Lantern Books, 2002). The title is derived from a comment by Isaac Bashevis Singer: "For the animals, it is an eternal Treblinka."

51. Coetzee, *The Lives of Animals*, p. 21.

52. Ibid., pp. 34–5.

53. Ibid., pp. 44–5.

54. Ibid., pp. 60–61.

55. Ibid., pp. 63–4.

56. Ibid., p. 58.

57. Ibid., p. 69.

58. Raoul du Pre, *NRC Handelsblad*, August 21, 2009.

59. The philosopher Ned Hettinger reflects on the issue of civil disobedience, of which eco-terrorism is a part, in his essay "Environmental Disobedience," in Dale Jameson, ed., *A Companion to Environmental Philosophy* (Malden, MA: Blackwell, 2001).

60. H. A. van Riessen, quoted in Rutgers, *Het wel en wee der dieren: ethiek en diergeneeskundig handelen [The Weal and Woe of Animals: Ethics of Veterinary Practice]*, p. 1.

61. Dirk Boon, *De eigenrichting van Pluk en het dier in de rechtspraak [Civil Disobedience, Animals, and Jurisprudence: Taking the Law into One's Own Hands]*, (Lelystad: Koninklijke Vermande, 1998), pp. 10 and 16.

62. Ibid., p. 16.

63. Ibid., p. 21.

64. An explanatory note to the article states: "In his actions the veterinarian often has to balance interests against each other. For this the veterinarian is personally responsible. This also applies to the management of veterinary-technical and veterinary-ethical norms, in the course of which the veterinarian must realize that societal views about these may be subject to change." The responsibility and the criteria for a balancing of interests, in which the animal is only one of many parties, are placed by the veterinarian against the social background. However, even if the great majority in a society believes that factory farming (or slavery) is ethically permitted, that is still not a sound argument. Sound arguments are independent of the question whether such an argument has a social basis.

65. Bernard E. Rollin, *An Introduction to Veterinary Medical Ethics: Theory and Cases*, 2d ed. (Ames, IA: Blackwell Publishing, 2006), p. 32.

66. Ibid., p. 55.

67. Ibid., p. 56.

68. Charles Darwin, *The Descent of Man, and Selection in Relation to Sex*, 2 vols. (London: J. Murray, 1871). About the theory of evolution, the origins of species, and their implication for an image of humanity and the world, *see* Richard Dawkins, *The Ancestor's Tale: A Pilgrimage to the Dawn of Evolution* (Boston: Houghton Mifflin, 2004); Richard Dawkins, *Climbing Mount Improbable* (New York: W. W. Norton, 1996);

James Rachels, *Created from Animals: The Moral Implications of Darwinism* (Oxford and New York, Oxford University Press, 1990); Daniel Dennett, *Darwin's Dangerous Idea: Evolution and the Meanings of Life* (New York: Simon & Schuster, 1995).

69. Richard Sorabji, *Animal Minds and Human Morals: The Origins of the Western Debate* (Ithaca, NY: Cornell University Press, 1993).

70. In her book *The Dreaded Comparison: Human and Animal Slavery* (New York: Mirror Books, 1996), Marjorie Spiegel compares the treatment of animals in our society with slavery.

71. Jacques Diouf, "Opening Statement," World Summit on Food Security, Rome, November 16-18, 2009. http://www.fao.org/fileadmin/templates/wsfs/Summit/Statements_PDF/Monday_16_AM/K6628e-DG-statement.pdf.

72. *See* http://www.mefeedia.com/watch/30022050

73. The philosopher Frederic L. Bender writes about a "biological holocaust" in his book *The Culture of Extinction: Towards a Philosophy of Deep Ecology* (Amherst, NY: Humanity Books, 2003).

74. Jeffrey Sachs, *The End of Poverty: Economic Possibilities for our Time* (New York: Penguin Press, 2005), and *Common Wealth: Economics for a Crowded Planet* (New York: Penguin Press, 2008).

75. *See* Frederic R. Siegel, *The Exploding Population Bomb: Societies Under Stress, Corrective Strategies and Solutions* (n.p.: CreateSpace, 2010).

76. Charles Clover, *The End of the Line: How Overfishing Is Changing the World and What We Eat* (London: Ebury, 2005).

77. Carol Kaesuk Yoon, "Iconoclast Looks for Fish and Finds Disaster," *New York Times,* January 21, 2003.

78. William McDonough and Michael Braungart, *Cradle to Cradle: Remaking the Way we Make Things* (New York: North Point Press, 2002).

79. *See* Gerbens.

80. *See* P. W. Gerbens-Leenes, *Natural Resource Use for Food: Land, Water, and Energy in Production and Consumption Systems* (University of Groningen: published PhD dissertation, 2006).

81. United Nations, *Universal Declaration of Human Rights* (1948) http://www.un.org/events/humanrights/2007/hrphotos/declaration%20_eng.pdf.

82. Anne Frank (Author), Otto H. Frank (Editor), Mirjam Pressler (Editor), Susan Massotty (Translator), Francine Prose (Introduction). *The Diary of a Young Girl.* (London: Everyman's Library, 2010).

83. Austin Dacey, personal remark to the author. *See* his book *The Secular Conscience: Why Belief Belongs in Public Life* (Amherst, NY: Prometheus Books, 2008).

84. Etty Hillesum, *An Interrupted Life: The Diaries, 1941-1943; and Letters from Westerbork*, trans. Arnold J. Pomerans (New York: Henry Holt, 1996).

85. Gerhard Durlacher, *Stripes in the Sky: A Wartime Memoir*, trans. Susan Massotty (London: Serpent's Tail, 1991).

86. Primo Levi, *If This Is a Man*, trans. Stuart Woolf (London: Orion, 1960); *The Reawakening: A Liberated Prisoner's Long March Home Through East Europe*, trans. Stuart Woolf (Boston: Little Brown, 1965).

87. A. C. Grayling, *What Is Good? The Search for the Best Way to Live* (London: Orion, 2004).

88. A. C. Grayling, *Among the Dead Cities: The History and Moral Legacy of the WWII Bombing of Civilians in Germany and Japan* (New York: Walker & Company, 2006), pp. 276–77.

89. Harry Mulisch's *The Stone Bridal Bed* (trans. Adrienne Dixon (1962 [1958]), uses war-damaged Dresden and recollections of its bombing. Len Deighton's *Bomber* (1970) describes a bombing raid from various points of view, in the air and on the ground, in Britain and Germany. Kurt Vonnegut's absurdist *Slaughterhouse-Five* (1969) describes the bombing of Dresden and its aftermath the point of view of a US soldier held as a POW near the city.

90. Grayling, *Among the Dead Cities*, p. 274.

91. Ibid.

CHAPTER 4: THE OPEN SOCIETY

1. Paul B. Cliteur, *Moderne Papoua's. Dilemma's van een multiculturele samenleving [Modern Papuans. Dilemmas of a Multicultural Society]*, De Arbeiderspers, Amsterdam, 2002.

2. "Two million girls and women are subjected to female genital mutilation each year." Jessica Williams, *50 Facts that Should Change the World* (New York: The Disinformation Company, 2004), p. 190.

3. Abraham Maslow pioneered the concept of a hierarchy of needs, of which self-actualization is the highest, in *Motivation and Personality*, 2d. ed. (New York: Harper & Row, 1970 [1954]).

4. *See* Carl Sagan, *The Demon-Haunted World: Science as a Candle in the Dark* (New York: Random House, 1995).

5. Anthony Storr, *Feet of Clay: Saints, Sinners, and Madmen: A Study of Gurus* (New York: Free Press, 1996).

6. Heinrich Dumoulin, *Zen Buddhism*, vol. 1, *India and China*, trans. James W. Heisig and Paul Knitter (New York: Macmillan, 1988).

7. Janwillem van de Wetering, *The Empty Mirror: Experiences in a Zen Monastery* (New York: St. Martin's Griffin, 1999 [1973]), p. 21.

8. Yukio Mishima's *Spring Snow,* trans. Michael Gallagher (New York: Knopf, 1972), is a wonderful novel set in the Japan of the 1920s and 1930s, when militarism and nationalism, coupled with Shintoist ideas of purity, reigned supreme.

9. For a fine cultural-historical overview of Buddhism, *see* Heinz Bechert and Richard Gombrich, ed., *The World of Buddhism: Buddhist Monks and Nuns in Society and Culture* (London: Thames and Hudson, 1984).

10. Aleksander Korshenkov, *Zamenhof: The Life, Works and Ideas of the Author of Esperanto,* ed. Humphrey Tonkin, trans. Ian M. Richmond (Mondial Books and the Universal Esperanto Association, 2010).

11. *See* the dramatic documentary *Jesus Camp,* filmed in an evangelical Christian summer camp. The indoctrination methods are shocking. This is child abuse. http://www.imdb.com/title/tt0486358/.

12. Aleid Truijens, column in *De Volkskrant,* August 18, 2009.

13. Christopher Lloyd, *What on Earth Happened? The Complete Story of the Planet, Life & People from the Big Bang to the Present Day* (New York: Bloomsbury USA, 2008). And: *Cynthia Stokes Brown, Big History: from the Big Bang to the Present,* revised ed. (New York: New Press, 2012); Fred Spier, *Big History and the Future of Humanity,* (Malden, MA: Wiley-Blackwell, 2011).

14. Office of the United Nations High Commissioner for Human Rights, *Convention of the Rights of the Child,* 1989, Article 13, http://www2.ohchr.org/english/law/crc.htm.

15. Herman Philipse, *Verlichtingsfundamentalisme. Open brief over Verlichting en fundamentalisme aan Ayaan Hirsi Ali* [*Enlightenment Fundamentalism: Open Letter to Ayaan Hirsi Ali about the Enlightenment and Fundamentalism*] (Amsterdam: Bert Bakker, 2005).

16. *See* Ayaan Hirsi Ali, *The Caged Virgin: An Emancipation Proclamation for Women and Islam* (New York: Fress Press, 2006); also: *Infidel* (New York: Free Press, 2008).

17. Richard Bellamy offers a lucid introduction to the meaning of democratic citizenship. He defines citizenship as follows: "Citizenship is a condition of civic equality. It consists of membership of a political community where all citizens can determine the terms of social cooperation on an equal basis. This status not only secures equal rights to the enjoyment of the collective goods provided by the political association but also involves equal duties to promote and sustain them—including the good of democratic citizenship itself." *Citizenship: A Very Short Introduction* (Oxford and New York: Oxford University Press, 2008), p. 17.

18. Although they are highly successful authors in the Netherlands and, in translation, in several other European countries, millions of copies of their books having been sold (a million of *A Flight of Curlews* alone), Jan Wolkers (1925–2007) and Maarten 't Hart (b.1944) are largely unknown in the English-speaking world.

Both grew up within orthodox Calvinism, reacted against its restrictions and austerity, and abandoned it.

19. Nigel Barley, *The Innocent Anthropologist: Notes from a Mud Hut* (London: Penguin Books, 1983).

20. Office of the United Nations High Commissioner for Human Rights, *Convention of the Rights of the Child*, Article 29.

21. Erik van Ree, "Het belang van vrij debat [The Importance of Free Debate]," *De groene Amsterdammer*, January 19, 2002, p. 24.

22. Tinkebell and Coralie Vogelaar, *Dearest Tinkebell* (Amsterdam: Torch Gallery, 2009). http://vorige.nrc.nl/international/Features/article2243400.ece/Artist_publishes%20_hate_mail_received_after_killing_her_cat.

23. http://www.imdb.com/title/tt0432109/.

24. Matthew Campbell, "Woman Artist Gets Death Threats over Gay Muslim Photos," *Sunday Times*, January 6, 2008. http://www.timesonline.co.uk/tol/news/world/europe/article3137510.ece.

25. Council of Europe, *Convention for the Protection of Human Rights and Fundamental Freedoms* (1950), Article 10. http://conventions.coe.int/treaty/en/Treaties/Html/005.htm.

26. Kingdom of the Netherlands, *Wetboek van Strafrecht* [Criminal Code], Article 137c. http://www.wetboek-online.nl/wet/Sr/137c.html.

27. Canada, *Criminal Code*, Section 319. http://www.efc.ca/pages/law/cc/cc.319.html.

28. Paul B. Cliteur, *Moreel Esperanto. Naar een autonome ethiek [Moral Esperanto: Towards an Autonomous Ethics* (Amsterdam: De Arbeiderspers, 2007).

29. http://www.rokerskerk.nl/.

30. http://www.rokerskerk.nl/overdekerk/.

31. http://www.venganza.org/.

32. Joop Boer quoted in *NRC Handelsblad*, September 2, 2006. American writer Colin Beavan experiences with living a no impact life in New York. He published an interesting and inspiring book about it: *No Impact Man: The Adventures of a Guilty Liberal Who Attempts to Save the Planet, and the Discoveries He Makes About Himself and Our Way of Life in the Process* (2008). Also a documentary has been created about the experiment of him and his family, titled *No Impact Man* (2008).

33. In an e-mail Joop wrote to me: "I don't see myself as a wise man, if only that were true. What often bothers me is that people say and think: 'The way that man lives, I can't come close to that, but that makes sense, because he is a very special person.' That is nonsense, of course, because everyone can do what I do. I live a lot more luxuriously now than I did in my youth in the 1950s and also a lot more luxuriously than approximately 3 billion other people on earth."

34. Ruut Veenhoven, *Conditions of Happiness* (Dordrecht: D. Reidel, 1984).

35. James Garvey, *The Ethics of Climate Change: Right and Wrong in a Warming World* (New York: Continuum, 2008), p. 140.

36. David L. Parker, *Before Their Time: The World of Child Labor*, Foreword by Senator Tom Harkin (New York: Quantuck Lane Press, 2007). "Compiled over 15 years, long-time activist Parker's stark photographs of underage laborers shine a necessary if disturbing light on the pathetic working conditions endured by those too young to defend themselves or to know better. By Parker's count, 320 million children under the age of 16 toil under hazardous conditions. This compilation of photos highlights six egregious industries that particularly exploit children, including farming, bricklaying and garbage picking. Intriguingly, for every horror shot Parker includes—such as the close-up of a Guatemalan boy's mutilated arms—he also includes tragicomic portraits of smiling circus performers, prostitutes and cotton pickers oblivious to any other life. Interspersed between the chapters are brief introductions (and a foreword by Sen. Tom Harkin) that point out the out-of-frame dangers his subjects face: asbestos clouding the air of miners, noxious gases polluting leather tanners or rabid dogs ready to devour stricken garbage pickers. Parker's grainy, black and white images allude to the realist photojournalism style of the 1930s, as if to demonstrate what little progress has been made in the past century."

37. On page 2 of her book *50 Facts that Should Change the World* Jessica Williams writes: "It's not too late to change the way our world works. But we need to act soon. Some of the facts need major shifts in thinking, while others require governments to start taking their responsibilities to the international community seriously. Neither of these things will be easy to achieve." As inspiration she quotes the anthropologist Margaret Mead: "Never doubt that a small group of thoughtful, committed people can change the world. Indeed, it is the only thing that ever has."

38. Henry Spira, quoted in Peter Singer, *Ethics in Action: Henry Spira and the Animal Rights Movement* (Lanham, MD: Rowman & Littlefield, 1998), pp. 197–98.

39. "Nudism," *Encyclopedia Britannica*, http://www.britannica.com/EBchecked/topic/422093/nudism. *See* Philip Carr-Gomm, *A Brief History of Nakedness* (London: Reaktion Books, 2010).

40. In the Netherlands there are plenty of wellness spas with sauna facilities where nude people of both sexes mix freely.

CHAPTER 5: TOWARD A BETTER WORLD

1. Herman E. Daly, "The Steady-State Economy in Outline," in G. Tyler Miller, Jr., *Living in the Environment: Principles, Connections, and Solutions*, 12th ed. (Belmont, CA: Wadsworth/Thomson Learning, 2002), p. 698.

2. David Schmidtz and Elizabeth Willott, "The Tragedy of the Commons," in R. G. Frey and Christopher Heath Wellman, eds., *A Companion to Applied Ethics* (Oxford: Blackwell Publishing, 2005), p. 672.

3. James Garvey, *The Ethics of Climate Change: Right and Wrong in a Warming World* (London and New York: Continuum, 2008), p. 1.

4. Intergovernmental Panel on Climate Change, *Climate Change 2007: Synthesis Report. Summary for Policymakers,* http://www.ipcc.ch/pdf/assessment-report/ar4/syr/ar4_syr_spm.pdf.

5. Annemarie Opmeer, interview with Marc van Roosmalen in *Milieudefensie Magazine,* 7/8 (2009).

6. Bill Devall and George Sessions, *Deep Ecology: Living as if Nature Mattered* (Layton, UT: Gibbs Smith, 2000), p. 74.

7. Bill McKibben, "Introduction," *The End of Nature* (New York: Random House, 2006 [1989], p. xviii.

8. Devall and Sessions, *Deep Ecology,* p. 74.

9. It is possible to say that we human animals apply the concept of intrinsic value to things we consider to be important, even though we know that we don't take the concept of intrinsic value literally.

10. *See* Paul Taylor, *Respect for Nature* (Princeton, NJ: Princeton University Press, 1986).

11. Or deep ecology could lead to "green terrorism," which takes the greatest polluters as targets.

12. Quoted in Devall and Sessions, *Deep Ecology,* p. 75.

13. Daly, "The Steady-State Economy in Outline," p. 699.

14. I deal with the subject of *moral* atheism in my book *Hoe komen we van religie af?* I hope it will appear soon in an English translation under the title *Beyond Religion: An Inconvenient Liberal Paradox.*

15. Peter Singer, *Practical Ethics,* 3d. ed. (Cambridge: Cambridge University Press, 2011), p. 20.

16. John Stuart Mill, *On Liberty,* quoted in: John Skorupski, *Why Read Mill Today?* (London: Routledge, 2007), p. 42.

17. Garvey, *The Ethics of Climate Change,* p. 145.

18. *See* Mathis Wackernagel and William E. Rees, *Our Ecological Footprint: Reducing Human Impact on the Earth,* illus. Phil Testemale (Gabriola Island, BC: New Society Publishers, 1996).

19. Animals used in food production, such as cattle, sheep, goats, pigs, geese, turkeys and chickens.

20. *See* Peter Singer, *Animal Liberation,* new rev. ed. (New York: Avon Books, 1991).

21. Note that in this case "deep" is negative and not positive as in deep ecology and deep vegetarianism.

22. http://www.lnt.org/index.php.

23. http://en.wikipedia.org/wiki/Leave_No_Trace.

24. *See* his article 'Aquacolypse' in *New Republic,* September 28, 2009: http:// www.newrepublic.com/article/environment-energy/aquacalypse-now?page=0,2#. *See also* Charles Clover, *The End of the Line: How Overfishing Is Changing the World and What We Eat* (London: Ebury, 2005 [2004]); Callum Roberts, *The Unnatural History of the Sea* (Washington, DC: Island Press, 2007); Stephen Sloan, *Ocean Bankruptcy: World Fisheries on the Brink of Disaster* (Guilford, CT: The Lyons Press, 2003).

25. Duane Elgin, *Voluntary Simplicity: Toward a Way of Life that Is Outwardly Simple, Inwardly Rich,* 2d. ed. (New York: Harper Collins, 2010); Jim Merkel, *Radical Simplicity: Small Footprints on a Finite Earth* (Gabriola Island, BC: New Society Publishers, 2003).

26. *See* John Naish, *Enough: Breaking Away from the World of More* (London: Hodder & Stoughton, 2008).

27. Arne Naess, *Ecology of Wisdom: Writings by Arne Naess,* ed. Alan Drengson and Bill Devall (Berkeley, CA: Counterpoint, 2008), p. 310.

28. Lester W. Milbrath, 'Envisioning a Sustainable Society," in G. Tyler Miller, Jr., *Living in the Environment: Principles, Connections, and Solutions,* 12th ed. (Belmont, CA: Wadsworth/Thomson Learning, 2002), p. 751.

CHAPTER 6: ECO-HUMANIST MANIFESTO

1. All sorts of wonderful manifestos and declarations exist concerning all kinds of noble (and sometimes less noble) objectives, such as *The Earth Charter: Toward a Sustainable World.* I see the eco-humanistic manifesto above all as a complement to the *Humanist Manifesto 2000,* drawn up by Paul Kurtz, in which he sketches a concrete image of a socially just world and how we would have to strive for it. It is still very anthropocentric, hence my complement to his document. This also connects with the 2006 *Freethinkers Manifesto,* which I helped to draw up. It makes a plea for animal welfare and an immediate global abolition of factory farming. It is a utopian statement, but for that reason not less ethically correct. To be right is not the same thing as getting your way. That is the tragedy of every world improver and activist. Power can get its way by force even without being right.

2. James Garvey, *The Ethics of Climate Change: Right and Wrong in a Warming World* (London and New York: Continuum, 2008), p. 28.

3. Harald Welzer, *Klimakriege: Wofür im 21. Jahrhundert getötet wird (Climate Wars: What People Will Kill for in the 21st Century)* (Frankfurt am Main: S. Fischer Verlag, 2008), p. 10 ff.

4. *See* Tim Flannery, *We Are the Weather Makers: The History of Climate Change,*

adapted by Sally M. Walker (Somerville, MA: Candlewick Press, 2009). Alfred Wallace introduced the idea of an aerial ocean in his book *Man's Place in the Universe* (1903): "The great aerial ocean which surrounds us, has the wonderful property of allowing the heat-rays from the sun to pass through it without being warmed by them; but when the earth is heated the air gets warmed by contact with it, and also to a considerable extent by the heat radiated from the warm earth because, although pure, dry air allows such dark heat-rays to pass freely, yet the aqueous vapour and carbonic acid (CO_2) in the air intercept and absorb them."

5. United Nations World Commission on Environment and Development, *From One Earth to One World: An overview by the World Commission on Environment and Development*, para. 27, http://en.wikisource.org/wiki/Brundtland_Report/From_One_Earth_to_One_World#I._The_Global_Challenge.

6. Herman E. Daly, "The Steady-State Economy in Outline," in G. Tyler Miller, Jr., *Living in the Environment: Principles, Connections, and Solutions*, 12th ed. (Belmont, CA: Wadsworth/Thomson Learning, 2002), p. 698.

7. *See* Fred Pearce, *When the Rivers Run Dry: Water—the Defining Crisis of the Twenty-First Century* (Boston: Beacon Press, 2006); Steven Solomon, *Water: The Epic Struggle for Wealth, Power, and Civilization* (New York and Toronto: Harper, 2011).

8. See *Charles Moore: The Great Pacific Trash Island*, http://www.youtube.com/watch?v=en4XzfR0FE8. Also: Jesse Goossens, *Plastic Soup* (Rotterdam: Lemniscaat, 2011).

9. Data from Goossens, *Plastic Soup*.

10. The biologist Edward O. Wilson writes about this in his books *The Future of Life* (New York: Alfred A. Knopf, 2002) and *The Creation: An Appeal to Save Life on Earth* (New York: Norton, 2006).

11. According to Jean-Michel Cousteau, almost 30 percent of coral reefs have already disappeared and unless action is taken another 30 percent of all coral reefs will have disappeared by 2030. "Foreword," *Another World: Colors, Textures, and Patterns of the Deep* (New York: Prestel Publishing, 2005).

12. In his book *In Defense of Dolphins: The New Moral Frontier* (Malden, MA: Blackwell, 2007), philosopher Thomas I. White argues that dolphins should be seen as nonhuman *persons* and therefore should be treated as persons on the basis of their social, cognitive and emotional capacities. For concrete action *see* www.wilddolphin.org, in which White is also involved. The slogan "in their world, on their terms," draws attention to the fact that we humans have to take care not to think anthropocentrically. We should protect dolphins against the harmful effects of human action, but we must allow them their freedom and individuality. Dolphins must not become pets. After all, if dolphins are persons, the imprisonment of a dolphin is a form of slavery. This also applies to the higher primates, who can also be seen as persons. Killing a dolphin or a higher primate is akin to murder.

13. *See* www.greatapeproject.org. On this website you may signal your support by signing the World Declaration on Great Primates.

14. www.savejapandolphins.org.

15. *See* Mark B. Tauger, *Agriculture in World History.* (London and New York: Routledge, 2011): 'Thus perhaps most people in the world [today—FvdB] live on foods produced, processed and transported with fossil fuels. While certain foods have been transported increasingly since the sixteenth century, no major population has ever been this dependent for food on another non-food resource before.' (p. 164).

16. In 1962 Rachel Carson published *Silent Spring*, which drew attention to the disastrous environmental consequences of the "wonder pesticide" DDT. One result of DDT use was that egg shells became so thin that they broke during brooding. That meant a drastic reduction of the number of birds, and hence a silent spring. Carson's book is seen as one of the first volumes that raised alarms about the environment. Although DDT use has been halted in many countries, and the book succeeded in that way in conveying the message, lots of other problems have cropped up. *See*, for example, Bridget Stutchbury, *Silence of the Songbirds: How We Are Losing the World's Songbirds and What We Can Do to Save Them* (New York: Walker & Company, 2007). A large-scale sustainable ecological consciousness, in so far as it exists, has not (yet?) been translated into worldwide action.

17. Along the Indian coast ships sent to be scrapped are broken up by low-paid workers who are not properly protected against the asbestos and other dangerous materials used in the ships.

18. The sociologist Duane Elgin has carried out research into the experience of happiness among people who live according to the principle of voluntary simplicity and reports on it in his book *Voluntary Simplicity: Toward a Way of Life that Is Outwardly Simple, Inwardly Rich* (New York: Morrow, 1981). *See* also his website www.awakeningearth.org.

19. Here are a few of the many guides to better living, most of which envisage a greener, environment-friendly life: Yvonne Jeffery, Liz Barclay, Michael Grosvenor, *Green Living for Dummies* (New York: Wiley, 2008); Ellis Jones, Ross Haenfler, Brett Johnson, *The Better World Handbook: From Good Intentions to Everyday Actions* (Gabriola Island, BC: New Society Publishers, 2007); Linda Catling and Jeffrey Hollender, *How to Make the World a Better Place: 116 Ways You Can Make a Difference* (New York: W. W. Norton, 1995); Matt Ball and Bruce Friedrich, *The Animal Activist's Handbook: Maximizing our Positive Impact in Today's World* (Brooklyn, NY: Lantern Books, 2009).

20. *See* http://www.fairtradetowns.org/about/. My own small town, Bunnik, has become a Fair Trade Town in 2011.

21. *See* Maria Rodale, *Organic Manifesto. How Organic Food Can Heal Our Planet,*

Feed the World and Keep Us Save. (New York: Rodale, 2010) and David Holmgren. *Permaculture. Principles & Pathways Beyond Sustainability.* (Hepburn, Victoria, Australia: Holmgren Design Services, 2011 (2002)).

22. *See* Bill McKibben, *Maybe One, A Case for Smaller Families.* (London & New York: Plume, 1998).

23. *See,* for example, the humorous book by Peter Cave, *Humanism: A Beginner's Guide* (Oxford: Oneworld, 2009); Paul Kurtz, *What Is Secular Humanism?* (Amherst, NY: Prometheus Books, 2007); Paul Kurtz, *Multi-Secularism: A New Agenda* (Piscataway, NJ: Transaction Publishers, 2010); Bill Cooke, *A Wealth of Insights: Humanist Thought since the Enlightenment* (Amherst, NY: Prometheus Books, 2011).

24. http://www.americanhumanist.org/. *See* Stephen Law, *Humanism: A Very Short Introduction* (Oxford: Oxford University Press, 2011).

25. *See* "The Parable of Earthland" earlier in this book.

26. In his book *The Transcendental Temptation: A Critique of Religion and the Paranormal* (Buffalo, NY: Prometheus Books, 1986) Paul Kurtz consciously draws no distinction between faith and superstition. Faith is institutionalized superstition.

27. W. K. Clifford, *The Ethics of Belief and Other Essays* (Amherst, NY: Prometheus Books, 1999 [1877]), p. 74.

28. The Committee for Skeptical Inquiry (www.csicop.org), publishes the *Skeptical Inquirer.* The mission of the Committee for Skeptical Inquiry is to promote scientific inquiry, critical investigation, and the use of reason in examining controversial and extraordinary claims.

29. *See* Nicholas Humphrey, "What Shall We Tell Our Children?" *The Mind Made Flesh: Essays from the Frontiers of Psychology and Evolution* (Oxford: Oxford University Press, 2002).

30. Bertrand Russell, *Sceptical Essays* (London: Unwin Paperbacks, 1977 [1928], p. 11. Russell continues: "I must, of course, admit that if such an opinion became common it would completely transform our social life and our political system." In any case I hope that Russell's adage comes to be commonly held among humanists.

31. *See* Richard Dawkins, *The God Delusion* (Boston: Houghton Mifflin, 2006); Daniel C. Dennett, *Breaking the Spell: Religion as a Natural Phenomenon* (New York: Viking, 2006); Sam Harris, *The End of Faith: Religion, Terror, and the Future of Reason* (New York: Norton, 2004); Christopher Hitchens, *God Is Not Great: How Religions Poison Everything* (New York: Twelve, 2007). *See also* Paul Cliteur, *The Secular Outlook: In Defense of Moral and Political Secularism* (Hoboken, NJ: Wiley-Blackwell, 2010).

32. Hivos is an international development organization guided by humanist values: http://www.hivos.org.

33. Bill Cooke, *Dictionary of Atheism, Skepticism, & Humanism* (Amherst, NY: Prometheus Books, 2005).

34. http://www.secularhumanism.org/index.php?section=main&page=manifesto.

35. http://www.humanistfederation.eu/index.php?option=com_content&vie w=article&id=161&Itemid=27.

36. Peter Singer, *Animal Liberation: A New Ethics for Our Treatment of Animals* (New York: Random House for New York Review, 1975).

37. Bill Cooke, *A Wealth of Insights. Humanist Thought since the Enlightenment* (Amherst, NY: Prometheus Books, 2011), p. 440.

38. Ibid., p. 23.

39. Ibid., p. 15.

40. Ibid., p. 11.

41. Ibid., p. 269.

42. Ibid., p. 341.

43. Ibid., p. 438.

44. Ibid., p. 439.

45. Ibid., p. 417.

MEDIAGRAPHY FOR A BETTER WORLD

"Create all the happiness you are able to create;
remove all the misery you are able to remove."
—Jeremy Bentham in a birthday letter
to a friend's young daughter

During my bibliographical research and the compilation of this mediagraphy, it constantly struck me how much information, knowledge, and wisdom is available for use in making the world more pleasant, just, beautiful, happy, healthy, free, animal friendly, peaceful, and sustainable. The books that are the key to a better world are easily obtainable in bookstores or, more often, on the Internet. Aside from books there are websites, documentaries, and periodicals. Why then is there such a wide gap between that better world and the world in which we live?

This mediagraphy is an invitation and an encouragement to further reading in the project of making the world better and more sustainable. I have divided it into five categories: (1) philosophy and humanism, (2) human-animal relations, (3) human-environment relations, (4) relations among humans, and (5) documentaries and videos. The divisions are not always tidy, but I hope their advantages outweigh their disadvantages.

PHILOSOPHY AND HUMANISM

Carroll, Robert T. *Becoming a Critical Thinker. A Guide for the New Millennium.* (Upper Saddle River, NJ: Prentice Hall, 2000). Thinking critically is a skill that requires practice and knowledge.

Cave, Peter. *Humanism. A Beginner's Guide.* Oxford: One World, 2009. Nice, humorous introduction to humanism, with ample attention to its philosophical underpinnings.

Clifford, W. K. *The Ethics of Belief and Other Essays.* Amherst, NY: Prometheus Books, 1999 (1877). Introduction by Timothy J. Madigan.

Cliteur, Paul B. *The Secular Outlook: In Defense of Moral and Political Secularism.* Hoboken, NJ: Wiley-Blackwell, 2010.

Cooke, Bill. *Dictionary of Atheism, Skepticism & Humanism.* Amherst, NY: Prometheus Books, 2006.

———. *A Wealth of Insights: Humanist Thought Since the Enlightenment.* Amherst, NY: Prometheus Books, 2011.

Dawkins, Richard. *The God Delusion.* London: Bantam Press, 2006.

Dennett, Daniel C. *Breaking the Spell: Religion as a Natural Phenomenon.* London: Allen Lane, 2006.

———. *Darwin's Dangerous Idea: Evolution and the Meanings of Life.* New York: Simon & Schuster, 1995.

Freeman, Samuel, ed. *The Cambridge Companion to Rawls.* Cambridge: Cambridge University Press, 2003.

———. *Rawls.* London: Routledge, 2007.

Gay, Peter. *The Enlightenment: An Interpretation.* Wildwood House, 1973.

Graham, Paul. *Rawls.* Oxford: Oneworld Publications, 2006.

Grayling, A. C. *Ideas that Matter: A Personal Guide for the 21st Century.* London: Weidenfeld & Nicolson, 2009.

Hochsmann, Hyun. *On Peter Singer.* Belmont, CA: Wadsworth, 2001. A concise introduction to Singer's philosophy.

Israel, Jonathan I. *Enlightenment Contested: Philosophy, Modernity, and the Emancipation of Man, 1670-1752.* Oxford: Oxford University Press, 2008.

———. *Radical Enlightenment: Philosophy and the Making of Modernity, 1650–1750.* Oxford: Oxford University Press, 2002. A history of the emancipation of philosophy from the shackles of theology.

———. *A Revolution of the Mind. Radical Enlightenment and the Intellectual Origins of Modern Democracy.* Princeton and Oxford: Princeton University Press, 2010.

Kurtz, Paul. *Living without Religion: Eupraxophy.* Amherst, NY: Prometheus Books, 1994.

————. *What Is Secular Humanism?* Amherst, NY: Prometheus Books, 2006.

Law, Stephen. *The Philosophy Gym: 25 Short Adventures in Thinking.* New York: Thomas Dunne Books, 2003. An introduction to philosophy using concrete problems, such as the question whether it is morally permissible to eat meat.

————. *Humanism: A Very Short Introduction.* Oxford. Oxford University Press, 2011.

Mautner, Thomas. ed. *A Dictionary of Philosophy.* 2nd ed. London: Penguin Books, 2005. A clearly written reference work. It includes an interesting philosophical self-portrait by Peter Singer.

Rachels, James. *The Elements of Moral Philosophy.* 2d ed. New York: McGraw-Hill, 1995. A good introduction to ethics.

Russell, Bertrand. *A History of Western Philosophy.* London: Routledge, 1990 (1945). This history is rather dated, of course, and lacks applied ethics, among other matters. But Russell shows clearly how the search for knowledge and freedom has proceeded over time. His history is itself philosophy.

————. *Sceptical Essays.* London: Unwin Paperbacks, 1977 (1935).

Van den Berg, Floris, *Harming Others: Universal Subjectivism and the Expanding Moral Circle.* Leiden University, 2011. PhD dissertation that is the academic version of *Philosophy for a Better World.*

————. *Hoe komen we van religie af? Een ongemakkelijke liberale paradox [How to Get Rid of Religion? An Inconvenient Liberal Paradox].* Antwerpen and Amsterdam: Houtekiet and Atlas, 2009.

————. "Proposal for a Moral Esperanto. An Outline of Universal Subjectivism." In *Think* 9, no. 24 (Spring 2010): 97–107.

HUMAN-ANIMAL RELATIONS

Armstrong, Susan J., and Richard G. Botzler, eds. *The Animal Ethics Reader,* 2nd ed. London & New York: Routledge, 2008).

Bekoff, Marc. *Animals Matter: A Biologist Explains Why We Should Treat Animals with Compassion and Respect.* Foreword by Jane Goodall. Boston & London: Shambala, 2007.

Cavallieri, Paula, and Peter Singer, eds. *The Great Ape Project: Equality Beyond Humanity.* New York: St. Martin's Press, 1994. *See also* the website www.greatapeproject.org. Jane Goodall: "Only if we understand can we care; only if we care will we help; only if we help shall they be saved."

Coetzee, John M. *The Lives of Animals,* ed. Princeton, NJ: Princeton University Press, 2001. Introduced Amy Gutmann. An impassioned literary pamphlet about human-animal relations. Coetzee employs the notorious Holocaust comparison. An example of how philosophy can be given a literary life and thereby gains in forcefulness.

Corbey, Raymond. *The Metaphysics of Apes: Negotiating the Animal-Human Boundary*. Cambridge: Cambridge University Press, 2005. A philosophical discussion of the differences among the great apes.

Darwin, Charles. *The Descent of Man*. London: Penguin Classics, 2004 (1871).

———. *On the Origin of Species*. London: Penguin Classics, 2009 (1859).

Dawkins, Marian Stamp. *Animal Suffering: The Science of Animal Welfare*. London: Chapman and Hall, 1980. Anyone who doubts whether animals are capable of suffering can find here an overview of the findings of scientific research that indicates that they are. (Oxford: Oxford University Press, 2012).

Dawkins, Richard. *The Ancestor's Tale: A Pilgrimage to the Dawn of Evolution*. London: Weidenfeld & Nicolson, 2004.

———. *Climbing Mount Improbable*. London: Penguin Books, 1997.

DeGrazia, David. *Animal Rights: A Very Short Introduction*. Oxford: Oxford University Press, 2002. A brief, clear introduction to the philosophy of human-animal relations and a plea for activism. "Considering both numbers of animals involved and the extent to which they are harmed, *factory farming causes more harm to animals than does any other human institution*," (p. 71, italics in the original).

———. *Taking Animals Seriously: Mental Life and Moral Status*. Cambridge: Cambridge University Press, 1996.

Diamond, Jared. *The Third Chimpanzee: The Evolution and Future of the Human Animal*. London: Harper Perennial, 2006 (1991).

Ellis, Richard. *The Empty Ocean*. Island Press: Washington, DC, 2004.

Foer, Jonathan Safran. *Eating Animals*. New York, Boston, London: Little, Brown and Company, 2009.

Fox, Michael Allen. *Deep Vegetarianism*. Philadelphia, PA: Temple University Press, 1999. Fox used to be a proponent of the use of animals for human purposes (*see* his book *The Case FOR Animal Experimentation: An Evolutionary and Ethical Perspective*. Berkeley: University of California Press, 1986) but has changed his views in the light of reason. This book is the most comprehensive philosophy of veganism I know and discusses all arguments for and against.

Friedrich, Bruce, and Matt Ball. *The Animal Activist's Handbook: Maximizing Our Positive Impact in Today's World*. Lantern Books: Brooklyn, NY, 2009.

Hawthorne, Mark. *Striking at the Roots: A Practical Guide to Animal Activism*. Changemaker Books, 2008.

Joy, Melanie. *Why We Love Dogs, Eat Pigs and Wear Cows: Introduction to Carnism. The Belief System That Enables Us to Eat Some Animals and Not Others*. San Francisco, CA: Conari Press, 2010.

McEwan, Ian. *Saturday.* London: Anchor, 2006. A novel in which the blind spot with
regard to the suffering of sea animals is identified and then ignored.

Nussbaum, Martha C. *Frontiers of Justice: Disability, Nationality, Species Membership.*
Cambridge, MA: Belknap Press of Harvard University Press, 2007).

Nussbaum extends the theory of Rawls in three areas: the handicapped, world citizens, and animals. The environment and future generations are much less
prominent. Veganism is not promoted.

Patterson, Charles. *Eternal Treblinka: Our Treatment of Animals and the Holocaust.* New
York: Lantern Books, 2002. An entire book about the comparison of factory
farming with the Holocaust. Anyone who finds the comparison persuasive will
look in a different way at the sabotage committed by animal activists such as
the Animal Liberation Front. Who the villains are and who the heroes are will
depend on your ethical perspective.

Rachels, James. *Created from the Animals: The Moral Implications of Darwinism.* Oxford:
Oxford University Press, 1999. A wonderful historical and philosophical analysis of the human-animal relationship and how humans have quite improperly
put themselves on a moral pedestal. Rachels pleads for a drastic moral recon-
sideration of human-animal relations.

Regan, Tom. *The Case for Animal Rights,* rev. ed. Berkeley: University of California
Press, 2004 (1983). Together with Peter Singer's *Animal Liberation,* this book is a
pioneering work in the animal rights movement. In Regan's view, the killing of
the higher mammals is murder.

Rollin, Bernard E. *Farm Animal Welfare: Social, Bioethical and Research Issues.* Hoboken,
NJ: Wiley-Blackwell, 1995. Rollin doesn't see "the 800-pound gorilla in the
room," the animal suffering in factory farming to which veterinarians are
accomplices.

———. *An Introduction to Veterinary Medical Ethics: Theory and Cases,* 2nd. ed. Hoboken,
NJ: Wiley-Blackwell, 2006. A very mildly applied critique of professional practice. In this book, too, Rollin fails to spot the gorilla.

Singer, Peter. *Animal Liberation,* 2nd. ed. London: Pimlico, 1995 (1975). Amply illustrated with photos of animal suffering, this book applies philosophy to human-
animal relations and comes to the gruesome discovery of the discipline's blind
spot where animal suffering is concerned. This volume is the bible of animal
welfare activism. Academic philosophy still finds it hard to accept that this is a
great book.

———. *Ethics into Action: Henry Spira and the Animal Rights Movement.* Lanham:
Rowman & Littlefield Publishers, 1998. An inspiring biography of an animal
rights activist. Spira successfully puts Singer's philosophy into action.

Singer, Peter, and Jim Mason. *The Way We Eat: Why Our Food Choices Matter.* Emmaus,

PA: Rodale Books, 2006. Singer is not too proud to carry out empirical research into the food industry. Among his stories is one about a day spent as a casual laborer, artificially inseminating turkeys.

Sloan, Stephen. *Ocean Bankruptcy: World Fisheries on the Brink of Disaster*. Guilford, CT: The Lyons Press, 2003.

Sorabji, Richard. *Animal Minds and Human Morals: The Origins of the Western Debate*. Ithaca, NY: Cornell University Press, 1995. A classicist shows that speciesism was already propagated by philosophers in the ancient world, who assigned moral status on the basis of capacity for rational thought.

Spiegel, Marjorie. *The Dreaded Comparison: Human and Animal Slavery*. (New York: Mirror Books, 1997). Like the Holocaust comparison, the comparison to human slavery is a motive for drastic measures to end animal suffering in factory farming.

Tannenbaum, Jerry. *Veterinary Ethics: Animal Welfare, Client Relations, Competition, and Collegiality*. 2nd. ed. Maryland Heights, MO: Mosby, 1995. Much ado about very little. Tannenbaum, too, fails to see the gorilla in the room.

Waal, Frans de. *Our Inner Ape: A Leading Primatologist Explains Why We Are Who We Are*. New York: Riverhead Trade, 2005.

White, Thomas I. *In Defense of Dolphins: The New Moral Frontier*. (London: Blackwell Publishing, 2007). Discourse about the social intelligence of dolphins and a plea to take them into the circle of morality on the basis of their capacities. A gripping combination of marine biology, philosophy, and activism. White does for dolphins what Jane Goodall did for chimpanzees.

HUMAN-ENVIRONMENT RELATIONS

Arthus-Bertrand, Yann. *The New Earth from Above: 365 Days*. New York: Abrams, 2009. Translated from the French by Anthony Roberts. Beautiful but disturbing and deeply affecting photographs of what humans are doing to the earth, supplemented with well-documented information about the ecological crisis. Arthus-Bertrand links his artistic vision to environmental activism. He is the model of the involved artist and, as far as I am concerned, a philosopher.

Bender, Frederic I. *The Culture of Extinction: Toward a Philosophy of Deep Ecology*. Amherst, NY: Humanity Books, 2003. A well-argued work of philosophy. Bender does not recoil from using tough language; the title of chapter one is "Ecocide," and another chapter has the title "Biological Holocaust." Bender pleads for a cultural change from anthropocentrism to ecocentrism.

Carson, Rachel. *Silent Spring*. Boston, MA: Houghton Mifflin Company, 2002 (1962).

One of the first books to raise an eco-alarm, this one about the effects of DDT use.

Catling, Linda, and Jeffrey Hollender. *How to Make the World a Better Place: 116 Ways You Can Make a Difference.* New York: W. W. Norton & Company, 1995.

Chiras, Daniel D. 9th ed. *Environmental Science: Creating a Sustainable Future.* Burlington, MA: Jones & Bartlett Learning, 2009.

Clover, Charles. *The End of the Line: How Overfishing Is Changing the World and What We Eat.* Berkeley: University of California Press, 2008. A dramatic report on the fishing industry and fish stocks by an investigative journalist. A documentary with the same title and based on the book appeared in 2009.

Daly, Herman E. *Beyond Growth: The Economics of Sustainable Development.* Boston, MA: Beacon Press, 1996.

———. "The Steady-State Economy in Outline." In G. Tyler Miller Jr. *Living in the Environment: Principles, Connections, and Solutions.* 12th ed. Belmont, CA: Brooks/Cole, 2002.

DesJardins, Joseph R. 4th ed. *Environmental Ethics: An Introduction to Environmental Philosophy.* Belmont, CA: Thomson/Wadsworth, 2006.

Devall, Bill, and George Sessions. *Deep Ecology: Living as If Nature Mattered.* Salt Lake City: Gibbs Smith Publisher, 2007. An important explanation of the principles of deep ecology and the philosophy of Arne Naess.

Diamond, Jared. *Collapse: How Societies Choose to Fail or Succeed.* London: Penguin Books, 2006. In contrast with earlier societies that failed because of ecological mismanagement, we are aware of the danger that threatens us. Nevertheless it seems as if our present civilization, which is global in its reach, can be added as an appendix to Diamond's book at some point in the future, provided someone is around to do it.

Eisnitz, Gail A. *Slaughterhouse: The Shocking Story of Greed, Neglect, and the Inhumane Treatment Inside the U.S. Meat Industry.* Amherst, NY: Prometheus Books, 2006. On YouTube: Humane Society of the United States, "Slaughterhouse Investigation: Cruel and Unhealthy Practices." http://www.youtube.com/watch?v=zhlhSQ5z4V4.

Elgin, Duane. 2nd ed. *Voluntary Simplicity: Toward a Way of Life That Is Outwardly Simple, Inwardly Rich.* New York, Harper, 2010 (1981). Sociological research on people who voluntarily live frugal and green lives, and who are happier and more contented than when they still participated in our consumer society.

Flannery, Tim. *The Weather Makers: The History and Future Impact of Climate Change.* London: Grove Press, 2001.

Garvey, James. *The Ethics of Climate Change: Right and Wrong in a Warming World.* London: Continuum Books, 2008. A new direction in philosophy: reflections on the question of responsibility for climate change.

Gerbens-Leenes, P. W. *Natural Resource Use for Food: Land, Water, and Energy in Production and Consumption Systems.* Groningen: University of Groningen, 2006.

Hiskes, Richard. *The Human Right to a Green Future: Environmental Rights and Intergenerational Justice.* Cambridge: Cambridge University Press, 2009. His is a rare voice for the inclusion of the environment in human rights discourse. The perspective remains anthropocentric: the concern is for future generations. Other animals are not mentioned, so that blind spots remain.

Intergovernmental Panel on Climate Change. *Climate Change 2007: Synthesis Report.* Available at: www.ipcc.ch/.

Jamieson, Dale, ed. *A Companion to Environmental Philosophy.* Oxford: Blackwell Publishers, 2001. Most of the articles are valuable.

———. *Ethics and the Environment: An Introduction.* Oxford: Clarendon Press, 2008.

Jones, Ellis, Ross Haenfler, and Brett Johnson. *The Better World Handbook: Small Changes That Make a Big Difference.* Gabiola Island, BC: New Society Publishers, 2007.

Marcus, Erik. rev. ed. *Vegan: The New Ethics of Eating.* Ithaca, NY: McBooks Press, 2001.

May, Elizabeth, and Zoe Caron. *Global Warming for Dummies.* Mississauga, ON: John Wiley and Sons Canada, 2009.

McDonough, William, and Michael Braungart. *Cradle to Cradle: Remaking the Way We Make Things.* New York: North Point Press, 2002. This work is an example of technological optimism, which propounds the idea that there are technological solutions that will make problems disappear so that people won't have to change their present lifestyles. Although it makes sense to study technological solutions and implement them, the danger exists that these are bandages that won't cure the problems.

McKibben, Bill. *Deep Economy: The Wealth of Communities and the Durable Future.* New York: Times Books 2007.

———. *The End of Nature.* New York: Random House Trade Paperback, 2005 (1989). A wonderful book that is a joy to read but has a dramatic message: there is no place on earth that does not show human influence.

———. *Fight Global Warming Now: The Handbook for Taking Action in Your Community.* New York: Henry Holt and Company, 2007.

———. *Hope, Human and Wild: True Stories of Living Lightly on the Earth.* Minneapolis, MN: Milkweed Editions, 2007 (1995).

———. *Maybe One: A Case for Smaller Families.* New York: Plume, 1999. An entire book devoted to a subject that is a big taboo in discussing the environmental problem: limitation of the number of children.

Meadows, Donella H., Dennis L. Meadows, and Jørgen Randers. *Beyond the Limits:*

Confronting Global Collapse, Envisioning a Sustainable Future. White Rive Junction, VT: Chelsea Green Publishing Company, 1992.

Merkel, Jim. *Radical Simplicity: Small Footprints on a Finite Earth.* Gabriola Island, BC: New Society Publishers, 2003. *See* www.radicalsimplicity.org.

Milbrath, Lester W. *Envisioning a Sustainable Society: Learning Our Way Out.* Albany: State University of New York Press, 1989.

Miller, G. Tyler Jr. *Living in the Environment: Principles, Connections, and Solutions.* 12th ed. Belmont, CA: Thomson Books/Cole, 2007. A beautifully illustrated and comprehensive textbook introduction to environmental science.

Naess, Arne. *The Ecology of Wisdom: Writings,* ed. Alan Drengson and Bill Devall. Berkeley, CA: Counterpoint, 2008.

Naish, John. *Enough: Breaking Free from the World of More.* (London: Hodder & Stoughton Ltd, 2008).

Roberts, Callum. *The Unnatural History of the Sea.* Washington, DC, Shearwater Press, 2003.

Rees, William E., Mathis Wackernagel, and Phil Testemale. *Our Ecological Footprint: Reducing Our Human Imprint on the Earth.* Gabriola Island, BC: New Society Publishers, 1995.

Rodale, Maria. *Organic Manifesto: How Organic Food Can Heal Our Planet, Feed the World, and Keep Us Save.* New York: Rodale, 2010.

Schmidtz, David, and Elizabeth Willott. "The Tragedy of the Commons." In *A Companion to Applied Ethics,* R. G. Frey and Christopher Heath Wellman, eds. (Oxford: Blackwell Publishing, 2005).

Singer, Peter. *One World: The Ethics of Globalization.* New Haven, CT: Yale University Press, 2004.

Taylor, Paul W. *Respect for Nature: A Theory of Environmental Ethics.* Princeton NJ: Princeton University Press, 1986. A plea for biocentrism.

Wilson, Edward O. *The Creation: An Appeal to Save Life on Earth.* New York/London: W. W. Norton & Company, 2006.

———. *The Future of Life.* London: Abacus, 2002.

Wright, Ronald. *A Short History of Progress.* New York: Carroll & Graf Publishers, 2004. A pessimistic philosophical analysis of the human-environment relationship: "The most compelling reason for reforming our system is that the system is in no one's interest. It is a suicide machine."

RELATIONS AMONG HUMANS

Barley, Nigel. *The Innocent Anthropologist: Notes from a Mud Hut.* (Prospect Heights, Illinois: Waveland Press, 2000 (1983).

Bellamy, Richard. *Citizenship: A Very Short Introduction*. (Oxford: Oxford University Press, 2008).

Bentham, Jeremy. *An Introduction to the Principles of Morals and Legislation*. Amherst, NY: Prometheus Books, 1988 (1789).

Bryson, Bill. *African Diary*. New York: Broadway, 2002. An evocative report on life in the African slums.

Chesler, Phyllis. *The Death of Feminism: What's Next in the Struggle for Women's Freedom*. Basingstoke: Palgrave Macmillan, 2005. Influenced by postmodernism, modern feminism has been infected with cultural relativism, which has led many feminists to side with women-oppressing cultures at the cost of the freedom of individual women.

Clapham, Andrew. *Human Rights: A Very Short Introduction*. Oxford: Oxford University Press, 2007.

Donnelly, Jack. *Universal Human Rights in Theory and Practice*. Ithaca, NY: Cornell University Press, 2002). A sound account of human rights, and a plea against cultural relativism. No discussion about animals, environment, or future generations.

Frey, R. G., and Christopher H. Wellman, eds. *A Companion to Applied Ethics*. Hoboken, NJ: Wiley-Blackwell, 2003.

Glover, Jonathan. *Humanity: A Moral History of the Twentieth Century*. New Haven and London: Yale University Press, 2001. The moral history of the bloodiest century in history prompts misanthropy and despondency. We must try to learn lessons from the past and put individual freedom at the center.

Grayling, A. C., *Among the Dead Cities: The History and Moral Legacy of the WWII Bombing of Civilians in Germany and Japan*. New York: Walker & Company, 2006. A good example of making moral judgments about the past.

———. *Toward the Light of Liberty: The Struggle for Freedom and Rights that Made the Western World*. New York: Walker & Company, 2007.

———. *What Is Good? The Search for the Best Way to Live*. London: Phoenix, 2004.

Haddon, Mark. *The Curious Incident of the Dog in the Night-Time*. London: Vintage, 2003. A novel about an autistic boy.

Hirsi Ali, Ayaan. *The Caged Virgin: An Emancipation Proclamation for Women and Islam*. Translated by Jane Brown. New York: Free Press, 2006. She writes on misogyny and intolerance in Islam.

———. *Infidel*. New York: Free Press, 2008.

Hochschild, Adam. *Bury the Chains: Prophets and Rebels in the Fight to Free an Empire's Slaves*. Boston/New York: Houghton Mifflin Company: 2005. A piece of history about the expanding circle of morality.

Holland, Jack. *Misogyny: The World's Oldest Prejudice*. London: Robinson, 2006. A gripping history of women's oppression. Many great philosophers turn out to have been misogynists. "All misogynists, from Plato and Aristotle, to Tertullian and St. Thomas, to Rousseau, Nietzsche and Hitler, have in one way or another sought to prove that it is possible for man to reassert the uniqueness of his relationship to God or to the cosmos—or however he chooses to describe the ultimate truth he identifies with his destiny. It creates a kind of dualism in which the woman is the lesser truth, tethered to sexuality that keeps getting in the way." (279)

Humphrey, Nicholas. "What Shall We Tell Our Children?" In *The Mind Made Flesh: Essays from the Frontiers of Psychology and Evolution.* Oxford: Oxford University Press, 2002.

Kurtz, Paul. *The Courage to Become: The Virtues of Humanism.* Westport, CT: Praeger, 1997.

———. *Forbidden Fruit: The Ethics of Humanism.* Amherst, NY: Prometheus Books, 1988.

———. *Toward a New Enlightenment.* ed. by Tim Madigan and Vern Bullough. Pascataway, NJ: Transaction Publishers, 1994. A plea for the completion of the Enlightenment project: demystification of society through critique of religion and other claims to transcendental knowledge, individual freedom, and a scientific worldview.

Layard, Richard. *Happiness: Lessons form a New Science.* London: Penguin Books, 2005.

McKibben, Bill. *Maybe One. A Case for Smaller Families.* London & New York: Plume, 1998.

Mill, John Stuart. *On Liberty.* Edited and introduced by Gertrude Himmelfarb. London: Penguin Book, 1985 (1859). The most important treatment of the idea of freedom in the history of philosophy. It is the foundation of the open society as it has taken shape in the Western world, in which individual freedom is a central concept.

More, Thomas. *Utopia.* Translated by Paul Turner. London: Penguin Books, 1965 (1516).

Narisetti, Innaiah. *Forced Into Faith: How Religion Abuses Children's Rights.* Amherst, NY: Prometheus Books, 2009. The human rights perspective on religious views on child rearing.

Palmer, R. R., Joel Colton, and Lloyd Kramer. *A History of the Modern World.* 10th ed. New York: Knopf, 2006.

Popper, Karl. *The Open Society and Its Enemies.* Princeton NJ: Princeton University Press, 1971 (1945).

Rawls, John. *A Theory of Justice.* rev. ed. Cambridge, MA: Harvard University Press, 1999. Not an easy read, but a landmark study that has fundamentally changed political philosophy.

Ryan, Alan. *Bertrand Russell: A Political Life.* (Oxford: Oxford University Press, 1988). Russell was a philosopher who worked actively for a better world by championing individual freedom as well as the emancipation of various groups, among them conscientious objectors during World War I and women.

Sachs, Jeffrey D. *Common Wealth: Economics for a Crowded Planet.* London: Allen Lane, 2008. Sachs is an incorrigible optimist who sees practical and achievable solutions everywhere. And indeed, if we wanted to, the world could easily become a good deal more just and less miserable.

Sachs, Jeffrey D. *The End of Poverty: Economic Possibilities for Our Times.* London: Allen Lane, 2005.

Schaer, Roland, Gregory Claeys, and Lyman Tower Sargent, editors. *Utopia: The Search for the Ideal Society in the Western World.* 2000.

Singer, Peter. *How Are We to Live? Ethics in an Age of Self-Interest.* Amherst, NY: Prometheus Books, 1995.

———. *The Life You Can Save: Acting Now to End World Poverty.* New York: Random House, 2009. Singer argues that it is a moral duty to donate to charitable organizations that prevent people from dying of hunger or lack of medicine. The money you spend to go to the movies could have paid for lifesaving medicine for African children. He proposes you donate at least ten percent of your income to charitable organizations.

———. *Practical Ethics.* 3rd ed. Cambridge: Cambridge University Press, 2011 (1980). A turning point in philosophy. Singer demonstrates that thinking philosophically can have highly concrete results. He applies his version of utilitarianism to a number of areas, among them medical ethics (euthanasia, abortion, "infanticide"), animal welfare, and the problem of hunger.

———. *Rethinking Life and Death: The Collapse of Our Traditional Ethics.* New York: St. Martin's Press, 1996.

———. *Writings on an Ethical Life.* London: Harpers Collins Publishers, 2001. A collection of Singer's essays that offer a clear view of how he illuminates different subjects in his quest to diminish suffering.

Singer, Peter, and Renate Singer, eds. *The Moral of the Story: An Anthology of Ethics Through Literature.* Oxford: Blackwell Publishing, 2005.

Skorupski, John. *Why Read Mill Today?* London and New York: Routledge, 2006. The author shows why Mill's insistence on individual freedom continues to be important and how it can be given political effect.

Taylor, Richard. *Good and Evil.* Amherst, NY: Prometheus Books, 1999. A thought experiment about the basis of morality, using the island parable.

Unger, Peter. *Living High and Letting Die: Our Illusion of Innocence.* New York: Oxford University Press, 1996. With the help of thought experiments Unger demon-

strates the deficiencies of our moral intuitions and argues that we have a grave
duty to donate money to mitigate suffering.

Vonnegut, Kurt Jr. *Slaughterhouse-Five*. New York: Dell Publishing, 1991 (1969). In
Vonnegut's absurdist novel the World War II bombing of Dresden occupies a
central place.

Williams, Jessica. *50 Facts That Should Change the World*. Cambridge: Icon Books, 2004.
The journalist Williams lists fifty shocking facts that destroy the notion that we
live in a just world. Of course we know this already, but Williams confronts us
painfully with the facts by stating them in well-documented form. The question
is whether this will actually lead to activism and change. Let's hope it does.

DOCUMENTARIES AND VIDEOS

Armstrong, Franny. *The Age of Stupid*. 2009. "Will people in the future call our time
the age of stupid?"

Arthus-Bertrand, Yann. *Earth from the Air*. 2006. Breathtakingly beautiful images with
a disturbing message. A photographer, Arthus-Bertrand reveals himself to be an
environmental activist. In his documentaries and books he shows what damage
humans are doing to the earth. You have to see this.

———. *Home*. 2009. This documentary will enthrall you. Armand Amar's music creates
an emotional thrill. *Home* is a hymn to the earth and the story of our lightning-fast
destruction of it. The beautiful images—even the destruction looks breathtaking
from above—the enchanting music and the tragic tale of what humanity is doing
to the earth combine for an overwhelming emotional experience. This raises a
philosophical question: can anything so tragic and gruesome be beautiful?

Bowman, Ron. *Six Degrees Could Change the World*. 2007.

Bozzo, Sam. *Blue Gold: World Water Wars*. Based on the book by Maude Barlow and
Tony Clarke, *Blue Gold: The Fight to Stop the Corporate Theft of the World's Water*.
New York: New Press, 2003. The world is becoming drier, the population is
increasing, and the demand for water is growing. This will lead to great problems and to conflicts.

DiCaprio, Leonard. *The 11th Hour*. 2007. An alarming film about the environmental
crisis.

Ewing, Heidi, and Rachel Grady. *Jesus Camp*. 2006. Powerful documentary about
children victimized by Christian propaganda.

Francis, Marc, and Nick Francis. *Black Gold: A Film about Coffee and Trade*. 2006. An
analysis of the ethics of coffee production and the coffee trade. Since seeing
this film I have been drinking only fair-trade coffee.

Gabbert, Laura; Schein, Justin, *No Impact Man*. 2008.

Geyrhalter, Nikolaus. *Our Daily Bread*. 2005. A documentary about the provenance of our daily food. Features factory farming, pesticide use, monoculture, and more. Food production in no way resembles the idyllic images of packaging and advertising.

Giordana, Marco Tullio. *The Best of Youth*. 2003. Marvelous film about an Italian family during the second half of the twentieth century. The change in psychiatry toward a more humane treatment of patients emerges clearly.

Global Warming: The Signs and Science. 2005. Television documentary.

Gogh, Theo van. *Submission*. 2004. With its script by Ayaan Hirsi Ali, this is the documentary about the misogynic passages in the Koran that led directly to the Amsterdam film-maker's murder by a young Muslim in 2004.

Guggenheim, Davis. *An Inconvenient Truth*. 2006. A documentary about Al Gore's campaign to give publicity to global warming.

Hall, Mark, *Sushi. The Global Catch*. 2012. A shock documentary about how the popularity of sushi worldwide leads to overfishing of the tuna stocks. The movie also shows how cruel fishing is for the animals who suffer.

Kenner, Robert. *Food, Inc.* 2008.

Levinson, Barry. *Rain Man*. 1988. Film about an autistic man.

Monson, Shaun. *Earthlings*. 2005. A documentary about the keeping of animals and the dependence of humankind on animals for food, clothing, entertainment, and experiments. An extensive piece of research into abuses of animals in pet stores, puppy mills, pounds, factory farming, leather and fur trades, sport and entertainment, and the world of medicine and science. Using hidden cameras and not previously shown images, the film shows the day-to-day course of events in several of the largest industries in the world that exploit animals for profit.

Moore, Michael. *Bowling for Columbine*. 2002. About the disastrous consequences of America's permissive gun legislation.

———. *Sicko*. 2007. About the inferior healthcare system in the United States where low-income earners are concerned.

Murray, Rupert. *The End of the Line: Imagine a World Without Fish*. 2009.

Nicolas G. Pierson Foundation (Party for the Animals, Netherlands). *Meat the Truth*. 2008.

———. *Sea the Truth*. 2010.

Planet Earth. 2006. Television series narrated by David Attenborough and Sigourney Weaver.

Planet Earth: The Future. 2006. Three-part television documentary.

Psihoyos, Louie. *The Cove*. 2009. A shock documentary about the killing of dolphins in Japan.

ReRun Productions. *The Call of the Mountain: Arne Naess and the Deep Ecology Movement.* 1997.

Riley, J. P. *Act Naturally.* 2011. Documentary movie on nudism in the United States. The existence of a flourishing subculture of nudism is an indication of a measure of freedom in society.

Singer, Peter. *One Man's Way: A Peter Singer Documentary Honoring Animal Rights Activist Henry Spira.* 1996. *http://www.youtube.com/watch?v=0Kip4XVDYlE.*

Stenberg, Michael, Johan Soderberg, and Torell Linus. *The Planet.* 2006.

Wagenhofer, Erwin. *We Feed the World.* 2005. An Austrian documentary that takes a long moral look at the food industry, which is dominated by multinational companies that act in highly questionable ways.

ACKNOWLEDGMENTS

I am grateful to many people and organizations that have helped to make the English translation and publication of this book a reality. Despite my sometimes misanthropic inclinations—those who have read the book will understand what I mean—I find solace in the friendship and cooperation that I have experienced.

First and foremost I must thank my friend and mentor Paul Cliteur, author of *The Secular Outlook,* who has put a lot of effort into fundraising and securing other support. In April 2011 I obtained my doctorate for *Harming Others: Universal Subjectivism and the Expanding Moral Circle,* prepared for Leiden University under his supervision. *Philosophy for a Better World* is a popular version of my dissertation.

I wish to thank the Dutch Foundation for Literature, and especially Maarten Valken, for its substantial contribution to the book's publication in English. I would also like to thank the following organizations for their generous financial support: the Remonstrantse Kerk in Bussum, the Belgium humanist association Humanistisch-Vrijzinnige Vereniging Gent, the Dutch Radar Foundation ("for equal treatment; against discrimination"), and Alain van Nieuwenburg of the Belgium humanist organization Vrijzinnig Vilvoorde. Henk Engelsman, board member of *De Vrije Gedachte,* kindly helped with the financial administration of the project.

Without publisher Leo De Haes of Houtekiet Publishing there would not have been a book to translate. Leo encouraged me to work on my book and helped to improve the text. I would also like to express my gratitude to Steven L. Mitchell, editor-in-chief of Prometheus Books, for his support and friendly communications.

I am honored and grateful that Paul Kurtz, one of my intellectual heroes, was willing to write the foreword but sadly was unable to do so before his passing. During my studies at Leiden University, more than a decade ago, Paul Cliteur suggested that I read Paul Kurtz's *Toward a New Enlightenment.* This book sparked my interest in humanism and the philosophy of humanism. In 2005 I had the opportunity to attend the Center for Inquiry conference "Toward a New Enlightenment" in Amherst, New York. At that time Paul consented to be interviewed. After that I got involved with the Center for Inquiry. In the summer of 2006, I was a visiting scholar a Center for Inquiry Transnational in Amherst, New York, during which I worked on my theory of universal subjectivism. In 2007 Paul offered me the opportunity to set up the Center for Inquiry Low Countries. The two Pauls, Cliteur and Kurtz, have coached me in my philosophical studies and humanist endeavors. Both became friends along the way.

In recent years I had two short conversations with Peter Singer. He inscribed my copy of *Practical Ethics* with the words: "Best wishes for your philosophical studies!" I hope he will think that this to my mind "Singerian" book indicates that my studies are off to a good start. There is no philosopher, past and present, with whom I feel more affinity. Singer's approach—applying philosophy to achieve a better world—and his personal vegan lifestyle are my motivation for persevering in the arduous study of philosophy and for getting involved in activism for a better world.

Michiel Horn, a Dutch-born professor emeritus of history at York University, Toronto, has translated this book. It was a stimulating experience to work with him, trying to improve the book and to adapt it for a North American audience. I wish to thank him for his meticulousness and persistence. Thanks also go to Michiel's wife, Cornelia Schuh, for her editorial corrections and suggestions.

Furthermore, I wish to thank my colleagues in the Utrecht University Copernicus Institute of Sustainable Development, who provide a stimulating environment in which I feel at home.

I thank my parents, André and Elly, for their unremitting support in so many ways. My sons, Julius and Hugo, are used to seeing their dad seated behind his desk, a book-laden island in the living room, as he struggles with self-imposed moral problems. Their bold questions have stimulated me to think harder and formulate my answers clearly.

Last but emphatically not least, I wish to thank the love of my life, Annemarieke Otten, to whom this book is dedicated. Not only does she offer emotional and moral support, but she is also my intellectual sparring partner. The ideas in this book originate from our many conversations and debates. Annemarieke constantly overwhelms me with newspaper articles and Internet sources relating to this project. She manages to make ideas concrete, to turn lofty ideals into a way of living. In many ways this book is one of gloom and doom. In stark contrast, my life with her is one of love and happiness.